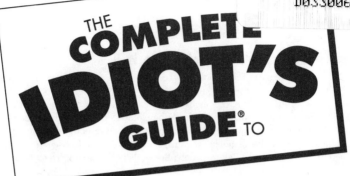

THE **COMPLETE** **IDIOT'S** **GUIDE**® TO

Getting and Owning a Dog

by Sheila Webster Boneham, Ph.D.

ALPHA

A Pearson Education Company

For Reno, my hero dog and muse.

Copyright © 2003 by Sheila Webster Boneham, Ph.D.

International Standard Book Number: 0-02-864284-8
Library of Congress Catalog Card Number: 2002110184

04   03   02   8   7   6   5   4   3   2

Interpretation of the printing code: The rightmost number of the first series of numbers is the year of the book's printing; the rightmost number of the second series of numbers is the number of the book's printing. For example, a printing code of 02-1 shows that the first printing occurred in 2002.

Printed in the United States of America

For marketing and publicity, please call: 317-581-3722

The publisher offers discounts on this book when ordered in quantity for bulk purchases and special sales.

For sales within the United States, please contact: Corporate and Government Sales, 1-800-382-3419 or corpsales@pearsontechgroup.com

Outside the United States, please contact: International Sales, 317-581-3793 or international@pearsontechgroup.com

Publisher: *Marie Butler-Knight*
Product Manager: *Phil Kitchel*
Managing Editor: *Jennifer Chisholm*
Senior Acquisitions Editor: *Randy Ladenheim-Gil*
Development Editor: *Michael Thomas*
Senior Production Editor: *Christy Wagner*
Copy Editor: *Michael Brumitt*
Illustrator: *Chris Eliopoulos*
Cover/Book Designer: *Trina Wurst*
Indexer: *Julie Bess*
Layout/Proofreading: *Angela Calvert, John Etchison*

Contents at a Glance

Contents

Foreword

Dogs are such wonderful companions. I am not surprised you have made the decision to share your life with one. Like all decisions, the choice to have a dog involves careful thought, planning, and management of both time and money. The initial cost of the dog, whether it be an adoption fee from a shelter or a breeder's price, is only the first in a long line of continuing health care, including food, veterinary care, and shelter. By picking up this book, you have made the first step in the right direction.

When it comes to choosing your new best friend, it's essential that you look at all the options available. Making a wrong choice can result in years of heartache caused by your dog's health problems or serious behavior problems that can literally be the death of your dog down the road.

The Complete Idiot's Guide to Getting and Owning a Dog, by Sheila Webster Boneham, Ph.D., covers the basics, such as finding the right breed for you and your lifestyle, and the not-so-basics, like health and genetics in breeding and pedigrees. It is written in easy-to-understand language and form and is liberally sprinkled with interesting facts and important warnings. Rather than simply stating "Don't buy from a pet store," it describes in detail the reasoning behind the warning. It even tells you how to look for clues in the ads that a breeder is not what he is representing himself to be.

Reading this book will give you excellent insight into what it takes to choose your dog and bring him up to be a good canine citizen. Although written for the average dog-owner-to-be, *The Complete Idiot's Guide to Getting and Owning a Dog* contains enough information to appeal to veteran dog owners as well. Addressing issues ranging from the time before you buy a puppy or adopt an adult dog to that final good-bye, and everything in between, this book will help any dog owner to cultivate that unique bond between a man (or woman) and his dog.

In all my experience as a pet owner, nothing has ever come close to the love and devotion a dog brings his owners. The selfless love a dog gives has continued through the ages to bring joy to millions of people, and even in this day and age, dogs constantly surprise us with their capabilities. Ordinary companion animals with no specialized training continue to fill the news with heroic deeds and sacrifices. Tasks formerly thought to be exceedingly difficult if not impossible are now performed and completed with the aid of a dog's superior senses.

With such devotion before us, how can we not strive to be the best owners we can be?

Krista Mifflin
Dogs Guide at About.com
dogs.about.com

Krista Mifflin is a long-time dog fancier who specializes in rare breeds and special-needs pets. She has been raising and training dogs for seven years. She has raised dogs with epilepsy and canine hip dysplasia, as well as dogs with socialization issues. Krista was educated and still lives in her hometown of Schreiber, Ontario. Aside from raising children and dogs, Krista maintains and writes for a website on About.com that is a complete online resource for the dog lover, owner, and owner-to-be.

Introduction

Over the past decade I've come into contact with hundreds of people with questions about dogs. Some have asked questions about getting a dog:

- 🏠 What kind of dog will suit me and my family?
- 🏠 Which is better, purebred or mixed-breed?
- 🏠 Are females better pets than males?
- 🏠 Where should I get my dog?

Some people have questions about canine health care:

- 🏠 What can I do to keep my dog healthy?
- 🏠 How can I best manage my dog's chronic illness?
- 🏠 What should I do if my dog is injured?
- 🏠 What sort of food and exercise does my dog need to stay healthy and fit?

Training and behavior questions are common, too:

- 🏠 What's the best way to train my dog?
- 🏠 How do I keep my dog and kids safe with one another?
- 🏠 Why does my dog do things I don't like, and how can I make him stop?
- 🏠 What sorts of fun things can my dog and I do together?

Puppyhood and the prime years give way to old age all too soon, and people have questions about their aging dogs, too:

- 🏠 What special care does my dog need in his senior years?
- 🏠 What changes should I expect in my dog as he grows older?
- 🏠 Should I get another dog before my old dog dies?
- 🏠 How will I know when it's time to say farewell?

I've wrestled with most of these questions myself over the years. Before I bought the first purebred dog of my very own, I spent hours figuring out what kind of dog I wanted and learned about good and bad breeders. Before I taught puppy kindergarten and obedience classes, I had to learn how to train my dog. As my dogs have aged or been sick or hurt, I've had to learn how to make them better or more comfortable. Hardest of all, I've had to search my soul to decide when it's time to let them go.

After teaching, working with rescue organizations and shelters, talking to many people about puppies and adult dogs, and spending untold hours on Internet discussion lists and bulletin boards, I decided to write this book. I've covered a lot of information. Some of the material is very basic, and some is more complex and advanced. I've tried to make this a book that I would want on my own bookshelf and I hope you'll want it on yours as a guide and a reference for years to come. May it help you get the dog of your dreams and live with him happily.

What's in This Book

I've tried to make this a book with something for the first-time dog owner as well as the more experienced one. If you're part of the latter group, you may want to skip over some of the more elementary information—or not, since I've found that there's always something new to learn or think about when it comes to dogs!

I've divided the book into seven parts. **Part 1, "Dogs 101,"** begins with a hard look at what it's like to own a dog responsibly. Then it guides you through the maze of decisions you'll need to make before you get your dog, and looks at your obligations as a dog owner in your community.

In **Part 2, "Where, Oh Where, Can Your Special Dog Be?"** you'll learn about good and bad places to buy a dog, and about adopting a dog in need. You'll also learn how to prepare for the big day—the day your new puppy or dog comes home.

Part 3, "Keeping Your Dog Healthy," focuses on routine health care, nutrition, and exercise for your dog, as well as health problems and emergencies.

Part 4, "Living with Your Dog," is about living with your dog, who, like you, is a social animal. The chapters in this part address basic manners your dog needs to learn as well as grooming and things to consider if you want to breed your dog.

In **Part 5, "Educating Fido,"** I talk about training your dog and dealing with problem behaviors.

Part 6, "Things to Do with Your Dog," introduces many activities for you and your dog, whether you have a competitive or adventurous streak or just want to have some quiet good times with your canine companion.

Part 7, "All Good Things Must End," talks about what to expect and what to do as your dog grows old and approaches the end of his life here with you.

Extras

Throughout the book you'll find a variety of sidebars. Some of them contain explanations or reminders about important points I mention in the text, and others give you additional information about things canine.

Doggerel _____
"Dog people" speak a whole language of our own! You'll find definitions of terms and concepts related to dogs in these Doggerel boxes.

Grrrrowls _____
Watch out! These boxes contain warnings so you and your dog can steer clear of dangers and pitfalls.

Chew on This

This is where you'll find tips and other goodies to chew on mentally!

BowWOW

These boxes are full of surprises—interesting canine facts and trivia about things canine.

Tail Wags (Acknowledgments)

Writing a book is like breeding a litter of puppies. Each is a creative effort that requires planning, research, time, love, work, and a lot of cleanup. I couldn't do either without my predecessors and my peers, and I can't possibly thank everyone by name who contributed to this book. If you've ever taught me or asked me about dogs, or argued with me and made me think, thank you! My friends Dorothy Montano, Pat Robertson, Hope Schmeling, and Vicki Webb all made helpful comments on parts of the manuscript. Thanks, gals, for putting up with my yapping and whining over the years, and for being my faithful friends. Treats to you all! Good editors, like good dog trainers, make all the difference in the finished product. Thanks to Randy Ladenheim-Gil for her positive reinforcement through creation of the book, and to Michael Thomas for vetting the manuscript with a gentle hand. Love and kisses to my husband and best friend, Roger, for giving me a safe, warm den while I wrote. Maybe someday you'll get me trained! Special belly rubs for Annie, Dustin, and Rowdy, the seniors in our pack, for hanging out in my office while I wrote and for reminding me to play. Last, first, and always, my thanks to the family of dogs. Your beauty, courage, versatility, forgiveness, and friendship are my inspiration.

Trademarks

All terms mentioned in this book that are known to be or are suspected of being trademarks or service marks have been appropriately capitalized. Alpha Books and Pearson Education, Inc., cannot attest to the accuracy of this information. Use of a term in this book should not be regarded as affecting the validity of any trademark or service mark.

Part 1

Dogs 101

You think you want a dog. Great! We'll start out by taking a look at what's involved so that you can be sure a real live dog is what you want—a dog is so much more than just a cute, fluffy puppy! If you're still sure after looking at the messy side of dog ownership, I'll show you the vast variety of characteristics you need to consider when choosing your dog—after all, looks aren't everything in a long-term relationship.

I'll explain what "papers" really are—and are not—and tell you about the documentation that should accompany a dog when you buy or adopt. Then we'll take a look at the place of dogs and dog owners in modern society and what you can do to keep peace with your neighbors while protecting your rights as a responsible dog owner.

Chapter 1

Are You Sure You Want a Dog?

In This Chapter

🏠 Knowing what to expect from dog ownership

🏠 Committing your resources to responsible care

🏠 Evaluating the real costs and benefits of dog ownership

🏠 Deciding whether you *really* want a dog in your life

Dogs have been sharing their lives with people for at least 12,000 years. Cave paintings show dogs with people, and we've been together ever since. Dogs have served us as hunters, guardians, early warning devices, and beasts of burden. Most of all, dogs have been our friends.

Your dog is a lot like a child. He relies on you to provide for nearly all his needs and to protect him from danger and disease. He demands your attention. He gets into things, breaks things, dirties things. He's always ready for fun. He consoles you and takes your mind off your troubles. He makes you cry. He loves you no matter what.

Chew on This

"He is your friend, your partner, your defender, your dog. You are his life, his love, his leader. He will be yours, faithful and true, to the last beat of his heart. You owe it to him to be worthy of such devotion."

—Author unknown

That's the good stuff, the bundle of pluses that inspire people to go out and get a dog. Before you do, though, keep in mind that responsible dog ownership requires a commitment. You need to spend time and energy—lots of it!—training, socializing, and exercising your dog, as well as playing with him, grooming him, and just being with him. Remember, dogs are social animals. They can exist without loving interaction, just as we can, but what a sad existence.

(Photo by Close Encounters of the Furry Kind)

Dogs demand attention and love, and return both tenfold.

You also need to spend money. Your dog needs food, veterinary care, toys, and obedience class. It's important to be realistic about the cost of owning a dog responsibly. You don't need to be wealthy, but lack of money is no excuse for failing to provide proper nutrition, routine and emergency veterinary care, safe shelter, training, and adequate companionship.

If you're not ready, willing, and able to provide for your dog's material and social needs, then please consider waiting until you have more money and time at your disposal. Remember, your dog will rely entirely on you for his physical and emotional needs. He can't go out and get a job. He can't divorce you and look for a new person with more time to spend with him. If you get a dog, he'll consider you his best friend. Make sure you can do right by him.

Do You Have Time for a Dog?

No doubt about it, a dog needs your time. If you get a puppy and you want him to develop into a well-adjusted, well-mannered dog that's a pleasure to live with, you need to invest a lot of time in the first year or two. Puppies aren't born knowing how to behave any more than children are. Your pup will need to be taught how to live properly in human society. Besides, he's a social animal and that means he will thrive on companionship, friendship, and love.

Puppies, and many adult dogs, need to go through at least one obedience class. Many people take their puppies through *puppy kindergarten* and then at least one obedience class. Most classes run from 6 to 12 weeks, and you should plan to spend at least a half-hour every day on doggy homework (which should really be called "doggy home play for education").

Doggerel

Puppy kindergarten classes are for puppies from two to five months in age, and emphasize socialization with other puppies and with people, leash control, and a few simple obedience commands.

You'll also need to spend time exercising your dog. How much time you'll need will depend on the kind of dog you have. Many sporting, herding, and working breeds need at least an hour of serious exercise a day—some need more than that! If you're gone during the day, plan to get up early enough to exercise your dog before you leave, and plan to spend at least an hour in the evening walking him, playing ball, or otherwise giving him a chance to run

off energy. Lack of exercise leads to boredom, which leads to many problem behaviors. If you aren't willing to spend that kind of time exercising a dog, then choose an older dog or a breed that doesn't need so much exercise.

 BowWOW

Puppies learn faster between seven and eight weeks of age than at any other time in their lives. If you can spend time with your puppy in several short, positive training sessions each day, he can learn a lot in this one week. At this age he can learn simple commands, including Sit, Down, Stand, and Come, and he can learn to walk quietly on a leash.

Many families get a dog for the kids, but don't really think about how much time is available for the dog. I have a lovely Labrador Retriever who was returned to her breeder by her first purchasers. They bought her because they thought a Lab would be great for their "active family"—but they forgot that their activities (baseball and soccer practice, gymnastics, music lessons, and Mom and Dad's clubs and sports) wouldn't accommodate an active puppy. Fortunately, they realized early that the dog didn't fit in, and their lack of planning has been my good fortune for the past nine years. But many dogs in similar situations end up in shelters, and many of those wind up dead.

 Grrrrowls

Dogs are not appliances. Don't get a dog as a status symbol. Don't get a dog as a "mate magnet" to attract members of the opposite sex. Don't get a dog because your friend or neighbor has one. Get a dog because you truly like dogs, for better and for worse, in sickness and in health.

If you love dogs, then time spent with the dog is its own reward, whether you're outside throwing sticks and balls or inside reading with a soft, fuzzy muzzle on your lap. But it's important to realize that dogs aren't furniture or appliances. They miss you when you're not there, and they need great chunks of your time. If your schedule is full right now, then please wait until you have the time a dog deserves. No dog should live lonely.

Do You Have Room for a Dog?

The vast majority of American dogs are house dogs. That's because most people get a dog first and foremost to be a friend and companion. Many dogs also participate with their people in dog shows, sports, leisure activities, and even some kinds of work, but the rest of the time (which usually means most of the time) the dog does what he does best—he's a buddy. But even if he's content to lounge around watching TV with you in the evenings, he still needs room to stretch his legs.

A small dog can often get all the exercise he needs in a small apartment, with on-leash outings thrown in for variety. Some large breeds are very sedate as adults and may also do fine in smaller homes or even apartments. A truly dedicated dog owner can probably do well with nearly any breed in a small home, but in most cases an active medium to large dog will do better in a reasonably large house with a reasonably large, fenced yard where he can exercise safely, and where you won't trip over him every time you turn around.

The key to success, then, is to be realistic about how much activity from what size dog your home and yard can accommodate, and how much you will be able to take the dog out for additional exercise if the home space is insufficient.

Does Your Family Want a Dog?

A recent study by the American Animal Hospital Association confirmed what most of us already know: Mom is the primary caretaker for most pets, even the ones the kids just had to have and swore to take care of no matter what. If Mom didn't really want the dog and resents the extra work of caring for it, the situation usually results in strained family relationships. The dog is nearly always the big loser because either he stays but gets less than his fair share of love and attention, or he loses his home. He may actually end up in a better home if he's the rare lucky one. More likely he'll wind up dead after spending some time alone and frightened in a shelter but terminally unadopted.

Try to include all family members in the decision to get a dog. Spend time together learning about dogs in general and about different breeds. This is a great opportunity to teach children to be careful and thoughtful when making decisions that affect other living beings. Remember, too, that children's interests change. The dog-crazy 10-year-old may be too busy with other things at 15 to give much time to the dog, but the dog will still need everything he needed before.

If you live with a roommate, be sure he or she is open to the presence of a dog before you get one. If not, it's probably best to wait until you can move or replace your roommate before you bring in a dog.

Can You Afford a Dog?

Most people underestimate the real cost of owning a dog. The purchase price is usually minimal compared to the cost of taking proper care of a dog for a decade or more. Costs for an individual dog vary, of course, depending on many factors. Food, medicines and veterinary care, professional grooming, outside boarding, and larger toys, beds, bowls, collars, and crates cost more for big dogs than for little ones. If the dog happens to be a puppy, some of these things will have to be replaced at least once as he outgrows them, or chews them up (it happens in the best of doggy families!).

A dog that requires professional grooming every four to eight weeks costs more than a "drip-dry" dog. And a poorly bred dog of any size or breed—including mixed-breeds—is likely to need a lot more costly veterinary care in the long run than a dog from a careful breeder (see Chapters 3, 5, and 6 for more information on buying purebred and mixed-breed dogs).

During the initial year, puppies and some adult dogs have higher veterinary expenses than they should during the following years. Puppies need a series of vaccinations to stimulate their immune systems to protect them from disease. So do some adult dogs that haven't had proper health care in the past. Altering (spaying or neutering) is normally done around six months of age, although, again, an adult adoptee may also need to be altered. Then there's training, of course—puppy kindergarten, basic obedience, maybe more.

Adult dogs continue to have expenses. Every dog should have an annual veterinary exam, and depending on the vaccination schedule you and your vet implement (see Chapter 9), you may need to add the cost of vaccinations. A dental checkup and possibly professional cleaning under anesthesia needs to be scheduled once a year, or more frequently if your dog is prone to tartar build-up.

What Do You Want from Your Dog?

The most important questions you need to ask yourself are these two: What do you want from your dog? What role will he play in your life?

If you're like most people, you want a dog for companionship, and that's a role that many dogs can fill successfully. But it's important to realize that, although most dogs can make good companions in the right situation, not every dog will suit *your* situation. Maybe you want a dog to be your partner in competitive or noncompetitive sports—an agility or obedience partner, a friend for jogging or hiking, or a hunting partner. Maybe you'd like a dog to protect your family and your home. All of these factors will influence the kind of dog you need to choose for a successful relationship. If you want a long-distance running partner, clearly a Bulldog or Chihuahua will be a poor choice for you. But that high-energy sporting or herding dog that suits you to a tee probably won't work well for your neighbor who prefers to walk once around the block and then settle in for a quiet evening.

Chew on This

Many people underestimate the cost of owning a pet dog. The following figures are rough estimates. They may be higher in some urban areas and slightly lower in others.

First Year	Each Year	After First Year
Purchase/Adoption	$0 to 2,000	N/A
Food	$120 to 500	$120 to 500
Supplements*	$0 to 100	$0 to 100
Food/water bowls	$10 to 40	$0 to 25
Treats	$20 to 200	$20 to 200
Dental/chew toys	$20 to 200	$20 to 200
Routine veterinary exam	$45 to 200	$20 to 100
Vaccinations	$20 to 150	$20 to 150
Emergency veterinary care	$0 to 2,000+	$0 to 2,000+
Heartworm test**	$0 to $20	$0 to 20
Heartworm prevention	($0) $24 to 120	($0) $36 to 132
Fecal exams	$10 to 30	$10 to 20
Worming	$10 to 25	$10 to 25
Spaying/neutering	$35 to 200	N/A
Professional teeth cleaning	$0	$60 to 100
Collar(s)	$7 to 50	$0 to 40
Leash(es)	$10 to 50	$0 to 50
Obedience training	$30 to 250	$0 to 200
Grooming tools	$20 to 250	$0 to 25
Professional grooming	$20 to 360	$20 to 360
Shampoo	$5 to 50	$5 to 50
Fence***	$0 to 2,500	$0 to 2,500
Stain/odor removers	$10 to 100	$10 to 100
Doggy bed(s)	$25 to 100	$0 to 100
Crate(s)	$20 to $250	$0 to 250
Toys	$10 to 200	$0 to 200
Boarding per day	$15 to $30	$15 to 30
	$462 to 9,975	$426 to 7,552

*Do not supplement your dog's diet without consulting your veterinarian.

**Heartworm tests and prevention are not required where there is no risk of exposure.

***If you move at any time during your dog's life, you may need to put in a fence for his safety.

Once you have a general notion of what you want from your dog, you still need to narrow your options. Would you prefer to vacuum up hair from a drip-dry sort of dog whose grooming you can do yourself? Or would you rather your dog have a standing appointment with a professional groomer but not leave telltale dog hair on your clothes and carpets? If you plan to hunt, will you be after upland birds or water fowl, or a combination? If you like to hike, do you want a fairly large, strong dog that can help haul you up steep terrain, or a medium-size dog you can hoist over obstacles when necessary? These and other factors that enter into smart choices will be covered in Chapter 2.

Grrrrowls

Although regular dental care is important, there are always risks with anesthesia, particularly for young puppies, older dogs, dogs with certain medical conditions, and some breeds. If your dog needs more than one procedure that requires anesthesia, have them done at the same time if possible.

Do You *Really* Like Dogs?

The dog you bring home will hopefully be a part of your life for a decade or more. If you have never had a dog, or haven't had one or been around dogs for a long time, you might want to take a little time to be sure you like the reality of dogs before you take the ownership plunge.

Grrrrowls

If you want a dog for protection, be careful what you choose. For most people, the best protection is a dog that is alert and that will let you know there's someone there so that, if necessary, you can call 911. Large "protection" breeds are not suitable for the average dog owner. Unless you're willing to put in lots of time working with the dog and trainer yourself and learning how to handle him properly, such a dog can be a tremendous liability. A large, forceful dog that you and other family members can't control is much like a loaded gun. In the right hands, it's useful. In the wrong hands, it's dangerous.

One advantage you have as a "researcher" is that dog owners love to talk about their dogs. In fact, you can't shut a lot of us up! So talk to people with dogs—no, wait—don't talk so much, but listen carefully and pay attention. You need to know if the breed you think is oh-so handsome or cute is also a slobberpuss, needs four hours of running exercise a day, is prone to doggy odor, or is otherwise a breed you just won't enjoy.

Talk to serious breeders, to pet owners, and to veterinarians and groomers. Join a discussion list or two on the Internet (see Appendix C). There are thousands of dog-oriented websites, discussion lists, and bulletin boards. Some are devoted to dogs in general, others to individual breeds, and still others to training and dog sports, health issues, and just about anything else "doggy" you can imagine. Ask about dogs in general and about the breeds you think you might like in particular. Pay attention!

(Photo by Close Encounters of the Furry Kind)

Your dog should be part of your life for a decade or more, so choose carefully for both your sakes.

Consider volunteering a few hours a week for your local shelter. If you zero in on a specific breed but aren't absolutely sure about making the long-term commitment to dog ownership, consider volunteering for a rescue organization for your chosen breed. Most groups are in need of foster homes. They will, of course, screen you and your family to be sure you will be a good temporary harbor for a dog looking for a permanent home. But if you've done your pre-dog homework and think you're ready, chances are they will, too. Be sure you understand the requirements and terms of fostering for that particular organization—get references just as you would for a breeder. If all checks out, you could give needed shelter, love, and attention to a dog in need, and decide for yourself whether dog ownership really is for you. Be forewarned, though—a lot of people fall in love with their foster dogs and wind up adopting them. That's okay—everyone loves a happy ending.

Do some reading as well. Your public library and bookstores should have lots of books on dogs. If not, see Appendix C for online sources. There are also several excellent magazines devoted to dogs as well as specialized periodicals for most breeds. Read more than one source—several if possible. Sometimes writers make mistakes, and some books are inaccurate, so double-check what you've read. The time and money you invest in learning about dogs before you run out and get one will save you a lot of money and heartache in the long run. You may even decide not to get a dog, or not to get the kind you thought you wanted, and that's okay, too! Better to make such decisions before getting the dog rather than after.

If you get a dog, it should be one that will fit into your life and make both of you happy. Most people can realistically find the right dog in any of several breeds. But as we'll see in Chapter 2, no single breed of dog is appropriate for every person, or even for the same person at different times in her life.

The Least You Need to Know

🏠 Dogs and people have been enhancing each others' lives for more than 12,000 years.

🏠 Owning a dog responsibly requires commitment.

🏠 The cost of purchasing a dog is a small portion of the cost of that dog over the years.

🏠 Take your time, and be sure you and your family or roommate really want a dog *before* you get one.

Chapter 2

Size and Other Big Decisions

In This Chapter

- Deciding what you want from your dog
- Understanding purebreds and mixed-breeds
- Choosing specific traits that you like in a dog
- Being clear about traits you don't like or can't live with
- Putting it all together to choose the right kind of dog

No other species of animal comes in as many forms as *Canis familiaris*, the domestic dog. We have teensy-weensy and enormous, hairy and bald as a cue ball, cuddly and aloof, clingy and independent. So if you meet the minimum requirements to qualify as a "dog person," then there's a breed (or mixed-breed) for you. All you have to do is find it! For some people, that's a snap. For others, it's a bit more difficult. But it's well worth the extra time and trouble to get the right sort of dog. Remember, this will be *your* best friend—not your Uncle Joe's or your neighbor's. Let's look at some of the steps

Grrrrowls
Choose the kind of dog that suits *you*, not someone else.

you can take to increase the odds that the breed you select is truly the one for *you* (for resources to help you learn about specific breeds, see Appendixes B, C, and D).

What Do You Want from Your Dog?

Probably the most important question is this: What do you expect your dog to contribute to your life? Do you want a jogging partner or a fellow armchair athlete? Do you want a smart dog that will learn quickly—not just what you want him to learn, but also what you'd rather he didn't know (like how to open his crate)? Or would you rather have a C student who takes a little longer but is generally happy to let you do his thinking for him? Are you willing to spend lots of time grooming or to pay someone else to do it, or would you be happier with a wash-and-wear sort of dog? Can you afford to feed a giant dog, or would your budget do better with a smaller pet? Can you tolerate hair, hair, everywhere, or would you prefer a dog that doesn't shed? Are you experienced enough to manage a dominant dog, or do you need one that won't challenge your authority? Let's face it—there are as many questions as there are dog breeds and mixes!

Your chances of finding the right breed and the right individual dog will be much better if you're honest with yourself, and with breeders, rescuers, or shelter workers, about what you want and, maybe more important, do *not* want in a dog. Be realistic about your budget—not just for getting the dog, but for taking care of him properly for the next decade or more. Be realistic about the amount of time you can devote to training, exercising, and just being with your dog. Be realistic about how much mess you're willing to live with. Then look for a dog that is most likely to fit into your life.

So What's a Breed, Anyway?

These days most dogs are kept as companions and are not expected to do the work they were designed to do. But it's still important to understand the original purpose of any breed you think you'd like to live with, because most dogs still have at least some of those characteristics.

Dogs bred for hunting tend to be friendly working companions with lots of energy and stamina. Dogs designed to work all day long herding livestock are usually very high-energy, intelligent dogs that need physical and mental exercise. Dogs bred to pull vermin out of holes are usually scrappy, active, and determined to dig. Dogs bred to be guardians are often independent, tough, and sometimes standoffish or even aggressive with people and dogs they don't know. All these varying traits are useful and all manageable *in the right environment*. But in the wrong home, any of these traits can be a problem. That's why it pays to do your homework before choosing a breed.

So how did the various breeds end up with different characteristics? Over the centuries, individual dogs with traits that people wanted were bred to one another, and over generations the traits became stronger and stronger. Breeding for specific traits is called selective breeding and is still practiced by responsible breeders. Selective breeding eventually resulted in the wide range in size, abilities, behaviors, forms, colors, coats, and personalities we see in modern dogs.

Eventually, selective breeding resulted in animals that *bred true*, meaning that they consistently produced offspring that were like the parents in most respects. If you breed an Irish Setter to an Irish Setter, you get Irish Setters. But if you breed an Irish Setter to an Irish Terrier, who knows what the pups will look like? And more to the point, we can't predict what their grandpups will be like, but we can be reasonably sure they won't be like the grandparents or the parents because the genes are just too assorted to produce consistent puppies. It takes generations of carefully selecting dogs with desired traits and breeding them together to achieve consistency—in other words, to create a breed. A *breed* is a group of animals within a species that are fairly homogeneous in terms of size, form, instincts, temperament, and other traits.

(Photo by Close Encounters of the Furry Kind)

Dogs come in all sizes, from big as a pony to these tiny Chihuahuas.

Standards were eventually established for individual breeds. A *breed standard* is a document created by members of a breed club to establish a set of characteristics that define a breed. The standard describes a correct member of the breed in terms of size, proportion, head, muzzle, eyes, ears, nose, teeth, neck, topline, tail, forequarters, hindquarters, coat, color, gait, and temperament. It also identifies traits that disqualify a dog of that breed from the show ring and, in the hands of responsible breeders, from breeding. Dogs that don't adhere to the breed standard can be wonderful pets, but they should be spayed or neutered.

When you decide on a breed, look for a breeder who breeds only dogs that come close to the breed's standard and, of course, have the health clearances recommended for the breed. What's the point of researching breeds, choosing one, and then getting a dog that isn't a good representative of the breed?

Purebred or Mixed-Breed?

Purebred dogs, *cross-bred* dogs, and *mixed-breed* dogs all make excellent companions. If you're looking for a dog for a specific purpose—say hunting, sheep-herding, or top-level obedience competition—then you probably want to choose a breed that typically excels in that area. It may be, too, that a cross of specific breeds will give you the traits you want. For instance, a Labrador Retriever × Golden Retriever cross will likely be a good-natured dog that likes water and loves to retrieve.

Doggerel
A **cross-bred** dog is the offspring of two purebreds of different breeds. **Mixed-breed** (also called random-bred or, less flatteringly, a mutt or mongrel) usually refers to a dog with more than two breeds in its background.

Don't be duped into thinking that mixing breeds will result in healthier offspring. The truth is that puppies, whether purebred or mixed, inherit genes from each parent. If the parents pass along the genes for a hereditary disease, the pups stand a good chance of having that disease. Hybrid vigor—the idea that unrelated parents produce healthier offspring—works only if natural selection is in operation. In the wild, a dog with clinical symptoms of a debilitating disease such as hip dysplasia or epilepsy would not be able to survive, and so would not pass on its genes. But in the modern world, with reasonable veterinary care and a constant food source, dogs with serious, even deadly, problems do survive long enough to produce lots of pups.

If you or someone in your family is limited in some way by health issues, you may need to consider that when choosing a breed.

Perhaps allergies or a respiratory condition mean you need a dog that sheds very little or not at all. It would be hard to predict how much a mixed-breed pup might shed when it grows up, but some breeds are known to shed very little and, in a few cases, not at all. Other limitations, such as lack of strength to manage a big, energetic dog, could also make it more important to have some ability to predict what a puppy will grow into.

I don't suggest choosing a dog strictly by its looks. That would be as silly as choosing a spouse just because of blue eyes! You live with the whole package, including energy, temperament, and interests, not just looks. But I do think we should enjoy looking at our companions. If you really like long, flowing hair, use that as a trait you desire, and then research the other characteristics of the many breeds with lovely long coats. There may well be one with *all* the traits that will make a good choice for you. A mixed-breed adult may also fit the bill, but mixed-breed puppies often grow up to look a bit different from what their baby faces lead us to expect!

Temperament and behavioral traits are also much more predictable with purebreds. This doesn't mean that all dogs of a certain breed act the same. As with members of a human family, there can be variations in individual personalities, energy levels, behaviors, and looks within a single litter, let alone the whole breed. But still, responsibly bred purebred dogs do tend to have certain basic traits that are highly predictable. You might prefer an outgoing dog that likes everyone. Or perhaps you prefer a dog that will bark to alert you when someone is around. If a busy dog that's always on the move would drive you bonkers, then you need to select for calmness. But if you want a dog that's always ready to join you in active outdoor pursuits, you need to find one with more get up and go.

Again, many mixed-breed dogs will fit either bill. Just remember that it's harder to predict how a mixed-breed puppy will act as an adult unless you know for sure the breeds in its background. If specific behavioral traits are important to you, then find a properly bred purebred pup of an appropriate breed and from appropriate lines within the breed (more on that in Chapter 5).

You may have heard that purebred dogs are "inbred" and therefore plagued with inherited health problems as well as flaky, high-strung dispositions. To some extent, this is true of poorly bred purebreds. The reality is that *all* living things are prone to inherited problems, and dogs are no exception. Purebred dogs do inherit problems, but so do mixed-breeds. There are advantages to a responsibly bred—let me repeat that, because it's really important—*responsibly bred* purebred. First, you can look for a breeder who tries to breed away from problems known in the breed. Failing that, you can make an informed decision. If you know that a breed is prone to early death from cancer, you can decide whether that is a risk you can live with and whether the short life expectancy is outweighed by the pleasure that a dog of that breed will give you.

Who Registers Dogs?

The American Kennel Club (AKC), the oldest and largest purebred dog registry in the United States, registers some 150 breeds. Every breed is assigned to one of seven groups based to some extent on the use for which the breed was developed: Sporting, Hound, Nonsporting, Working, Toy, Terrier, and Herding. Breeds newly recognized by the AKC are initially placed in the Miscellaneous class and are later moved to an appropriate group. The AKC sanctions *conformation* shows as well as tests and competitions for dogs involved in obedience, agility, field-work, herding, earthdog, hunting, and tracking.

The United Kennel Club (UKC) is the second oldest and second largest all-breed dog registry in the United States. The UKC registers some 250,000 dogs annually. Some breeds are eligible for registration with both the UKC and the AKC; some are not. The UKC offers conformation

> **Doggerel**
> **Conformation** refers to a dog's form, essentially his size and shape, or how he is conformed. At a conformation show (sometimes called a "breed" show), dogs are judged according to how closely they conform to the breed standard.

shows, obedience trials, agility trials, coonhound field trials, water races, night hunts and bench (conformation) shows, hunting tests for the retrieving breeds, beagle hunts and bench shows, and other events.

The American Rare Breed Association (ARBA) registers some 160 breeds that are relatively rare in the United States. ARBA offers conformation shows and classifies breeds into various groups, including Companion, Herding, Hounds, Spitz and Primitive, Sporting, Terrier, and Working.

BowWOW

Several registries, including the AKC and the UKC, now have DNA programs in place that enable them to verify a puppy's parentage. The rules and requirements change periodically as the programs develop. For current information, contact the AKC or the UKC, or visit their websites (see Appendix C).

As a puppy buyer, you need to be aware that registration alone does not indicate the quality or health of a dog or puppy, or even in some cases that it is the purebred it is supposed to be (see Chapter 3). The registries rely on the honesty and knowledge of breeders. Unfortunately, as in all walks of life, there are some shady and incompetent people producing dogs who shouldn't be. For now, understand that it's up to you to know what to ask and how to verify what you are told. We'll get to that in detail in Chapter 5.

Some puppies represented as purebred are not. Responsible, ethical breeders, of course, don't play this game. But all too many pups from pet stores, backyard breeders, and puppy mills are mixed-breeds represented as purebreds. The AKC will investigate complaints and may revoke registration if the puppies or adult dogs don't look like the breed they're supposed to be. If the parentage of a puppy is suspect, the AKC can require a DNA test.

Small, Medium, or Large?

When it comes to dogs, size does make a difference. Most big dogs don't belong in an apartment, or with people who can't manage them physically. Of course, energy and temperament also enter into the picture, but think carefully about the adult size before you get the puppy. One of the saddest things I remember seeing was a sign on the shelter cage of a sweet, normal-size (meaning enormous!) one-year-old St. Bernard. The sign stated the reason his owners gave him up: "He growed too big."

Size can have practical implications. If you travel with your dog, keep in mind that a bigger dog will need more room in the car. If you take his crate along, it will be bigger and heavier to move in and out of the car, motel rooms, or your relatives' homes (if they let you in!). For many people, the extra effort to own a large or even giant breed is worth it, but be honest with yourself and fair to the dog before you make the commitment.

A dog's size also affects the cost of maintaining him properly. A big dog's food bill will be higher. If you need to board him, that will cost more. He'll need a bigger crate, bigger bed, bigger toys—all more expensive than smaller ones. He'll also need larger doses of heartworm and flea preventative and other medications. Be sure you can afford a big dog before you get one.

Tiny, fragile dogs don't belong in homes with rambunctious kids. Your current pets may also be a factor in deciding whether to get a small dog. If you have a big, rowdy dog or two, or a dog with high prey drive, be sure that you and everyone in your family are committed to keeping a small dog safe before you bring one home.

More Hair or Less?

There's nothing prettier than a well-coifed dog with a beautiful coat, and nothing cuter than a terrier with his rough coat and spiffy whiskers. But dogs with impressive coats don't look that way by accident. Poodles, terriers, and some others may need professional grooming to keep their coats in good shape.

Dogs with longer coats usually need more grooming, especially if they spend time where they can pick up burrs and other bits of plant matter in their coats. Matting can be a problem, especially with silky coats that tangle easily. Some dogs need specialized grooming. If you choose a dog with a high-maintenance coat, be sure you understand and are committed to proper coat care. Many breeds, both long-haired and short-haired, shed. If you don't like to groom and vacuum, and can't stand dog hair on your clothes and your furniture, you'll probably do better with a dog that sheds less.

(Photo by Close Encounters of the Furry Kind)

Consider how much time you can devote to grooming before you pick a dog with lots of hair, like this Afghan Hound.

Shedding and brushing aren't the only considerations when it comes to coats. Some breeds have oily coats designed to protect the dog when he's working in wet conditions. Oily outer coats can develop a distinctly doggy aroma, especially if the dog gets wet. If you choose a breed with an oily coat, you'll probably want to bathe the dog more often (unless you're showing the dog, in which case you need to preserve the correct texture).

Jogger or Couch Potato?

Your activity level dictates to a certain degree what type of dog will best suit you. If you're an armchair athlete who wants a canine lap-warmer, you need a smallish dog that's content with minimal exercise. If you jog and want a canine partner, you need to choose a dog with enough energy and size to keep up. If the dog has to sit home while you go off to meetings, sports events, lessons, and jobs, you certainly don't need a high-energy, active breed. In fact, maybe you don't need a dog at all.

High-energy dogs require lots of exercise and training. For some breeds that means more than an hour every single day of hard exercise—running, playing fetch games, long walks, and so forth. Such dogs also require obedience training so that you can control the energy when you need to do so. Many of the dogs from the herding, sporting, and working groups fall into this category. The need for exercise applies particularly to young dogs, but some individuals retain their high energy well into adulthood. I live with a 10-year-old Australian Shepherd named Rowdy, who still lives up to his name! A high-energy dog who doesn't get the exercise he needs is not a pleasant companion or

Chew on This

Herding, Sporting, Hound, and Working breeds have energy and stamina to spend long days in the work for which they were developed. Most dogs from these groups need owners who are committed to giving their dogs an hour or two of exercise every single day.

housemate, and is likely to develop behavioral problems out of boredom and frustration.

If you have the time to spend with your dog, there are plenty of activities for the two of you to pursue. Hiking, jogging, backpacking, and playing long games of "fetch the tennis ball" are fun. If you and your dog enjoy training, you might consider obedience or agility competition or tracking (see Chapters 22 and 23 for more on activities). You might also be interested in activities that test your dog's instinct for whatever his breed was developed to do. Training for and participating in herding, lure coursing, earthdog events, sporting tests and trials, and other sports will create a wonderful bond between you and your dog, and help channel all that energy into having fun.

Social Butterfly or One-Man Dog?

One of the best reasons to choose a purebred dog is that you have a pretty good idea what to expect in terms of the dog's temperament. Let's face it—temperament (what people sometimes call "disposition") is essential in our day-to-day life with a companion. That's another good reason to buy from a responsible breeder who considers temperament to be as important as physical health. Responsible breeders don't knowingly breed dogs with poor temperaments, and they pay attention to variations within their litters. A good breeder will want you to have a dog whose personality meshes with yours.

It's important to remember, though, that each individual dog is exactly that—an individual. Golden Retrievers are not supposed to be quarrelsome or show hostility toward other dogs or people under normal circumstances, but I've seen the occasional Golden Retriever attack another dog. The Australian Shepherd is supposed to be "reserved in initial meetings," but I know a few who are regular social butterflies.

If you're drawn to breeds that tend to be one-person or one-family dogs, be sure you understand what that means for day-to-day living in your circumstances. If you have lots of people, particularly children, in and out of your home, a standoffish, protective dog may not be your best choice for a pet.

Obedient Dog or Independent Thinker?

A lot of people think they want an intelligent dog. If that's what you think, please be sure you understand a few things about canine intelligence. First, smart dogs are not necessarily obedient dogs. They're not necessarily disobedient, either. In short, there's just no correlation between intelligence and *biddability*.

Some breeds are easy to train, and some are difficult. In general, breeds that were designed to work independently of their handlers tend to need more patient and persistent training, while breeds developed to work closely with people tend to be easier to train.

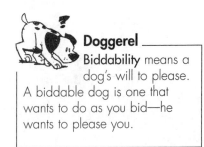

Doggerel
Biddability means a dog's will to please. A biddable dog is one that wants to do as you bid—he wants to please you.

Terriers, hounds, and the northern breeds are notoriously difficult to train because they're smart and independent. Sporting and herding breeds tend to be easier to train, although their high energy also makes them a handful, especially while they're young. Toys and Nonsporting breeds vary a lot in trainability.

If you don't have the time and patience to train a puppy, consider an older dog from a rescue program or breeder (see Chapter 5). If you do have time for a puppy but not a lot of dog-training experience, then select a breed that is generally more easily trained.

A Puppy or an Adult?

If you're like most people, when you think of getting a new dog, you think first of puppies. And why not? What's cuter or sweeter or funnier than a little puppy? Before you rule out an older dog, though, be sure you understand that there's more to a puppy than a cute face and puppy antics.

Puppies are babies, and they need a lot of attention. They have accidents on carpets. They have lots of energy, but not always at convenient times. They don't have much sense. The cute baby stage lasts only a few weeks, and then puppies turn into lanky adolescents—canine teenagers. Most stay that way for many months. A young dog will need you to devote lots of time to training so that he can develop into a well-adjusted, well-mannered adult.

If you've never had a dog before, a puppy may not be your best choice. If you're really devoted to learning as much as you can about training and caring for your puppy, if you have a responsible breeder who will guide you, and if you have a sense of humor even through late nights and messy cleanups, then maybe you are a puppy person. Ask your friends who have puppies or have had one recently and try to get a realistic view of what puppies, particularly puppies of your chosen breed, are like to raise. If it doesn't sound all that appealing, then do yourself and a dog a favor and adopt or buy an adult. You can always get a periodic puppy fix by visiting friends with puppies or by volunteering at your local shelter.

Aside from the chaos a puppy can bring into your life, consider some other factors as well. You can't predict exactly how a baby puppy will mature. An experienced breeder with a good eye can make an educated prediction, but lots of things can affect the outcome as a puppy grows. Starting with a puppy does give you more influence on its development, since you're in charge of socialization, training, nutrition, exercise, and everything else in his young life. The adult dog, like the adult person, is definitely the product of both its genes and its environment. In fact, that's why it's so important that you be committed to raising a puppy properly before buying one.

When you choose an adult dog, you pretty much get what you see. You can evaluate his basic temperament. You know how big he is. You can see his coat and have an idea of how much he sheds. If you adopt from a rescue or shelter, you may be able to arrange to have him checked and possibly x-rayed before you adopt him. If you get him from a responsible breeder, you may also get documentation of any health clearances he's had as well as his health history.

Why would an adult be available from a responsible breeder? Sometimes a show prospect just doesn't turn out to have what it takes for a successful competition career. Sometimes a breeder decides that a retired show or breeding dog would be happier as a pampered pet in a one- or two-dog family rather than as one of several dogs in the breeder's home. Sometimes a dog comes back to the breeder because of a problem in its home—perhaps divorce, illness, or death. Such a dog may be a good choice if the dog's history is important to you, but you don't think you're really a puppy person. (See Chapters 5, 6, and 7 for more on finding an adult dog.)

Pink Collar or Blue?

You may be wondering which makes a better pet, a male or female. A lot of people think that females (properly called *bitches*) make better pets than males (or *dogs*). Although there are some differences between the sexes—*vive la différence!*—the personality of the individual animal matters more than its sex. That is especially true of altered (spayed or castrated) dogs, and honestly, most dogs should be altered (see Chapters 9 and 17).

If you've decided on a purebred, ask breeders and owners of the breed about their experiences with males and females. In some breeds, males tend to be scrappier and females sweeter. In other breeds, males tend to be more affectionate and females more independent. But again, individual personality is far more important than gender.

The Least You Need to Know

- Think carefully about what you want from your relationship with your dog.

- Purebred dogs from responsible breeders offer a predictable range of traits within each breed.

- Mixed-breeds also make great pets, but it's more difficult to predict the size and temperament of the adult from the puppy.

- Size, energy level, grooming needs, and intelligence are all important factors in choosing the best dog for *you*.

- Males and females both make great companions, especially when neutered or spayed.

Chapter 3

Sniffing Along the Paper Trail

In This Chapter

- 🏠 Understanding registration
- 🏠 Reading a pedigree
- 🏠 Naming your puppy
- 🏠 Hunting for healthy dogs

We often hear about dogs with "papers." But what *are* papers? It's true that all sorts of paperwork accompanies a truly well-bred dog, but the simple claim that a dog "has papers" is meaningless in terms of the dog's quality. What most people probably mean when they say a dog has papers is that the dog has registration papers. Some people also mean that the dog has a *pedigree*, which is simply a family tree showing the dog's ancestors.

What Registration Papers Mean— and Don't Mean

The AKC is the first to say that AKC registration does not guarantee the quality of a puppy. Responsible breeders are honest about the parentage of their puppies and keen to keep their pedigrees accurate. But many puppies from puppy mills and careless puppy producers are also registered with the AKC and other registries. Such puppy producers use registration as a way to get more money for their puppies. In some cases, they don't know (and don't really care) who the sire is. From the looks of some of the dogs bred in these places, many are not even purebred. Why would you pay for a purebred puppy who will grow into a dog that doesn't look like the breed it's supposed to be—because it isn't?

Remember, too, that registration is no guarantee that a puppy will be a good representative of its breed in terms of appearance, behavior, or temperament, even if it is purebred. Registration doesn't tell you that the puppy's parents were checked for hereditary problems, or that the puppy was handled properly during the important developmental periods. Registration is a starting point and an entrée into the world of canine competition. You still need to check out the breeder as well as her dogs and their quality, health, and suitability for your situation.

What's a Pedigree, Anyway?

If you're interested in purchasing a purebred puppy, the breeder should provide the puppy's *pedigree* before you make a commitment. I've heard of buyers being told that they can have the pedigree when they buy the pup. That's completely backwards! The pedigree is one of the things a serious breeder uses to plan a litter. An educated buyer looks at the pedigree when deciding whether to buy a puppy, and a responsible breeder will be proud to show you the pedigree and explain it to you. She should know a lot about the dogs in that pedigree—in fact, she should know most of it by heart. If the breeder doesn't seem to know much about the pedigree, beware.

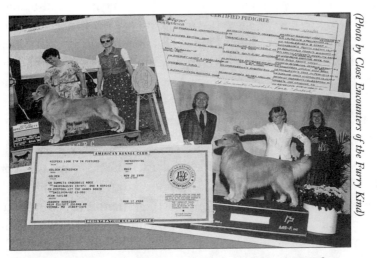

(Photo by Close Encounters of the Furry Kind)

Lots of paperwork accompanies a responsibly bred purebred dog—from left to right we have a registration certificate, pedigree, and photos of a puppy's parents.

Okay, so exactly what is this pedigree thing? It's quite simple—it's a family tree. Normally, a breeder will provide a pedigree showing four or five generations. The pedigree begins on the left with the individual dog or litter and moves one column to the right with each earlier generation, giving the registered names of the ancestors. Titles earned are shown on most pedigrees, and very often the pedigree will give additional information, such as the dogs' colors, Orthopedic Foundation for Animals (OFA) ratings, and special honors.

So why bother with a pedigree if you're looking for a pet, not a show or breeding dog? For several reasons. First, the pedigree gives you an indication of whether the breeder is a serious, responsible breeder of quality dogs, or just a puppy producer trying to make a buck. How can you, a novice in the world of canine pedigrees, tell the difference? First, look at the names of the dogs. Serious breeders have kennel names that appear in their dogs' names. In most breeds, you'll see names like "CH. Foxpacks Here's Lookin at You" or "Fallen Tree Cinderella CD, CGC," where Foxpack and Fallen Tree denote the respective kennels. You shouldn't see names like "Suzi Q. Jones" or "Big Tuff Guy." There are some exceptions, particularly in breeds that have only recently moved from strictly working status into the realm of show breeders. But overall, expect to see "fancy" registered names, and usually more than one dog with the same kennel name—maybe Foxpack's Here's Lookin at You is a son of Foxpack's Look the Other Way.

Next, look for initials before and after the dogs' names. These are abbreviations for titles earned in competition. For example, in "CH. Foxpack's Here's Lookin at You," the CH. denotes "conformation champion." If you don't know what the initials mean, ask the breeder. (If she doesn't know, walk away!) At least half the dogs in the first two generations (the puppies' parents and grandparents) should have titles or be on their way to titles. Most serious breeders are active in competition. In some breeds, it is very difficult to finish a championship. Still, some of the dogs in the pedigree should have performance titles (obedience, agility, herding, hunting, and so on—see Chapter 23) and points toward the champion title.

But hold on, you say. You just want a nice, healthy, reasonably well-behaved pet dog. Who cares about show titles or the breeder's goals? Well, to be honest, *you* should. Even champion parents and grandparents will produce some puppies that just don't have what it takes to compete successfully. Most of the time, whatever it is that keeps such a pup out of the game for breeders and competitors is insignificant for that pup's future as a wonderful companion. You may luck out and get a dandy puppy from a badly bred litter. But the odds are not in your favor. Looks, health, temperament, intelligence, and beauty are all influenced by a puppy's genetic background. Do yourself a favor—either buy a well-bred pup or adopt a dog in need from a shelter or rescue organization. Don't support bad breeding—you'll help no one if you do, least of all yourself or your dog.

Grrrrowls

"Champion bloodlines" are often claimed by puppy mills and other people who produce puppies like livestock to make a buck. The claim is usually based on some champions several generations back. Serious breeders breed litters whose pedigrees show many titled dogs among the parents and grandparents, as well as further back.

Naming Your Puppy

Registered dogs have two names. One is the *registered name* that appears on the dog's registration papers. The registered name is something like a person's legal name. The other is the dog's *call name*, the name that you call him. As the buyer, you will always have your choice of call name for your dog. Some breeders will also let you choose the registered name or at least participate in picking the name, whereas other breeders select all their puppies' registered names. The AKC registered name is limited to 28 letters and spaces, so consider that when choosing a name.

So how do you name a dog? Well, certain conventions apply when choosing a registered name. First, the breeder's kennel name usually appears as either the first word of the name or at the end of the name. The kennel name is rather like a signature or brand name, as it tells those in the know where that dog came from. Sometimes the breeder has a theme for names in a litter. For instance, I had a litter in August and the puppies were given "summer" names— Perennial Hot Sultry Summer, Perennial Hot August Night, Perennial Summer Surprise, Perennial Summer Skies. (Perennial is my kennel name.) Some breeders alphabetize their litters, so all the pups in the first litter have names beginning with A, the second litter with B, and so forth.

If the breeder doesn't have any specific guidelines, then you may want to find a name that reflects your aspirations for the dog (one of my agility pups is named Perennial In Flight), an event (my Lab was born on our anniversary, so her name is Anniversary Waltz), the dog's color (I'd like to name a blue merle Busy Being Blue), or something else with meaning for you. Play with the name for a few days before you send in the registration application. Sometimes a name that sounds great at first doesn't wear well. If you're short on inspiration, consider book, song, and movie titles; geographical places; or historical figures. Finally, remember that this is your friend you're naming. Don't give your dog an insulting or demeaning name, or one that suggests that the dog is dangerous. That would reflect badly on you, not your dog.

Your dog's call name will be up to you, although your breeder may make suggestions. Often the call name is linked to the registered name. For instance, the call names for the summer pups I mentioned are, in the same order, Summer, Gus, Susi, and Skye. Sometimes the call name just comes to you from watching the puppy—my Ted looked like a little teddy bear when he was a puppy, Ben was the biggest pup in the litter (Big Ben), and Mac just looked like a Mac!

Keep in mind that you'll be using the call name a lot, so make it something that's easy to say. Usually, names of one or two syllables work best—it's a lot easier to say "Jack, come!" than to spit out "Alphonsus, come!" Make the sound of the name unique in your household. If you have a dog named Mickey, don't name the puppy Nicky. And if your husband's name is Roger, don't name the puppy Raja! (When I married my husband, Roger, I did have a dog named Raja—which made for some very confused looks from people at times.)

Registering Your Puppy

When you buy a purebred puppy, you'll receive a registration application. You'll need to complete the form, sign it, and make sure it's signed by the breeder or breeders. Spell your puppy's new name exactly as you want it spelled on his registration certificate, because once the name is registered, it can't be changed unless the registrar made a mistake. Send the form to the registry with the appropriate payment, and you will receive your dog's registration certificate.

Your breeder can assign your puppy *full* or *limited* registration through the AKC. Limited registration is used for any puppy that the breeder sells with the understanding that it may not be used for breeding. A dog on limited registration is not eligible to compete in conformation shows, but may compete in all other areas (obedience, tracking, field trials, hunting tests, herding, lure coursing, agility, and earthdog—see Chapter 23). If you do breed a dog with limited registration, its offspring cannot be registered with the AKC. Some other registries have forms of registration similar to the AKC's limited registration. The limited registration option allows breeders to protect their breeding programs and their puppies, and only the breeder can later change a dog's registration from limited to full.

Long before you begin to think about naming and registering your puppy, though, you need to know what goes into making him a fine, healthy representative of his breed. Let's look at the basics of canine genetics, and then the paperwork used to document health screening in dogs.

Health Runs in Families

Heredity determines the shape of your dog's head, his color, the length and texture of his coat, his instincts, his basic temperament and behavioral tendencies, his size, and his sex. Heredity also determines whether or not he has any of a large assortment of physical and mental disorders that can be passed from parent to offspring. Some disorders are linked to specific breeds or even families within breeds, while others are widespread across breeds and mixed-breeds. Some inherited disorders are merely cosmetic—perhaps the ears stand upright when they should tip over, or the coat is fluffy when it should be smooth. Other disorders have serious negative effects on the length or quality of the dog's life and his ability to function around people and other animals. Some inherited disorders can be treated effectively. Others cannot.

We must realize that things can go wrong when dealing with nature and that problems can appear that we never suspected in a bloodline. But we can hedge our bets. Responsible breeders screen their breeding animals for inherited disorders to increase the chances that all puppies they produce will be healthy.

All breeds have one or more potential problems, as do all mixed-breeds. That doesn't mean that there are no healthy dogs or families of dogs within each breed. It does mean that the potential for problems exists, just as people have the potential to inherit defects from their parents and grandparents.

The impact of an inherited disorder on a dog's life—and the life of his human caretaker—varies. Some disorders are barely noticeable in a pet, although they should eliminate a dog from consideration for breeding. Among these are one or two missing teeth or a nonstandard color for the breed. Other problems are easily repaired with surgery, but again should eliminate the dog from consideration for breeding. These include hernias and monorchidism (a missing testicle). Other disorders are more serious. Some of these require surgical intervention. Some cause the dog considerable pain and may or may not be successfully treated. Some cause permanent disabilities.

Chew on This

Screening for inherited diseases is expensive, and breeders who screen their breeding animals charge more for puppies than those who don't screen. If you prefer not to pay the price of a carefully bred pup, and if you're willing to accept the risks of owning a dog whose parents were not screened, consider adopting a dog from a rescue organization or a shelter. Please don't support irresponsible breeding by buying poorly bred puppies.

The prevalence of specific inherited disorders varies from breed to breed, so do your homework. Learn as much as you can about your breed or breeds of choice so that you know the right questions to ask. Up-to-date information about genetic disorders inherent in your breed is available from the national breed club. A list of breed clubs is available from the AKC, UKC, Canadian KC, and other registries (see Appendix D).

(Photo by Close Encounters of the Furry Kind)

Like father, like son—these are German Shorthaired Pointers.

Why do dogs have inherited disorders? Partly because that is the nature of living things. Genetic disorders occur in all animals, including ourselves. However, we have to remember that dog breeds are founded on limited numbers of individuals, and even if the population of a breed has expanded to the thousands or even millions, the fact remains that all those individuals are related if we go back far enough into their pedigrees. Just as some inherited diseases are more prevalent among some groups of people, some inherited diseases are more prevalent within certain breeds of dogs. A responsible buyer learns about the problems in the breed she chooses and buys only from breeders who strive to produce healthy, sound pups.

Documents That Vouch for Health Screening

Not so long ago, the only way for a breeder to know what genes—good and bad—her dogs carried was to breed the dogs and watch the offspring. Now science has expanded the tools available to the responsible dog breeder. As more knowledge is gained, breeders will have better and better tools at their disposal to eliminate or control many serious inherited disorders from their dogs.

Whether we want to reduce the occurrence of a problem trait, or increase the occurrence of a desirable trait, we need to know its *mode of inheritance*—that is, how the trait is inherited. We also need to know how to identify the trait as early as possible in puppies. Sometimes that can be done just by looking at the puppy—if we're concerned about color or markings, we can see those very early in the puppies of most breeds. Your dog's underlying genetic makeup is his *genotype*. The traits that we can physically see make up the dog's *phenotype*. Phenotype usually reflects a combination of genes and environmental factors that affect development. For instance, your dog's potential adult size is determined by his genes. But his adult size is also affected to some extent by the quality of food you give your dog, his general health during his growth phase, and sometimes other environmental factors.

The modes of inheritance have not yet been determined for many traits thought to be inherited. Interestingly, some traits that appear in more than one breed are not always inherited in the same way in the different breeds, and the traits sometimes behave differently from one breed to another. Finally, although many problems occur in multiple breeds, some occur only in a handful of breeds, and some breeds simply never inherit certain disorders.

> **Doggerel**
> The **mode of inheritance** is the way in which a trait is passed from parent to offspring. If a trait is expressed, it occurs in the individual. (A person with blue eyes expresses the gene for blue eyes.) **Genotype** is an individual's genetic makeup, while **phenotype** is the individual's expressed traits, the ones we can experience with our senses.

New tests to detect problems are being developed every day, and the number of inherited disorders for which breeders can have their dogs screened is rapidly increasing. Until recently, it has been difficult (if not impossible) to eliminate diseases that are passed on by dogs who do not have the symptoms of the diseases. Now, however, DNA can be used to determine not only if a dog has some disorders, but also if he carries the genes for those disorders. As scientists learn more and expand the number of tests available, breeders will be able to screen all breeding animals and prevent transmission of many more inherited disorders.

Not all inherited disorders can be detected or prevented through testing, but you greatly increase your chances of getting a healthy pet if you insist on seeing the parents' screening test certificates. Let's look at the common inherited disorders for which tests are now available.

Hip Dysplasia

Dogs are prone to a number of inherited defects of the skeletal system. The most prevalent of them is *canine hip dysplasia* (*CHD*), a malformation of the hip joint. CHD cannot be detected by watching the dog move, so don't be misled by anyone who claims she doesn't

> **Chew on This**
>
> Mixed-breed dogs are not necessarily healthier than carefully bred purebreds. A mixed-breed dog can, in fact, inherit the potential for all the diseases that occur in all the breeds in his ancestry. Hip dysplasia, epilepsy, allergies, and other disorders that occur in many breeds are not uncommon in mixed-breed dogs.

need to x-ray her dogs since she can see that they're okay. Not all breeds are prone to CHD, but many are. If you've chosen a breed in which CHD occurs, be sure to see certification showing that the parents are free of hip dysplasia. Preferably, the puppy's grandparents and great-grandparents will also be certified free of CHD, as well as siblings in each generation and prior offspring if they have any. In other words, you want to see as many relatives as possible certified free of CHD.

The OFA rates hip structure by evaluating x-rays. The dog must be at least 24 months old when x-rayed in order to be certified, although preliminary evaluations can be made earlier. Dogs that are considered free of CHD are rated Excellent, Good, or Fair. Dysplasia is also ranked at three levels of severity.

The Pennsylvania Hip Improvement Program (PennHIP) uses a different method, also requiring x-rays, and can evaluate puppies as young as four months. PennHIP provides two numbers. First, they provide a distraction index for each hip that indicates the laxity, or looseness, of the hip joint. Laxity is considered an accurate predictor of degenerative joint disease. Second, PennHIP provides a percentile score showing where an individual dog ranks in relation to all members of his breed that have been evaluated by PennHIP. The percentile ranking may change as more dogs are tested, but the laxity index will not.

Some breeders now use PennHIP, but most use OFA. A few use both systems. Several other programs are also available, a few of them limited to single breeds, so once again, you need to do some research to determine what's appropriate for your chosen breed.

Whatever system is used, your breeder should show you an original certificate or copies of original certificates verifying that the parents are free of CHD. You can also use your potential puppy's pedigree (which the breeder should be happy to provide prior to selling you a pup) to verify OFA or PennHIP certification (see Appendix D).

Other Orthopedic Problems

Elbow dysplasia refers to inherited elbow disease, consisting of one or more problems in the elbow joint. Usually, a dog with elbow dysplasia in one elbow has it in both. Symptoms of elbow dysplasia include lameness, faulty movement as the dog tries to compensate for elbow pain by turning his front toes inward, and limited range of motion in the elbow. Symptoms usually appear in puppyhood; the exact age depends on the individual's particular problems as well as environmental influences, such as weight and exercise. In breeds that are prone to elbow dysplasia, breeding animals should be x-rayed and found free of elbow dysplasia before being bred.

A cushion of cartilage protects the ends of a dog's long leg bones. Although it protects the bone, the cartilage itself can be injured, particularly in a large, active, young dog. If the cartilage in the joint cracks and tears, the dog has *osteochondrosis* (*OC*). If bits of cartilage break free and float in and around the joint, the dog has *osteochondrosis dissecans* (*OCD*). OCD usually affects the shoulder or elbow, but may also occur in the hip or knee, causing inflammation of the joint (arthritis), lameness, and swelling of the joints (especially after exercise). OCD is usually quite painful. Symptoms usually appear when the dog is between four months and one year old. Research suggests that a dog must inherit a predisposition for OCD, which is then brought on by trauma, usually in the course of normal exercise.

As I write this, the OFA is conducting research on OCD, but at present there is no standardized screening test for the disease. If you're considering a breed in which OCD commonly occurs, ask the breeder about the incidence of the disease in your potential puppy's relatives. Your best bet is a pup with no close relatives affected by the disorder.

The *patella*, or kneecap, is located in the *stifle* joint in the dog's hind leg. If the patella luxates, it slips out of its normal position and locks the leg straight, which is painful and potentially crippling. *Patellar luxation* is a problem in many toy breeds as well as some larger breeds. A veterinarian can check for patellar luxation even in young puppies. Dogs with luxating patellas should never be used for breeding. If you're considering a breed prone to this disorder, ask to see either OFA certification or a letter from a veterinarian certifying that the parents have normal patellas. If possible, ask that your puppy be examined by a vet before you bring him home, or retain the option of returning him for a full refund within a certain time if your own vet finds his patellas to be abnormal during his first puppy exam.

Other orthopedic problems occur in some breeds and affect different parts of the skeletal system, including the spine and various joints. Learn about your breed, and if it is prone to any of these disorders, insist on seeing the appropriate documentation before you buy your puppy.

Inherited Eye Disease

Inherited eye disorders affect many breeds. If eye diseases are a problem in your chosen breed, be sure to see documentation of an eye examination within the previous year. Ask about the grandparents of the puppy as well; hopefully, there is evidence that they also passed yearly eye examinations until at least six or seven years of age. In some breeds, the puppies, too, should have their eyes examined at a specific age, so find out whether that is recommended for your breed. All eye examinations should be done by an American College of Veterinary Ophthalmologists (ACVO) board-certified specialist. General practice vets don't have the special training or the equipment necessary to administer a thorough eye examination.

The Canine Eye Registry Foundation (CERF) maintains a registry of purebred dogs that have been examined by ACVO Diplomats (members) and found to be free of major inherited eye disease. CERF also issues certificates to those owners who submit the results of the ophthalmologist's exam. However, many breeders prefer to see the actual examination form rather than a CERF certificate, because the ophthalmologist may note certain conditions that would not prevent a dog from getting a certificate, but which are of concern to careful breeders. In any case, you should see originals or copies of either a CERF certificate or a certification of eye examination by a veterinary ophthalmologist.

Testing for Other Inherited Disorders

So is that it? Watch out for orthopedic and eye problems and you're home free? Well, no, not quite. Some breeds are prone to inherited heart defects; blood disorders; kidney, liver, and lung disorders; diabetes; and deafness. The incidence of cancer is very high in some breeds. Idiopathic (inherited) epilepsy occurs in a number of breeds. A few breeds even have their very own inherited disorders that occur in no other breeds.

Unfortunately, no tests have been developed yet for some of these problems. Your best approach is to read as much as you can about the breed, find a breeder you trust (see Chapter 5), and ask her what she's doing to control the problem in her puppies. Ask for evidence of testing where that is possible, and find out as much as you can about relatives of the pup you're considering.

Remember, though, that there *are* healthy dogs out there! It's well worth the extra time and effort it takes to find a breeder who does everything humanly possibly to produce healthy pups from healthy parents. More about that will be covered in Chapter 5. First, though, Chapter 4 looks at the social and legal side of dog ownership.

The Least You Need to Know

- A registered dog is not necessarily a high-quality dog.

- Pedigrees tell you a lot about dogs and their breeders.

- Your dog's name should be special, honorable, and meaningful for you.

- Just like people, dogs inherit good and bad genes from their ancestors.

- Health screening greatly increases the chances that you'll get a healthy pup.

Chapter 4

The Human Side of Dog Ownership

In This Chapter

- 🏠 Being a good neighbor
- 🏠 Protecting your rights as a dog owner
- 🏠 Keeping dogs safe at home
- 🏠 Understanding dog-ownership laws

Half the fun of having a dog is doing things together. Your dog will enjoy a daily walk or two, visits to friends, and errands in the car in cool weather (and in warm weather if you don't have to leave him in the car—see Chapter 21). Sadly, dogs are no longer welcome in all too many public places because a few people have behaved as if the rules of common courtesy don't apply to them. But if the rest of us behave ourselves, we can keep the privileges we still enjoy as dog owners and maybe even regain some of those we've lost. We have four important tools to help us be responsible dog owners—a leash, a fence, training, and pooper scooper bags.

(Photo by Close Encounters of the Furry Kind)

Half the fun of having a dog is doing things together.

Your Dog and Your Community

Most people like dogs, or at least tolerate them. So why are dogs so often a source of friction among neighbors? Probably because too many dog owners allow their dogs to disturb the neighbors in various ways. Some don't know that their dogs are causing problems. (A few don't seem to care.) But it's our responsibility to know, and to prevent our dogs from annoying people.

One of the biggest problems caused by neighborhood dogs is continuous or frequent barking. We used to have neighbors who let their three dogs bark from 5:30 in the morning until 10 at night. I have a very high annoyance threshold when it comes to dogs, but let me tell you, that barking made me nuts—especially when I found out that some neighbors thought it was my dogs making all the noise! Most people won't mind an occasional bark to alert you to something or

Chew on This ___ Train your dog so that he behaves calmly and politely in public places as well as at home. People appreciate a well-behaved dog—you'll be amazed at how many of them compliment the two of you.

while your dog is playing. But no one should have to listen to your dog yap yap yapping, and you're responsible for teaching him to be quiet (see Chapter 20).

Bodily waste is another problem caused by dogs with irresponsible owners. Frankly, I don't know anyone who enjoys picking up dog poop, but if you want a dog, cleaning up after him is part of the package. If you don't want to pick up your dog's feces and dispose of it properly, what makes you think anyone else does? It's no wonder that some places have pooper scooper laws that require owners to clean up after their dogs. Even if there is no such law where you live, please be considerate. Carry bags with you on walks, and use them so that other people don't have to deal with your dog's deposits on lawns and sidewalks (see Chapter 21). Don't let your dog urinate in people's gardens or on shrubs, flowers, mail boxes, and lawn decor. Your dog really doesn't need to pee every three feet on his walk, so train him to go only where appropriate.

Dogs can cause neighbors other problems as well. Aside from being at risk himself, if you let your dog run loose he can bother or kill your neighbors' pets, dig in your neighbors' gardens, or frighten or even bite your neighbors or their children (see "Dogs and the Law" later in this chapter).

BowWOW

Protect your rights as a dog owner by respecting your neighbors' rights.

- Don't let your dog raise a ruckus—keep him quiet or take him inside.
- Don't let your dog run around—keep him confined or on a leash whenever he's out of your house.
- Don't let your dog raise a stink—clean up your yard every day or two, and pick up after your dog on walks.

The bottom line is that if you have a dog, you're responsible for his well-being and you're responsible for his actions.

Dogs at Large

A dog running loose is a dog in danger. Dogs running the neighborhood can cause dissension among the neighbors, and the dog is often the one who suffers the consequences. Loose dogs can quickly become a nuisance, especially if they team up with other dogs and form packs. A pack of dogs can be a serious threat to livestock, pets, and even people, especially children. Dogs in packs are like people in mobs—they lose their individual inhibitions and do things they wouldn't normally do, things you might never expect. With or without a pack, a loose dog may be hit by a car, stolen, poisoned, shot, or worse. Your dog isn't a wild creature who needs his freedom. He's a domestic dog, and he needs the safety of home.

Your leash attached to a properly fitted collar on your dog is almost a miracle, it's so simple and effective. It keeps your dog safe from cars, from running away and getting lost, from other animals that aren't so friendly, and even from people who don't like dogs. Your leash also keeps other people's lawns, shrubs, gardens, pets, and children safe from your dog. You may love dogs and welcome their attention, but not everyone feels that way. Many people are afraid of dogs, so even if your pooch wouldn't hurt the flea that bit her, she shouldn't be the one who decides where she goes and whom she greets. Even those of us who do love dogs don't necessarily want *your* dog digging up our zinnias! So take your dog for lots of outings, but take her *on leash*.

Most states and local jurisdictions have laws against letting dogs run loose. But dogs don't stay home just because they're supposed to. They stay home because they have no choice or because nothing has been inviting enough to make them take off—yet. Whenever temptation beckons, most dogs will leave if given half a chance. If you think your dog knows the limits of his yard and will never cross them, you're kidding yourself and risking your dog's life.

Chew on This

If your dog gets lost, you can increase your chances of finding him by following a few simple steps:

- Have your dog wear a name tag, registration tag, and rabies tag attached to his collar so that anyone who finds him can also find you. Collars and tags can get lost, though, so a form of permanent identification (a tattoo or microchip) is a good idea, too.

- *Act fast.* The longer your dog is lost, the less chance you have of finding him.

- Run a lost ad in your local newspaper with a brief description of your dog. Consider running ads in newspapers from neighboring towns as well—you'd be surprised at how far a dog can wander in a short time.

- Call all shelters and veterinarians in your own county and adjacent counties. Some areas have multiple shelters, so call them all. Visit the shelters as often as possible and check for yourself. Shelter staff could overlook your dog among the many they take in. Don't assume they will recognize him by breed, even if his breed is common.

- Make up posters with a color photo of your dog, where and when he was lost, and your telephone number. Post them around the area where he was lost, at grocery stores and convenience stores, near schools, and in other well-traveled spots.

- Children often know more about what's happening at the "street level" in their neighborhoods than adults do. Call neighborhood schools and ask if you can hang your poster somewhere in the school.

The best way to contain most dogs is with a secure fence. Fencing is expensive, but if necessary you can fence just a portion of your yard for the dog. If you're putting in a new fence, make it high enough that your dog can't jump out of it. If you already have a fence, and your dog is able to get out of it, supports angled inward from the fence posts and strung with plain wire (not barbed) or with fence fabric will keep him from jumping or climbing out. You could also try a special harness made to keep the dog from jumping. If your dog is a digger, bury several inches of metal fence fabric or chicken wire underground, or set concrete footers around the edge of the fence. If your dog digs a hole, fill it with rocks or concrete.

Here are some of the common types of conventional fences used for dogs:

- Chain link is relatively expensive, but it's strong, especially if it's secured along the bottom with a tension line. Chain link comes in different heights and tends to hold up well. Most dogs can't get through chain link, although you need to be sure there are no gaps at gates or along the bottom that a puppy or small dog can slip through. One drawback is that kids (and adults) can poke fingers, sticks, and other things through chain link, so if your fence will border a sidewalk or street, you may want to block access with shrubbery or vinyl strips made to slide into the chain link mesh.

- Woven or welded wire farm fence is cheap and will hold large dogs, although smaller dogs can get at least their heads through and in some cases can get out. It comes in different heights and is relatively easy to install.

- Picket fences work well for most dogs, but very small puppies or dogs can sometimes slip their heads between the slats and get stuck. Picket fences are sometimes installed with a gap along the bottom because the rigid fence sections don't match the contours of the ground, so you may need to install wire fence fabric along the bottom to prevent a small dog from going under the fence. As with chain link, pickets are easy to breach with fingers and other objects.

- Privacy fences of wood or vinyl are expensive, block the view, and aren't allowed in some neighborhoods. On the plus side, they're high enough to hold most dogs, and the solid wall keeps your dog out of reach of fingers, sticks, and other dogs' noses.

🏠 Split-rail fences are relatively inexpensive, and they don't block your view. You'll need to fasten fence fabric along the inside of the fence to keep your dog from going between the rails or climbing the rails to get out.

A lot of people seem to be latching on to underground fencing as a relatively cheap, easy way to confine their dogs. An electrical wire attached to a transmitter is buried underground around the edge of the area where you want your dog confined. Your dog wears a collar with a receiver and electrodes that are in contact with his skin. When he approaches the boundary, the collar beeps a warning. If he gets closer, he gets an electric shock. He has to be trained to understand that the beep means a shock is coming and that he can prevent it by backing off.

There are some serious problems with underground electrical fences. If your dog has a high pain threshold or sees something that really motivates him, he'll risk the shock (or forget about it) and cross the wire. Once he's out, he won't want to cross back in because the motivation isn't strong enough to outweigh his fear of the shock.

Another problem is that an underground fence doesn't keep anything from coming into your yard. Your dog is vulnerable to attack by other dogs and teasing or even theft by kids and adults. You also open yourself up to legal and financial liability if someone comes onto your property and is bitten.

A dog charging up to the edge of a hidden fence system can be terrifying for people passing your property. When a dog charges a conventional fence, people know the fence will stop him. If he charges the edge of a hidden fence, a passerby may not know that he's fenced at all and cannot know for sure that the fear of a shock will hold him. This is particularly a problem for anyone walking by with a dog. Believe me, it's heart-stopping to have a dog charge you with no visible barrier in sight, and letting your dog do that is not a nice way to treat your neighbors.

If you must resort to an underground electrical fence, I suggest you keep the perimeter well away from sidewalks or other places where people walk or ride bicycles, and that you allow your dog to be out in the yard only when a responsible member of the family can be there with him.

Dogs and the Law

Four and a half million Americans are bitten by dogs each year. The law is nearly always on the side of the person who's bitten. It used to be that a dog was given "one free bite"—the dog's owner wasn't responsible unless he knew the dog was likely to bite. That's no longer true in many places, and if your dog bites someone, you could face legal and financial penalties even if the victim was trespassing or did something to provoke your dog.

BowWOW

According to the Humane Society of the United States, dogs that are not spayed or neutered are three times more likely to bite than dogs that are spayed or neutered.

About one fifth of total homeowners insurance liability payouts each year in the United States are for dog bites. If you own a dog, make sure that your homeowners or renters insurance policy covers your liability in case your dog bites or otherwise injures someone. Make sure you understand the terms of your policy and the amount of coverage you have.

Grrrrowls

If your dog is aggressive, you need to get professional help. But beware of self-styled dog trainers or behaviorists with no documented qualifications. Ask your veterinarian or obedience instructor for recommendations if you need professional help, and then check the person's educational qualifications, experience, and references from dog owners who have used his services.

Your best defense as a dog owner is prevention. Proper training and socialization will help your dog learn to be a well-adjusted, well-behaved member of his community. Spaying or neutering will also help prevent bites (not to mention unwanted litters of puppies). Seeing to it that your dog gets lots of exercise and attention will also help. Finally, you can hedge your bets by buying only from a responsible breeder who makes temperament a priority in breeding (see Chapter 5), or adopting from a rescue organization or shelter that carefully screens dogs before placing them (see Chapter 7).

Chew on This _____

Here are some simple steps you can take to lower the chance that your dog will bite someone:

- Have your dog altered (spayed or neutered). Altered dogs are less likely to bite.

- Don't let your dog run loose. In most places you are legally and financially liable if your dog bites or causes any damage, whether you're with him or not.

- Keep your dog's rabies vaccination current according to the law where you live.

- Protect legitimate callers from your dog. When you open the front door to someone, be sure your dog is restrained. Don't let your dog harass meter readers and others who have a legal reason to be on your property.

- Don't leave your dog in your yard alone unless you have a secure fence with locked gates. If a young child opens a gate, enters the yard, and is bitten, you are responsible.

- Don't chain or tie your dog. Chaining or tying promotes aggression.

If your dog behaves aggressively, threatens to bite, or does bite, get help immediately from a *qualified* person who is equipped to deal with aggressive behavior (see Chapter 20).

Common Types of Dog Laws

Most jurisdictions have laws affecting dog owners and ownership. Some of these laws make perfect sense, while others are ineffective

and potentially damaging to responsible dog owners and their dogs. Be sure you know your local laws and keep track of proposed laws. If you don't like them, let your voice be heard. Vote. Here are a few of the more common types of laws affecting dog owners.

Breed Bans

Laws banning certain breeds or mixes containing certain breeds have sprung up in recent years. Breed bans are usually passed in the wake of several attacks, or a single especially awful attack, by a dog or dogs of a particular breed. Concern and fear about vicious dogs are legitimate, to be sure. Unfortunately, breed bans don't address the real issue and they create problems of their own.

The real problem behind the bites and full-out attacks that prompt legislation banning specific breeds is not the breeds but the irresponsible owners of individual dogs. Some breeds, granted, are more likely than others to be big, strong, protective, or even aggressive. In the hands of responsible owners who socialize, train, and control them, most members of those breeds are less of a threat to their neighbors than the ill-tempered little "pet" dog that was never socialized or trained and bites the neighbor's child.

Chew on This _____

Officials who are charged with enforcing breed-specific bans are rarely knowledgeable enough about dogs to properly identify breeds. In one study, law enforcement officers and city council members contemplating a ban on "pit bulls" were shown photos of dogs and asked to pick out the Pit Bull Terriers. Among the dogs picked were a Boxer, a Pug, a Bulldog, a Labrador Retriever × Boxer cross, and a terrier mix.

A more effective approach is to hold owners responsible for the behavior of their dogs and to pass laws that put strict controls on ownership of aggressive dogs regardless of size or breed. Enforcement of laws already in place, including leash and confinement laws as well as license laws, would also help.

(Photo by Close Encounters of the Furry Kind)

A leash will keep your puppy safe when away from home, and still allow him to have lots of fun.

Leash Laws

Nearly every jurisdiction in the country has a leash law of some sort. A leash law is one that prohibits dog owners from letting their dogs run loose. In other words, dogs must be confined or leashed.

Why? Shouldn't dogs be able to follow their hearts and noses and live a life of carefree canine abandon? In a word—no! There may have been a time when dogs could run loose and live happy, carefree lives, although I doubt it. We should remember that most dogs lived short lives in the "good old days" and often died young of distemper, rabies, other diseases, infection, injury, and other causes. If they harassed livestock or threatened people, they were shot. Unwanted litters were drowned or otherwise dispatched. We've come a long way in humane care of animals (although there's plenty of room for improvement in today's society).

Leash laws are also meant to protect public health and safety. They prevent dogs from forming packs that can attack livestock, pets, and even people. Leash laws help prevent the spread of some diseases and parasites. Loose dogs in modern society can even present a traffic hazard if drivers try to avoid hitting them on busy streets. Above all, leash laws are in part a way to keep dogs safe.

Licensing

Many areas require dog owners to purchase licenses for their dogs. Revenue from dog licenses often goes to help support local animal shelters, although it usually amounts to only a small portion of the annual funding. A license attached to your dog's collar is one way of increasing the chances that you'll get him back if he gets lost. Licenses are also one way to promote rabies vaccinations, since proof of vaccination is nearly always required for a license.

Number Limits

Many communities place a limit on the number of pets a person can own. But again, such laws don't address the real problem—irresponsible owners. The laws are meant to prevent nuisances, but they don't. One little dog allowed to run loose, potty in the neighbors' yards, leap on the neighbors' kids, threaten or chase people, and otherwise wreak havoc is a nuisance. One dog left in the backyard to bark all night is a nuisance. On the other hand, a responsible person can manage quite a few dogs without letting them be a problem for neighbors at all—and a responsible person knows his or her own limits.

Pet limits are also difficult to enforce, and they encourage otherwise responsible dog owners to break the law. Laws limiting pet ownership solely on the basis of numbers have been challenged successfully in several communities around the country.

The Least You Need to Know

- 🏠 A good dog owner is responsible to his neighbors and community.
- 🏠 Dogs and people benefit when dogs aren't allowed to roam.
- 🏠 Legal and financial liability come with dog ownership.
- 🏠 Some laws pertaining to dogs and dog ownership don't solve the problems they're supposed to address.

Part 2

Where, Oh Where, Can Your Special Dog Be?

Dogs are available all over the place. I'll tell you why it's to your advantage—and your dog's—to deal with a responsible breeder, rescue organization, or shelter, and I'll show you why serious dog people are so down on pet stores, puppy mills, and casual breeders. I'll also talk about prices—when you buy a dog, a low price may not be any bargain at all.

Then we'll see what you need to do to get ready for your new family member, whether you've decided on a puppy or an adult. I'll give you a shopping list and a to-do-in-advance list. I'll explain the conventions of naming dogs (there can be quite a lot in a name!) and suggest some sources of inspiration if you're stumped. Finally, I'll tell you what you need to do to make the big day a smooth-running success, and the start of a long and happy relationship.

Chapter 5

Should You Buy from a Breeder?

In This Chapter

- 🏠 Knowing a responsible breeder when you see one
- 🏠 Getting to know your breeder
- 🏠 Evaluating puppy-buying paperwork
- 🏠 Understanding how dogs are priced
- 🏠 Picking *your* puppy

If you've decided on a purebred puppy and a breed, then your best source is a responsible breeder. In this chapter we'll learn about responsible breeders and what you should expect when looking for a well-bred puppy.

What *Is* a Breeder?

Responsible dog breeders are committed to the health and well-being of their dogs and their breeds. They work hard to produce healthy animals, to improve their dogs with each generation, and to raise their puppies carefully. They try to place each puppy in the right home and to be resources for their puppy buyer throughout the life of the dog.

Responsible breeders are involved in at least one sport or activity that tests their dogs' instincts, abilities, and quality. Some compete in dog shows or obedience or agility trials. Others are active in sports that test their dogs' talents in whatever the breed was developed to do. Noncompetitive activities such as search and rescue, dog-assisted therapy, hunting, or herding take up some breeders' time. Many are involved in dog clubs and in more than one activity.

Responsible breeders study individual animals, their parents and siblings, their previous offspring, and their pedigrees when planning a litter. They provide good prenatal care and a clean, warm, safe environment. They monitor their puppies and bitches closely before, during, and after the birth. They socialize their puppies and give them good veterinary care. They place their puppies carefully and turn away would-be buyers they find unsuitable. Their puppies aren't merchandise. They are little parts of the breeder's heart.

Finding a Responsible Breeder

Most puppies are cute. Darned near irresistible in fact! Please don't be seduced. The little puppy that you bring home with you is going to grow into a dog, and hopefully that dog will be part of your life for a long time. You'll both be happier if he has a good start in life. Buying from a responsible breeder increases your chances of getting a healthy canine companion that has the physique and personality you expect in the breed.

Let's begin your search for a responsible breeder. Start with your local kennel club or breed club. The American Kennel Club (AKC) has a list of clubs on its website at www.akc.org. A visit to a nearby dog show, sporting event, or herding trial will lead you to breeders and give you a chance to see lots of dogs. Just remember that you're the one who's there to gawk and talk—the breeders are there to compete with their dogs. For spectators, a dog show is a show, but to the participants it's competition. Some will be happy to talk while they prepare their dogs, but others may be preoccupied with what they're doing. Don't expect people to stop their preparations to chat with you. Buy a show catalog, cruise the vendor booths, watch the dogs, and enjoy yourself. Don't forget to visit the obedience and agility rings. The names and addresses of the owners and breeders of the dogs are in the show catalog. You can contact them after the show for more information and leads on puppies. For now, watch, enjoy, and learn.

BowWOW

More than 15,000 competitive events with approximately 2,000,000 entries take place each year under AKC rules. Dogs can earn more than 40 AKC titles in three general categories: conformation; obedience, tracking, and agility; and a variety of performance events. Additional competitive programs are offered through other registries.

But wait! You don't want to buy a show dog or a working dog, right? Just a nice pet. Why should you look at show dogs or dogs at sporting trials, or talk to their breeders? Because, as we saw earlier, serious breeders are involved in activities that prove their dogs' abilities. Not every well-bred puppy is a future competition star. In a litter from two champions, most of the pups will probably not be show material. So every litter is likely to have a few pups destined to be pets, not competitors—and that's a fine calling for a dog! The faults that keep them out of competition are usually minor—in fact, most people won't see them even if the breeder points them out. For instance, a puppy might have a splotch of white where he shouldn't, or a kink in his tail. The fact is that the least puppy from a well-bred litter will grow into a much better dog than the best pup from a badly bred litter.

You may be lucky enough to find a well-bred puppy through a newspaper advertisement, but most responsible breeders don't advertise in the newspaper (see Chapter 6 for more on newspaper ads). Magazines like *Dog Fancy* and *Dog World* feature breeder ads, but be careful. Some very appealing ads are placed by puppy mills and other sleazy characters.

Another good way to get a lead on a breeder is by referral. If you see a dog you like, find out where he came from. Ask about health problems and temperament. Ask how helpful and supportive the breeder was after as well as before the sale. If the dog came from a responsible breeder, contact her. Even if she doesn't have a puppy for you, she may be able to refer you to someone.

As you investigate breeders, it may be helpful to have a checklist handy. Here are some things to remember.

A responsible breeder …

- Keeps her puppies until they're seven weeks old or older.

- Answers your questions—and is happy that you're asking them!

- Welcomes you to visit her home or kennel, and meet her dogs.

- Asks about your lifestyle, your family, your experience with dogs, why you want this breed of dog, and lots more.

- Belongs to one or more dog clubs.

- Breeds only dogs that have been tested for hereditary diseases known to occur in the breed, and shows you the certificates.

- Knows about relatives of the sire and dam.

- Acknowledges that inherited problems occur and does not claim that her dogs' bloodlines are free of health problems (there's no such thing as a "clean line").

- Is cautious about selling you a breedable dog until you prove yourself responsible.

- Tells you about the downside of owning her breed.

- 🏠 Handles and socializes her puppies.

- 🏠 Keeps her dogs in a clean environment.

- 🏠 Knows every dog by name.

- 🏠 Knows every puppy as an individual.

- 🏠 Happily refers you to her previous buyers.

- 🏠 Asks for and checks your references.

- 🏠 Does not sell "purebred but unregistered" puppies and does not charge extra for "papers."

- 🏠 Does not pressure you to buy a puppy—in fact, she makes you prove you're worthy of owning one!

Making Contact

Each breeder you contact probably has several dogs to clean up after, groom, train, exercise, play with, and cuddle. She probably has a family, friends, work, and other obligations. For a responsible hobby breeder, breeding is exactly that—a hobby. It's not a business in the conventional sense, and she's not "on call" for you 24/7. You'll be much better received if you call at a reasonable hour, and understand if it's not a good time. Don't expect a breeder to call you back long distance at her expense. She may get a lot of calls, and the cost of returning them adds up. Either ask her to call back collect, or ask when you should call again.

Have questions ready, but hold a conversation, not an interrogation. If you don't understand an answer, ask for an explanation. Remember, she probably thinks, breathes, and talks dog all the time, and she may forget that you aren't fluent in the jargon of the dog world. If you feel uncomfortable with someone, trust your instincts. Thank her for her time, and move on to the next name on your list.

What should you ask? Start with general information. Find out how long the breeder has been in this breed and how many litters she's bred. Ask if she has any other breeds. Responsible breeders have one or two breeds, occasionally three (people with lots of breeds will be covered in Chapter 6). Don't write off a breeder just because she's new if she appears to be well informed and to have good quality dogs. By the same token, don't automatically equate longevity with knowledge. I know people who loudly proclaim their many years in their breeds, but who have accomplished nothing and apparently learned about the same.

(Photo by Close Encounters of the Furry Kind)

A breeder's facilities should be clean and her dogs well cared for.

Ask the breeder what her goals are, both for her breeding program and for the litter you're considering. Does she want to produce winning show dogs or obedience and agility stars? Or maybe she's striving for top-notch field trial or herding dogs, or all-around, versatile dogs that will perform well in several areas. She may not even be interested in competition, but rather in producing fine hunting companions or working dogs. These are all worthy goals. If she doesn't have any goals for her breeding program, or she bred the litter to supplement her income, or because Fluffy is so sweet, run the other way.

Ask about the dogs' bloodlines. Don't worry if the names don't mean much. The point is that serious breeders can rattle off pedigrees from memory, and they know lots about the ancestors of their puppies. What you're checking with this question is not how impressive the dogs are, but how impressive the breeders' knowledge of them is.

Grrrrowls

Unfortunately, not everyone who sells puppies is honest. Be sure to see proof of claims made by any breeder. Responsible breeders are happy to show you registration papers, health clearances, title certificates, pedigrees, and other paperwork on the parents of their litters and on the puppies where appropriate.

Finally, if you feel good so far about this person and her dogs, ask for names, telephone numbers, and e-mail addresses of people who have purchased pups from the breeder. She should be willing to give you lots of them. If she's new to breeding, ask for referrals to people who know her relationship to dogs; her veterinarian, dog club contacts, or training contacts might work.

If all this seems like overkill, remember two things. First, the pup you're going to buy will be with you a long time—a decade or more. You'll be a lot happier with him if he's sound of mind and body, and a good representative of his breed. Second, the breeder should be someone you trust for the life of your dog. She should be someone you can come to with questions and someone who will care when you brag about the dog. She should be a potential friend.

Visiting Breeders

Now, you've zeroed in on one or two breeders. It's time to meet them and their dogs. You should meet as many of your potential puppy's adult relatives as feasible. You should be able to meet the dam of the litter. Puppy care is a big job for doggy moms, so don't expect her to look her best. She may have had her belly hair trimmed to make it easier for the puppies to nurse, and she's probably covered with puppy spit. Pay attention to her temperament, but remember that it is normal for bitches in many breeds to be protective of their pups.

Doggerel

Dam (not "dame") refers to a dog's mother. Sire (not "sir") refers to the father.

If the sire is on the property, you should be able to meet him, too. However, often the sire is not owned by the breeder. Serious breeders use stud dogs owned by other people in order to bring new blood or traits into their kennels. The breeder should be able to show you pictures of him as well as copies of his health clearances, and she should be able to tell you why she chose this particular dog. If the reason is that a friend owns him or he's close at hand and her bitch was in heat, that's a sign that he wasn't chosen carefully. Stud dogs should be selected because they will contribute certain positive characteristics that the breeder wants in her pups.

If you don't like the parents, don't buy the puppy. Puppies are not little copies of their parents, but they do inherit many of their traits and will probably grow up to be a lot like one or the other, or a combination of the two—just like kids do.

Grrrrowls

It's easy to transmit deadly infectious disease and parasites from one kennel to another, even if everything looks clean. Never visit two kennels in a row without going home, showering, and changing clothes, including your shoes.

Look around. The facilities should be clean, and clear of potential dangers. The dogs should look healthy, with clear eyes and trimmed toenails. They should be reasonably clean and well groomed. Fresh water should be available, and the dogs should have room to move around and play. How friendly the dogs are depends on their breed, but they should accept you in the presence of their breeder.

The breeder should know every dog by name. Serious, responsible breeders do what they do because they love dogs. Love should be obvious in their interaction with their dogs. The breeder should know each puppy as an individual. She should know which is the dominant pup of the litter, and which is the sweetie pie. She should know the complainer (every litter has one), the troublemaker, and the comedian. If she hasn't spent enough time with the pups to know this much about them, then the puppies haven't spent enough time with her to be well socialized. Besides, if she cares so little about these wonderful young creatures in her care, how much do you think she'll care that you get the right one?

If you don't feel good about what you see at the breeder's place, move on. You can do better.

The Breeder-Buyer Relationship

Don't think of your breeder as someone you pay and never see again. When you buy a puppy, you should be starting a long-term relationship with the person who arranged for that puppy's conception, who watched him come into the world, who loved and cherished him for his first weeks, and who wants only the best for him all his life.

Questions You Should Expect

You've asked your questions. Now it's time to answer some. If a breeder doesn't ask you anything except for your credit card number, you need to consider whether she's really the breeder for you. A good breeder will ask you lots of questions.

She'll ask you where you live and whether you have a fence. She'll want to know who will care for the pup and where the pup will live, play, and sleep. She'll want to know about your experience with dogs, with this breed, and with other pets. She'll want to know what other pets you have now and why you want this puppy. She'll want to know whether you've ever bred dogs or other animals and whether you intend to breed your puppy. She'll want to know whether you've ever gotten rid of a dog and, if so, why. Be honest with the breeder. Don't tell her what you think she wants to know. The questions are aimed at making sure that the puppy will be well cared for, and that he will fit into your life.

A top-notch breeder wants this pup to grow up to be the dog of your dreams. Selling you a puppy who will have too much energy, too much hair, or not enough sociability for you won't do the breeder any good, and it sure won't do you or the dog any good. The breeder may tell you that her breed, or her specific dogs, aren't for you. Accept that. If several breeders of a particular breed discourage you from getting the breed, consider that they may be right. Be glad that there are breeders who care enough to do all they can to ensure a good match.

Contracts and Guarantees

Responsible breeders sell their puppies on contracts. A good contract is designed to protect the breeder, the buyer, and the puppy. Read the contract carefully, and be sure you understand the terms of the sale. Here are some things to look for in the purchase contract.

A responsible breeder will require you to have your pet spayed or neutered. She doesn't do this so she can hog the market. She does it to protect her puppy and the breed. If you think you want to breed dogs (more on that in Chapter 17), then do it right—buy a high-quality bitch, prove her value through competition or some other activity, educate yourself, and be a responsible breeder. Otherwise, be glad your breeder requires you to alter your pup. That shows her commitment to keeping the breed's future in good hands, and her concern for keeping puppies out of the clutches of puppy mills and backyard breeders. Be wary of any breeder who doesn't care whether her puppies will be used for breeding.

Most contracts will require you to give the breeder a chance to take the puppy back if you can no longer keep him. A responsible breeder will take the puppy back at any time in his life for any reason. Naturally, she'd rather place each puppy in a lifelong home, but if something goes wrong, she won't want the dog to pay the price.

The purchase contract should absolutely guarantee that your puppy is healthy when you take him home. Normally, the first 48 to 72 hours are covered. That's to give you enough time to take your pup to your veterinarian for a checkup, but probably not enough time for your puppy to contract an infectious disease after leaving the breeder.

Most of the literature on how to buy a puppy will tell you that the breeder should offer a guarantee against hereditary disease. I used to insist on that myself, but my experience as a breeder, buyer, and owner has made me change my stance a bit. The fact is that no one can guarantee that a puppy (or any living thing) will never have an inherited health problem. And puppy guarantees don't really guarantee that puppies will be free of problems. They guarantee that the breeder will do something to compensate the buyer if a problem arises.

Many breeders do guarantee their pups against the hereditary diseases common to their breed. But some responsible breeders do not do so, especially if a problem is nearly universal in the breed. Unfortunately, certain problems are widespread in some breeds. For example, some breeds are plagued by heart problems or cancer, others by hip dysplasia or eye disease (see Chapters 3 and 10). Responsible breeders are working hard to reduce the incidence of those problems, but until they do so, every puppy is potentially at risk for the disease. It would be foolhardy for a breeder to offer to replace every puppy in a breed where a problem is virtually universal. For some people, the pleasures of having a particular breed are worth the sorrow of the dog's shorter life expectancy. For others, longevity is more important. Only you know what's best for you. If you choose a breed with a widespread problem, then choose a breeder who does everything humanly possible to prevent the disease in her puppies, but realize that you have to assume some of the risk.

If your breeder does offer a guarantee against inherited disease, the terms of the guarantee should be clearly spelled out in the purchase contract. If the breeder offers to replace your puppy, be sure you understand how the replacement works. Will you have to return the first puppy? Will you have to take the second puppy within a certain period of time? Will the second puppy be closely related to the first puppy? (If so, do you really want another puppy from those parents?) Few breeders offer financial compensation instead of a replacement puppy. If you're not comfortable with the terms of the guarantee, or the terms aren't clear and the breeder won't clarify them *in writing*, look for another breeder.

Some breeders don't use written contracts. Many of them are honest, responsible people who will stand behind their puppies. The trouble is, unless you've been involved with the breed long enough to know the breeder's reputation, you have no way to know who's honest and who isn't. The saying that "a contract is only as good as the people who sign it" is thrown around a lot in the dog world. To some extent, it's true, since going to court to enforce a contract is expensive. But a well-written contract makes the terms of a sale clear, so that both parties understand the same terms and don't have to rely on memory if a problem arises after months or years. Be cautious about buying a puppy without a written purchase contract.

How Much *Is* That Doggy?

So how much is this puppy going to cost? And why do some pure-bred puppies cost more than others? Keep in mind that it's expensive to breed responsibly (see Chapter 17). Responsible breeders start with the best bitch they can afford and breed to quality stud dogs, who command higher stud fees than the pet dog down the road. Screening for hereditary disease is expensive. Proving the dogs in competition is expensive. If the puppies are cheap, chances are slim that their parents have been health screened or proven in any capacity except their ability to reproduce.

Prices for well-bred puppies vary from breed to breed, place to place, and breeder to breeder. Don't use pet store prices as a reference—pet stores usually charge premium prices for poorly bred puppies (see Chapter 6). By the time you've talked to several breeders, you probably have a feel for prices in your breed of choice. In general, a pet puppy from a breed that typically has easy deliveries and larger litters (5 to 10 puppies) will cost in the neighborhood of $500 to $1,000. A pet puppy from a breed that typically requires a C-section delivery, or that generally produces small litters (one to four puppies) may cost $1,000 or more. Some rare breeds command higher prices.

Now catch your breath! Yep, you're right; you can easily find a purebred puppy for $100. And yes, a $100 puppy may be a terrific, healthy pet. We all know people who have them. But the deck is stacked against you. The cost of trying to repair serious health or behavioral problems on a "bargain" puppy can easily run into hundreds or even thousands of dollars. Besides, a sloppy breeder isn't likely to offer you support and sound advice on training, behavior, and other questions you may have along the way. Penny-wise is definitely pound-foolish when buying a puppy. If you can't or prefer not to pay for a well-bred puppy, then why not adopt a dog from a shelter or rescue group, rather than support an irresponsible breeder by buying a poorly bred puppy?

Pick of the Litter

Okay, you've finally found a breeder you like and trust, and you like her dogs. Now you can get down to the business of choosing that special puppy—*your* special puppy. And I'll bet you're going to get all kinds of advice about picking a pup.

Someone's going to tell you to let the puppy choose you. That works sometimes, although sometimes that pushy guy who's the first to greet you is the dominant pup and not the one you need.

Someone is also going to tell you all about "testing" the pups, which is fine as far as it goes. Temperament and aptitude tests do give you some idea of a puppy's personality, but they aren't effective in predicting adult temperament. When you take a puppy home, you take home raw material. The rest is up to you. The dog your puppy grows into will be the product of his genetic makeup and the nurturing you do as he develops.

A good breeder knows a lot more about each puppy after weeks of observing them than you can learn in a visit or two. Let her pick your puppy, or pick two or three from which you can choose. If you've been honest and clear with her about what you want in a dog, she will know which puppy will work for you. She'll also know if none of them will. If that's the case, then accept that the puppy you're looking for isn't there. Better to take your time to find the right one than to buy in haste and regret at leisure.

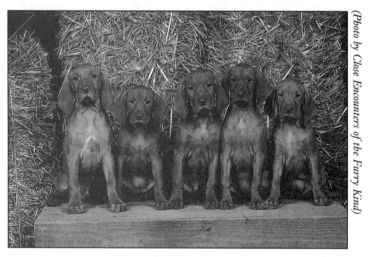

(Photo by Close Encounters of the Furry Kind)

Sometimes it's hard to decide which puppy will suit you best, so find a breeder you trust and let her help you choose your pick of the litter.

If you are choosing among puppies, watch each one as he plays with his littermates, his mother, and by himself. If you can't really tell what's what with puppy personalities, ask your breeder to interpret their behavior for you. If you're looking for a pet, look for a pup that is neither extremely dominant nor extremely submissive, and who seems interested in people. The breed will affect how interested the pups are in strangers (some breeds are more reserved and take longer to warm up), but if the puppy shows no interest in his breeder, whom he knows, he may be very independent. Clap your hands when the pup isn't watching you (not too loudly—the point is not to scare the little guy). He may startle, but should recover quickly, and maybe even come to investigate. Remember, though, that one-time tests like this don't mean much. You may see the pups when they're worn out from hours of play and think the wild child of the litter is quiet when in fact she's pooped. That's why it's important to have a breeder whose evaluation of the puppies you trust.

BowWOW

A healthy 7- to 12-week-old puppy ...

- Is solid and well proportioned.
- Is not excessively thin (ribs should not be visible on a baby puppy.
- Is not potbellied (a thin pup with a potbelly may be infested with roundworms).
- Has soft and glossy fur.
- Is free of fleas.
- Has healthy skin with no red, itchy, or bald spots.
- Has a clean rectal area with no sign of tapeworms (see Chapter 9) and no sign of diarrhea.
- Has bright, clear eyes.
- Has pink gums and healthy breath smelling only of the slightly musky odor of "puppy breath."
- Has a correct bite for his breed and properly aligned jaws.
- Has a damp but clean nose with no sign of discharge.
- Breathes normally with no sneezing, coughing, or wheezing.
- Has clean ears, free of odor, inflammation, dirty-looking buildup, or discharge.
- Moves well with no signs of lameness.
- Is happy and playful—unless he's sleeping!

Buying at a Distance

Perhaps you've done lots of research on the Internet and really like the dogs that a particular breeder has bred. Or maybe you're on some discussion lists and have confidence in a breeder whose posts you've read there. Maybe you belong to a breed club and have seen a particular breeder's dogs in the club's magazine and are drawn to them. Or you might know people, personally or online, who have recommended a specific breeder and her dogs. Many people successfully purchase puppies sight unseen.

If you decide to purchase a pup at a distance, go through all the steps we've already discussed, and a few more. Find other people who have had the breeder choose puppies for them, and ask how good the matches were. If you're straightforward about what you want and don't want, an experienced breeder can usually pick the right puppy—and, of course, will tell you if the right pup just isn't in the litter.

Puppies and dogs are shipped by air all the time, and although we hear hair-raising stories about mishaps, for the most part shipping is safe and the dogs do fine (see Chapter 23).

The Least You Need to Know

- Choose a responsible breeder for a purebred puppy or older dog with good health and a sound temperament.

- Be sure you understand and are comfortable with the terms of a breeder's purchase contract and guarantees.

- You get what you pay for, so don't let the purchase price be the most important factor when choosing a puppy.

- Puppies in a litter vary in personality, so let your breeder help you choose the right one for *you.*

Chapter 6

Where *Not* to Buy a Dog

In This Chapter

- 🏠 Sorting out the good breeders from the bad
- 🏠 Reading advertisements critically
- 🏠 Understanding why pet store puppies may have problems
- 🏠 Knowing what to look for and ask when puppy shopping

Now that we've looked at the good guys of the puppy world, let's look at some of the others. Some of these aren't so much bad guys as misinformed guys. The trouble is, what you don't know when breeding dogs can hurt the dogs and the people who get them as pets.

Backyard Breeders

Backyard breeder (known in the *dog fancy* as a *BYB*) is a term that means different things to different people. Sometimes it refers to someone who breeds several dogs, maybe several breeds, to make some money. She doesn't do any health screening, and she isn't active in any sort of competition or serious activity with her dogs, nor is she affiliated with breed clubs or other organizations.

Doggerel

The **dog fancy** refers to people who are devoted to competing with dogs and to breeding healthy, high-quality animals.

Doggerel

A **backyard breeder (BYB)** is a person who produces puppies, accidentally or on purpose, without health clearances for the parents or pups, and with minimal if any knowledge of the breed standard, genetics, or effective methods of raising puppies.

Sometimes BYB refers to the pet owner who has a sweet pet and breeds only one litter, maybe to make a little money or "to let the children experience the miracle of birth." But again, it's likely to be a litter bred with no health clearances on the parents or the puppies, with little knowledge of the breed standard or how to choose a proper sire for a litter. In fact, the litter may be an "accident" and the result of a decision made by the dogs themselves. A BYB may mean well, but may not know much about how to raise physically and mentally healthy puppies. In general, then, a BYB is a casual (one might say careless) puppy producer.

Chances are that the BYB's bitch is a sweet enough pet, but one with more or less serious faults in terms of the breed standard. She may carry hereditary diseases that she can pass along to the pups. Same for the stud dog, who is probably chosen because he's convenient and willing, not because he's a quality dog. In fact, responsible stud dog owners won't breed their dogs to bitches who lack health clearances and reasonable conformation and temperament. Sometimes a BYB produces a perfectly acceptable litter of pets. More often, though, the puppies develop into dogs with problems ranging from life-threatening or crippling to chronically annoying to dangerous.

Backyard breeders tend to advertise in newspapers. Occasionally, responsible breeders do as well, but be alert to terms in ads that tip you off that the advertiser isn't a serious, knowledgeable breeder. Let's look at some examples.

1. "Full-blooded Brittany Spaniel puppies. Papers available. OFA certified. Champion bloodlines."

2. "Registered Peek-a-Poos, five weeks old, weaned and ready to go. Both parents on premises."

3. "Rare silver Labs."

4. "Tea-cup Poodles."

5. "Puppies! Golden Retrievers, Poodles, Cocker Spaniels, Shih Tzus, Dalmations, St. Bernards."

6. "Golden Retriever puppies. Parents certified for hips, elbows, heart, eyes, vWB. Father OTCH, dam CD, WC, grandparents titled. Spay/neuter contract. Qualified buyers only."

Okay, let's look at #1. Knowledgeable dog people don't say "full-blooded." The proper term is "purebred," and in fact serious breeders don't usually even mention that in the ads. Why? Because if it is a Cocker Spaniel, it *must* be a purebred—otherwise, it isn't a Cocker Spaniel (or insert your favorite breed). But wait—it says Brittany Spaniels, not Cocker Spaniels. Wait again—the name of the breed is simply "Brittany"—the Spaniel part was dropped years ago, and serious fanciers of the breed know that. One of my favorite dopey ads was for "Registered Black Labs, yellow and black." There's no such breed as Black Lab. There are Labrador Retrievers, though—Labs—that come in yellow, black, and chocolate. Be sure that *you* know the proper names of any breeds you're considering, and beware of advertisers who don't.

Grrrrowls

Words like "tea-cup" are red lights that the pups may not be responsibly bred. Those terms are not used by responsible breeders, who breed to the standard for the breed, not for traits that are considered to be faults. Serious health problems often accompany extremes of size as well as unusual colors.

Keep in mind, too, that some people will say full-blooded to mean puppies whose parents are crosses of the same two breeds. It takes generations of careful breeding to create a breed. Puppies whose parents are both Peek-a-Poos (a cross between a Pekinese and a Poodle) are still mixed-breed puppies. Unless they are dedicated to a long-term, careful program of cross breeding to create a new breed for a specific purpose (which is how most modern breeds started), responsible breeders do not breed mixed-breed puppies.

What about that word "papers" in an ad? Again, responsible breeders don't mention that their puppies have papers because it goes without saying. If you buy a purebred puppy, you have a right to a copy of the pedigree (the litter's family tree) and to the registration application for the pup (see Chapter 3 for more information). You should not pay extra for a pedigree or for registration papers!

How about the "OFA certified" part? Nonsense. Puppies cannot have their hips formally rated by the Orthopedic Foundation for Animals (OFA) until they are two years old. The Pennsylvania Hip Improvement Program (PennHIP) will evaluate hips at four months of age, but most pups advertised in the newspaper are much younger than four months. (See Chapter 3 on health documentation.) The parents, on the other hand, should have OFA or PennHIP certification in most breeds. Exactly what the parents should have in the way of health clearances depends on the breed, so do your homework before you start puppy shopping. Finally, if the advertiser blanks out when you ask about OFA or Canine Eye Registry Foundation (CERF) (pronounced "surf"), run as fast as you can in the other direction. Same thing if he tells you something like "I don't bother with that stuff; my dogs don't have those problems" or "My vet says their hips are okay." Unless his vet is an orthopedic specialist and he is using x-rays, his evaluation doesn't mean anything.

Does "champion bloodlines" sound impressive? It's not. If you go back three or four generations, most purebred dogs—even those from puppy mills—have some champions in their background.

That's because, unfortunately, some people breed pet-quality dogs to make money, and some people breed the pet-quality offspring of those dogs. When you look at a pedigree, the dogs that matter most are the parents and grandparents of the litter. They don't all have to be champions, but about half the dogs in the first two generations (parents and grandparents) should have titles of some sort to show that their breeders were serious about proving the quality of the dogs, not just about filling their pockets.

How about those registered Peek-a-Poos in #2? That's not a breed, is it? No, it's not. But there are a few organizations around that will register anything for a fee. (I know someone who registered her daughter with one of them!) In the United States and Canada, the legitimate multibreed registries are the American Kennel Club (AKC), the United Kennel Club (UKC), and the Canadian Kennel Club (CKC). There are also a few registries that register only certain types of dogs (for instance, the National Stockdog Registry (NSDR) registers herding breeds) or only a single breed (Jack Russell Terriers, Cavalier King Charles Spaniels, and Australian Shepherds, among others, have independent single-breed registries). Again, do your homework so that you know what's legitimate for the breeds you're investigating.

BowWOW

If puppies are advertised as "registered," be sure it is with a legitimate registry. A number of so-called registries were formed so that people who have lost their registration privileges with the AKC and other legitimate registries can still have "papers" on their puppies. Know the standard registries for your breed of choice.

Now, the rest of ad #2. Five weeks old and ready to go? Yes, they may be weaned, but five weeks is way too young for a puppy to leave home (see Chapter 8). As for the presence of both parents, you'll have to use some judgment on that. Sometimes a breeder owns a dog and a bitch that truly suit one another in terms of individual physical and mental traits as well as pedigree. That's fine, if the breeder can tell you why she chose to breed these specific animals. It's great if you can see both parents, but don't be alarmed if the sire lives a plane ride away. Serious breeders often send their bitches to "outside studs"—studs owned by other breeders—because they want the specific traits offered by a specific dog. If a litter owner refers to her "breeding pair," or if she always uses the resident male for all her females, that's not a good sign. It usually means she's selecting the sire based on convenience and financial concerns (no stud fee), not on sound principles of selective breeding.

> **Chew on This**
>
> One of your best tools as a puppy buyer is a basic knowledge of the breed you want. Get a good book from the library or go to the website for the breed's parent club, and learn the basics so that you know what to ask.

Now, what about those "rare silver Labs" in ad #3 (or rare white Boxers or rare long-haired Rottweilers?) *Be careful* about ads for anything "rare" in dogs. There *are* rare breeds, and in some breeds there are less-common colors that are still acceptable. But again, know your breed! Often colors and other traits are rare because they are not allowed by the breed standard. Sometimes they are disallowed for reasons that have nothing to do with suitability as a pet (although you certainly shouldn't pay more for a pup with a fault). But some colors are disallowed because with them come health problems. Finally, some traits are rare because the genes for them simply do not exist in certain breeds—meaning that the dog who has the trait is actually a cross. Such is sometimes the case with Silver Labs, which are either very poor specimens or are Labrador Retriever × Weimeraner crosses. The same applies to terms like "tea-cup" that are not part of the terminology used by responsible breeders. "Tea-cup" anythings are just very small individuals, and they often have health problems directly related to their size.

How about ad #5, the ad for several breeds? Or the breeder who runs a perpetual ad for puppies of one or two breeds? Look out! Raising puppies properly is exhausting, time-consuming work (see Chapter 17). Responsible breeders have one or two breeds, occasionally three, and they don't have litters all the time. Ads like that just scream puppy mill or really ambitious backyard breeder. There's no way that pups can be properly raised under such conditions. Please don't support that kind of irresponsible breeding.

Now let's look at the last ad, #6. It definitely sends a better signal than the others. Titles on the parents and grandparents suggest that their owners and breeders are serious about proving the dogs' abilities in competition, and the appropriate health clearances show they are interested in breeding healthy puppies. (If you don't know what the abbreviations stand for, ask when you call. In this case, vWB is von Wilbrandts disease, a bleeding disorder; OTCH is Obedience Trial Champion; CD is Companion Dog, an obedience title; and WC is Working Certificate, meaning she's passed a test of her retrieving instinct.) Not only that, but they don't want their pet-quality puppies to be used for breeding, and they have some requirements for their buyers other than cash on the barrel.

(Photo by Close Encounters of the Furry Kind)

Beware of breeders whose dogs don't appear to be well cared for.

Puppy Mills

Puppy mills came into existence after World War II. The U.S. Department of Agriculture (USDA) encouraged farmers to raise puppies for supplemental income when traditional crops were failing. Retail pet stores sprang up, and a new group of puppy brokers began to act as middlemen. In the last half-century, commercial puppy production has grown into a multimillion-dollar industry.

Most puppy millers know and care little about choosing physically and mentally sound breeding dogs. Most have little in the way of capital, so they start their businesses with poor facilities and poorly bred dogs. They house their dogs in deplorable conditions. The dogs often live in filth and get little or no exercise. They are fed cheap, poor-quality food. They get substandard health care, no screening for inherited diseases, no proper prenatal care, and little if any socialization or affection. Bitches are bred every heat until they can no longer produce puppies. Then they are often killed, dumped, or just left to languish until they die. Millers usually keep a few male dogs, who are bred as much as possible as long as they are fertile.

Grrrrowls

People who buy puppies that have been bred and sold irresponsibly support cruelty and perpetuate the production of dogs with serious physical and mental problems. For the sake of the dogs, and yourself, please be informed and responsible when you get your new dog.

Make no mistake—puppy mill dogs are not beloved companions for their owners. They're money makers, and when they can no longer make money, they're of no use. Some states in the Midwest, as well as areas of Pennsylvania and other states, are notorious for puppy mills, but they exist throughout the United States and in other countries as well.

Doggerel

A **puppy mill** produces lots and lots of puppies with only one motive: to make money. Puppy mills are usually overcrowded with dogs, and the dogs are usually neglected and may be abused because there are just too many of them to be given proper attention and care. Puppy millers don't care where the puppies end up once they're paid for, and don't socialize the pups for proper mental and social development. **Pet wholesalers** (brokers) buy puppies in quantity from puppy mills and resell them, usually to pet stores.

Puppies from puppy mills are often damaged before they're even born. Poor nutrition for a pregnant or nursing bitch can cause permanent physical and mental problems in her unborn puppies. The puppies are often ill, infested with parasites, and improperly socialized. It's not a very good beginning for a dog chosen to fulfill your wishes for a healthy, happy companion.

Puppies from puppy mills are usually sold to pet wholesalers or brokers, who buy puppies in large numbers from puppy mills in the United States and abroad, and then sell or trade them to other wholesalers or to pet stores. When operating across state lines, brokers have to be licensed by the USDA, and they have to follow the shipping regulations provided for in the Animal Welfare Act. Those requirements, however, are minimal and not always strictly enforced. To a broker, puppies are strictly a commodity, like furniture and clothes.

One term that is confusing because it is used very differently by the USDA on the one hand and the AKC on the other is the term *hobby breeder*. The USDA defines a hobby breeder as someone who sells puppies directly to pet stores, but owns no more than three breeding bitches and who grosses less than $500 per year. USDA hobby breeders do not need to be USDA licensed, so there is no regulation of their facilities or practices except in the rare places where local laws are in place (and those aren't usually enforced unless someone complains).

Doggerel

The term **hobby breeder** is used in very different ways by different people. Some use the USDA definition, which is essentially a small-time breeder of puppies for distribution through pet stores. Others use the term to mean a responsible, serious breeder who places puppies carefully and directly with individual buyers. If someone tells you he's a hobby breeder, be sure you know which definition he has in mind.

The confusion arises because serious dog fanciers and breeders use the term *hobby breeder* in a very different way. For this group, a hobby breeder is someone who usually breeds only one breed (or possibly two), and who has a well-planned breeding program designed to protect and improve the breed. Such breeders usually have only one or two litters a year and may skip some years. They regard puppies as living, feeling beings and provide them with a clean, safe environment, proper food, health care, exercise, and socialization. They sell puppies directly to individuals whom they first screen to be sure the pup will be well cared for. So if someone tells you she is a "hobby breeder," be sure you find out what she means by the term.

Pet Stores

Please don't buy a puppy from a pet store. No responsible breeder ever sells puppies through a pet store. Regardless of what some stores claim, the truth is that pet stores get their merchandise—and that's exactly what puppies are to them—from commercial breeders, brokers, puppy mills, or backyard breeders. Responsible breeders do not think of puppies as merchandise, and they do not entrust the fate of their puppies to strangers. Pet store puppies are usually taken from their mothers and siblings when they're four or five weeks old, which is much too young for proper social development.

Pet stores rely on the cuteness of puppies as a selling point. They also rely on the emotional impulses of the people who walk in, cuddle a puppy, and can't bear to put him back in that cage. So out comes the credit card. Some people do luck out and get a reasonably good pet. But the odds are against it. People who are in the business of producing puppies for pet stores don't generally pay attention to health screening for hereditary disease. They match up sires and dams by availability (or sometimes by accident) rather than by careful selection. They don't bother to handle and socialize the puppies. How can they? There are just too many of them! No, the odds are that your pet store puppy will have health and temperament problems. To add insult to injury, pet store puppy prices often match or exceed the price of a responsibly bred puppy from a breeder. No, pet stores offer no bargains when it comes to puppies.

But don't they have to guarantee the pups they sell? Yes, most states have laws requiring a minimal guarantee or warranty, and most pet stores will take back a puppy within a certain time if certain conditions are met. Responsible breeders, in contrast, will take their puppies back at any time throughout their lives, because the puppy, not the dollar, comes first.

Pet store staff are usually not very well informed about the breeds they sell, but in my experience they rarely say "I don't know." I've had pet store personnel tell me that Labrador Retrievers have no hereditary health problems (they do! they do!) and that Australian Shepherds have personalities like Golden Retrievers (they don't! they don't!). In fact, pet stores offer virtually nothing in the way of support when it comes to training, behavior problems, health issues, or anything else.

All That Glitters Is Not Gold

There's another group of puppy producers you need to beware of as well. Unfortunately, some people who seem to meet the requirements of a responsible breeder at first glance don't stand up to a closer examination. An honest, ethical breeder is your best source for a healthy purebred puppy backed up by knowledgeable breeding. But you need to be cautious. Be cautious, and reread Chapter 5 about breeders—the good ones! Some of the snazziest websites and magazine ads belong to some of the sleaziest people, so don't be dazzled. Ask lots of questions and check references. There are excellent, honest breeders around, and one of them has the right pup for you. Being informed and patient will help you find her.

The Least You Need to Know

- Backyard breeders produce puppies for a variety of reasons, but rarely produce high quality.

- Puppies from puppy mills and commercial breeders are likely to suffer physical and emotional problems.

- Pet store puppies come from commercial breeders and usually lack proper socialization and health screening.

- Wise puppy buyers look beyond glitzy advertising.

Chapter 7

Adopting a Homeless Dog

In This Chapter

- 🏠 Adopting a rescued purebred dog
- 🏠 Adopting a dog from a shelter or pound
- 🏠 Adopting a dog from an individual
- 🏠 Rescuing and keeping a stray

Adopting a dog in need of a home can be a rewarding experience for both of you. Dogs who have lost their homes seem to understand and appreciate the opportunity for a loving new home. And as an adopter, you'll know that you've saved a life and gained a best friend in the process.

Purebred Rescue Programs

Rescue refers to the process of saving purebred or mixed-breed animals, particularly dogs. The individuals and groups who take in and foster rescued dogs and then place them in new homes are nearly always unpaid volunteers. They give their time, their knowledge, and their dog-handling skills because they love dogs. Most people have heard of Greyhound rescue, a network of groups that place retired racing Greyhounds into homes as pets. What many people don't realize is that rescue groups exist for nearly every breed of dog.

Why do purebred dogs need to be rescued? Sometimes a dog loses his home when his owner dies or experiences a serious change in circumstances that prevents his owner from caring for him any longer. Some rescued dogs are strays whose owners can't be found. Sometimes dogs are confiscated from puppy mills or other abusive situations and turned over to rescue volunteers for rehabilitation and placement. All too often, dogs find their way into rescue because their first owners didn't do their homework before buying, didn't train the dog once they had him, and finally got fed up with the dog's uneducated behavior.

BowWOW

Purebred rescue organizations are always looking for volunteers. You don't have to handle rescued dogs to help, and you don't have to give more than a few hours a month to be useful. There are lots of jobs that need doing, from making telephone calls to fund-raising to bookkeeping. If you'd like to help the rescue effort, contact a group and find out where you might fit in.

Rescued dogs tend to be older adolescents or adults, although occasionally puppies are placed through rescue programs. Some rescued dogs have behavioral problems due to lack of exercise, training, or socialization, but the majority of them blossom into terrific companions once they have proper care and training. Many rescued dogs have no problems at all, or just minor ones that are easily corrected with gentle training and lots of love. If you're not up to the work of raising a puppy properly, a rescued dog may be just what you need. And don't shy away from truly mature dogs—a healthy dog of five, six, or seven years, or even older, can be a wonderful, wise friend with lots of life still to live. Anyway, love and friendship are measured by their depth, not their duration.

Rescue volunteers nearly always foster the dogs for some time before placing them. Fostering gives rescuers a chance to evaluate each dog's temperament, behavior, and training needs in a household environment, which helps in placing each dog into a suitable home. Rescuers work hard to provide some basic house manners, and most recommend that adopters take their dogs through basic obedience classes. Rescued dogs are generally given physical examinations, and potential adopters are advised about possible health problems. All reputable rescuers require that every dog be spayed or neutered before he is placed or very shortly afterward. In general, rescue organizations will not place dogs with known histories of biting, aggression, or severe behavioral problems. If you contact a rescue group about adopting, ask what their policy is on these issues.

Doggerel

Rescue usually refers to dogs that are fostered and placed into new homes by volunteers who work with one or two breeds. **Search and rescue** (SAR) refers to dogs that are trained to search for victims of a disaster or for people who are lost.

If you want to adopt a rescued dog, you will be asked to complete a detailed application, provide references, and agree to a home visit by a rescue volunteer. These requirements are meant to ensure that you will get the right dog for your situation, and that each dog will be placed into a suitable home. When you adopt a dog, you will sign a contract requiring you to provide proper care. The contract will probably specify that if you ever find that you cannot keep the dog, you will return him to the rescue organization. You will probably pay an adoption fee, which can range from less than a hundred dollars to several hundred dollars. Some organizations ask only for a donation. If that's the case, please be generous. Without donations, organized rescue would cease to exist.

Most rescue groups provide postadoption support. They will give you information about the breed and about the individual dog. They are usually available to answer questions you may have. And don't forget to call and tell them how well your rescued dog is doing. That is the rescuers' main reward—knowing that a dog they saved is doing well and making someone happy. And indeed, rescued dogs make wonderful pets.

Chew on This

How do you find a rescue organization for the breed you're considering? The American Kennel Club (AKC) keeps a list of rescue contacts for all AKC breeds. Your local kennel club, as well as training schools or clubs, veterinarians, and breeders in your area, may be able to put you in touch with local rescue groups. The Internet is also an excellent source—just search for "[name of the breed] rescue" and you're bound to find some links.

You may have to wait for the right dog to show up, depending on the breed and your requirements. That's okay—good things are worth waiting for. Use the time to study the breed, locate a veterinarian and obedience class, and learn more about canine nutrition, health care, and training. If you have children, get a good book on dogs and look at it together so that they will be ready, too. Most kids are delighted to know that the dog they're getting is special, and that your family is doing a good thing by adopting a dog who needs you.

Shelters and Pounds

Good dogs often show up in animal shelters. Some are turned in by their owners for reasons much like those given in the rescue section you just read. Some are strays whose owners never bail them out. Many wonderful pets are adopted from shelters, but it pays to understand a bit about shelters and shelter animals before you adopt.

Adopting a dog from a shelter can be rewarding if you prepare ahead of time to select the right one. You save a life and gain a wonderful friend and companion. Adopting a shelter dog is usually less expensive than getting one from a breeder. Shelter dogs, especially those turned in by their owners, may already be housetrained and have some manners, although few have had much training. Most will be more than a year old and full grown; new owners won't have to wonder how big he'll get or how much grooming she'll need.

(Photo by Close Encounters of the Furry Kind)

Perhaps your best friend is waiting for you at your local shelter.

Most states require each county to maintain a facility for the impoundment of stray animals. Local law enforcement often works with these facilities to enforce laws against animal cruelty and neglect. These public shelters are sometimes run as government agencies or are contracted out to private organizations. They are usually funded by tax dollars, dog and cat licensing fees, loose-dog and other fines, donations, grants, and adoption fees.

Private shelters vary widely in their policies and practices. Some work much like public shelters, except that they don't receive public monies. Some accept any animal in need, but because space is limited, they must limit how long they can keep each animal before turning to euthanasia to make room for another. Others, sometimes called "no-kill" shelters, do not euthanize healthy animals to make room for others. That sounds great, but such shelters turn away many animals. The reality is that the paid staff and the volunteers in private animal shelters are nearly all there because they love animals. They work hard to find homes for the ones in their care, and they mourn the ones that must die or be turned away from their doors.

If you're looking for a dog from a shelter, you should be aware that although some shelter workers are knowledgeable about dogs, some are not. Shelter staff are usually dedicated and caring people, but some are not able to identify and differentiate breeds accurately. A dog doesn't have to be a purebred to be a great pet, but if you want to be reasonably certain of getting a dog with the traits typical of a specific breed, take along someone who knows the breed well to help you evaluate candidates.

Find out how dogs are evaluated when they arrive at the shelter, who does the evaluation, and what is included in the evaluation. Some shelters have all incoming dogs examined by a veterinarian and checked for heartworms and intestinal parasites. Some evaluate the dog's temperament and behavior in the shelter, and, when possible, keep notes about the dog's health care and behavior in his previous home. But many shelters lack the resources to provide such in-depth services and have to get by with minimal evaluations.

Not all shelter staff are able to evaluate canine behavior effectively or to assist adopters with difficulties after the adoption. If you're thinking of adopting, ask lots of questions. Find out whether anything is known about the dog's background, and ask what steps have been taken to evaluate his temperament. Many shelter dogs make great pets, but unfortunately some are there due to problems, such as aggression. Others will do well with the right owners, but may not be right for you. If you are the least bit uneasy about a dog's behavior, walk away. And if you don't feel that the shelter staff can offer you the advice and support you need, find another shelter or a rescue group.

Chew on This

If you're thinking of adopting a shelter dog, ask the shelter staff these questions:

- 🐾 What do you know about this dog's background?
- 🐾 Do you know why this dog was turned in?
- 🐾 Has he shown any behavior problems since he's been here?
- 🐾 Has he growled at anyone since he's been here? Has he bitten anyone?
- 🐾 Does he appear to be friendly with other dogs?
- 🐾 Do you know whether he's housebroken?
- 🐾 Does he appear to have any obedience training?
- 🐾 What health tests and vaccinations has he had?
- 🐾 Has he been wormed (see Chapter 9)? When, and for what kinds of worms?
- 🐾 Does he appear to be healthy now?
- 🐾 Has he been exposed to any contagious diseases since he's been in the shelter?
- 🐾 Has he shown any limping or other signs of orthopedic problems?
- 🐾 Is he a purebred, or do you know which breeds he has in him? Can someone at the shelter refer me to information about his breed or breeds?
- 🐾 Do you offer any postadoption help if he has behavioral problems?
- 🐾 Do you offer any obedience classes, or can you recommend an instructor?

When you visit the shelter, be alert to the physical environment. There will undoubtedly be a strong sense of dog in the air, but in general the place should seem clean. Ideally, dogs will not have physical contact with their neighbors, because nose-to-nose contact can quickly spread distemper, kennel cough, other diseases, and fleas. Feces spread from one kennel run to another can also spread diseases as well as intestinal parasites. Dogs in the adoptions area should appear fairly healthy. They may be thin and in need of a good grooming, but should not have discharge from their eyes or noses, and should not be coughing. Remember, if you adopt a dog that is ill, you can carry the disease home to any dogs you have and to your neighbors' dogs if they have contact or walk in the same areas.

If the shelter doesn't seem clean, or the dogs don't appear to be reasonably healthy, be cautious. Either adopt elsewhere or, if you really want a particular dog, consider taking him directly to your veterinarian for a thorough exam and possible quarantine before taking him home. Or quarantine him from your other dog at home until you're sure he isn't carrying any contagious disease. Many minor problems can be cleared up with good food, exercise, and care, but if you have another dog at home, it still pays to be cautious.

To adopt a dog from a shelter, you usually have to complete an application that asks for proof of residence and age, your experience as a pet owner, references, and, if you rent, the name and phone number of your landlord.

The next step is to choose your dog. A walk through the adoption area can be overwhelming—there are just so many dogs in need of homes. You can't take them all (really, you can't!), so before you go, make a list of the traits you want and the traits you don't want. Your list will keep you on track. Remember to include size (or potential size if you're looking at puppies), temperament, sex, type of coat and grooming required, and age. It's all too easy to lose your heart to every pair of big doggy eyes you see, so remember that many of those dogs are there because someone chose badly. For the sake of the dog, don't repeat the previous owner's mistake.

When you have chosen the dog you'd like to adopt, you usually have to wait from 24 to 48 hours before taking him home. This is to let you sleep on it and be sure this is the right decision, and to give your family time to talk over any concerns. It also gives the shelter staff time to check the information you provided. They want to be sure the animals they care for and send back into the world will be well cared for. You will probably pay an adoption fee, which may or may not include the cost of spaying or neutering your new buddy.

Dogs don't always appear at their best in a shelter environment. Many will be overly excited, or depressed and quiet, or downright scared. If you see a fellow you think you might like, ask if he can be taken to a quiet place where you can interact with him. Sit quietly for a while and see what happens. Maybe have a few treats in your pocket to show him you're a pretty good person. Your whole family should meet the dog before you decide for sure, but try to keep the initial meeting calm. Explain to your children that the dog may be a little afraid—kids are usually very sympathetic and gentle when they understand that.

(Photo by Close Encounters of the Furry Kind)

Adoption day is a happy one for everyone involved.

When you officially adopt your dog, you'll probably sign a contract that will require you to keep the dog as a pet; to provide proper housing, food, and veterinary care; to have the dog spayed or neutered if that hasn't already been done; to allow postadoption visits by shelter staff; and to return the dog to the shelter if you can no longer keep him or her.

Adoption fees vary from shelter to shelter, depending on what services the shelter provides prior to adoption and also on the shelter's funding and budget. If you're so inclined, all shelters appreciate a little extra donation.

Please be just as careful in choosing a dog to adopt as you would be if you were choosing a dog to purchase. You don't want to end up with the wrong sort of dog, and nobody wants the dog to end up back at the shelter.

Private Adoptions

Another option is to adopt an older puppy or young adult privately from a person who is trying to place him. You may see an ad in a newspaper or a card on a bulletin board at the veterinarian's office. Sometimes you can find a good dog this way, but proceed with caution. Very often people give dogs away because of behavioral or health problems. Some of these problems have been brought on by lack of training or proper care, and are fixable. Some problems, though, may be more serious. Unfortunately, people won't always tell you, even if the problem is serious, like a history of biting.

If you're considering a private adoption, be sure to ask why the dog is no longer wanted. Ask directly whether the dog has ever bitten anyone, snapped at anyone, or threatened to bite anyone. Ask whether the dog gets along with other animals. Even if you don't have another pet, you'll probably want to walk your dog in public places, and a truly aggressive dog can be a serious problem in public. Ask to see the dog's vaccination and examination record, and find out whether he has been on heartworm prevention. If no written record is available, ask for the name of the dog's vet, and call the office to verify the dog's health history. Explain that you're thinking of adopting the dog, and ask if there's anything you should know.

Watch the dog move, and look for signs of lameness. If the dog is a purebred, or a cross of two known breeds, do a little research before you visit so that you'll know what problems are prevalent in

the breed or breeds. If you look at a German Shepherd Dog ×
Labrador Retriever cross, and you know that both breeds are prone
to hip dysplasia, and you see that the dog limps on a hind leg, you
should be suspicious. Hip dysplasia may not be the problem, but
unless you're willing to take on the expense of a dysplastic dog, you
should be careful.

Ask whether the dog's owner would let you have the dog examined by your own veterinarian at your expense before you commit to
adopting him. Invite the owner along—they may not be too keen on
letting you take the dog away without them. Some people won't be
too keen on the idea anyway, and you may have to just go with your
instincts and decide to adopt or not.

Strays

Sometimes the most wonderful dog just shows up practically on
your doorstep. One of the best dogs I ever had was a Miniature
Schnauzer that I found late at night in an ice storm as I walked to
my car in a library parking lot. No one ever claimed her, and I suspect she was dumped. Even if you don't keep a stray, rescuing a dog
from the streets can be very rewarding. Here are some suggestions if
you find yourself trying to help a stray dog.

Unless someone else has already caught the dog, catching him
will be the first step. Even if a dog seems to be friendly, *be careful*.
Stray dogs are often frightened. The dog may also be injured and in
pain. Fear and pain can cause even the friendliest canine to bite.

Don't reach for a dog that growls, bares its teeth, or otherwise
warns you off. If he threatens to bite, believe him. A snare, which
consists of a loop of rope fastened to a pole, will allow you to catch
and control the dog without endangering yourself. Animal shelters
usually have snares, as do many veterinary offices. If you are not
experienced in handling frightened or aggressive dogs, get help from
someone who is. Remember that even if you cannot keep the dog
and he is taken to a shelter, even if he is euthanized, he's better off

than he would be left to fend for himself. The modern world is not a friendly place for stray dogs, and by removing the dog from life on the street, you have saved him from many horrors, including starvation, poisoning, cars, and cruel people.

Learn what you can about canine body language. Being able to "read" a dog will go a long way toward keeping you from being bitten. Few dogs bite with no warning at all, but if you don't understand the warning, it won't do you much good. If you are not confident that you can handle or confine the dog safely, *leave him alone*. Go for help or additional equipment, such as a snare or muzzle, or a *humane trap*. Don't take foolish risks. Dog bites are painful, and a dog does not have to be very large to inflict serious, permanent damage.

Grrrrowls

If a dog threatens to bite by growling and baring his teeth, believe him. Despite the old saying, barking dogs *do* bite. Be very cautious when trying to catch or handle a dog you don't know.

Sometimes you can walk up to a stray dog or get him to come to you with food or a soft voice. Even if the dog comes to you and allows you to touch him, don't try to guide the dog with your hands on his body, and don't carry the dog unless he is very small and quiet. Don't stand over the dog or back him into a corner—he may bite out of fear. Use a leash to lead the dog to where you want him. Your leash can be make-shift if necessary; a rope or belt will work. If the dog has no collar, you can improvise a slip collar with a leash, rope, or belt. A slip collar is difficult for a dog to duck out of and gives you more control.

If you plan to transport the dog in your vehicle, be sure you can confine him adequately. Although you might simply put a rescued dog in the back of a car and drive home without mishap, the potential for disaster is tremendous. You don't need a frightened dog leaping into your lap in traffic. A crate is the ideal means of confinement. It keeps the dog from moving or being thrown around the car. It limits the area with which the dog has physical contact, allowing for more effective cleaning and disinfecting—a good idea if you have other pets at home. If the dog has fleas, it keeps most of them and their eggs in the crate. Should the dog become ill or relieve itself, the mess is confined and more easily disposed of. Finally, a crate protects and restrains a traveling dog in the event of a traffic mishap.

Doggerel _____

A **humane trap** is a wire cage with a spring-loaded door. You put bait (food) inside the trap, and when the animal enters to get the bait, the door closes behind him. You can then transport him to a safe place. Many veterinarians and animal shelters have humane traps available at a nominal charge.

If you don't have a crate, the next best thing is to tie the dog, preferably in the back, away from the driver. If you must transport a dog in the back of a pickup truck, cross tie the dog, that is, use two leashes or ropes, fastening one to one side of the truck bed and one to the other side, to keep the dog from jumping or being thrown out of the truck.

A stray that has been on his own for any length of time will probably have internal and external parasites that can be passed to your dogs. He could also transmit disease. If you plan to take the dog home rather than turn him in to a shelter or rescue group, have him examined by a vet *before* you take him into your home if possible. An examination will cost some money, but if it keeps your dogs safe, it's money well spent. Be aware, though, that health examinations aren't foolproof. Some diseases have incubation periods, during which the dog may or may not be contagious. He may appear healthy when examined but become ill a few days later, and he could transmit the disease despite your precautions.

Whatever areas the dog has been in contact with during transportation should be cleaned and disinfected. If the veterinary examination showed no cause for concern about the animal's health, wash the crate with detergent, rinse with a 10 percent bleach solution followed by clear water, and dry carefully. Don't forget to wash all blankets, rugs, towels, and other items that have been in contact with the dog. If you use cedar or wood chips, straw, or newspaper, seal the bedding in a plastic bag for disposal. Spray all carpeting and uphol-stery in the car with flea spray and then vacuum.

If the veterinarian did find evidence of disease, ask her advice for safe cleanup. Don't forget to clean leashes, water bowls, and other equipment that may have been contaminated. Finally, don't forget to clean yourself and your clothing, including shoes, before handling your own or someone else's pets.

There's always a chance that a dog on the loose has a frantic owner somewhere looking for him. As soon as possible, check for tags on his collar. If he doesn't have a name tag, you may be able to trace the owner through a license number or through a rabies tag number issued by a veterinary hospital.

You should also check for permanent identification. First, look for a tattoo. Dogs are usually tattooed on the belly or the inner thigh, or occasionally on the ear. If the dog is hairy or has dark skin, the tattoo may be difficult to locate. If you find a tattoo, write down the number.

Microchips are becoming more and more common as a means of permanent identification, so have the dog scanned for a chip if possible. Check with area animal shelters, rescue groups, and veteri-narians to find someone with a scanner. Have the operator run the scanner over the dog's withers (the high point at the base of the neck where the shoulder blades stick up), his back, and down his sides to look for a reading. If the dog has a chip and if the scanner reads it, a number will appear on the screen. Unfortunately, not all scanners can read all microchips, although manufacturers are standardizing the technology for mutual readability.

If the dog does not have any identification that you can locate, you will have to resort to other ways of trying to find the owner. You can place a found ad in the local newspaper (they're often free), and post signs around the area where the dog was found. Even if you're running a found ad, be sure to read the lost ads. The Internet has also become an effective means of spreading the word about lost and found dogs, so post to a few canine bulletin boards or discussion lists—especially those for the specific breed, if you know it—and if possible check those same sources for lost notices.

BowWOW

Microchips are implanted under the skin over the withers, the high point at the base of the neck where the shoulder blades meet. But sometimes the chips slip down the neck or leg. If you're scanning a dog for a microchip, be thorough. Tattoo and microchip numbers are usually registered with various organizations. See Chapter 8 for a list.

If you place an ad, give out only enough information to avoid irrelevant calls. For instance, include the breed if you know it, or a brief description of the dog: "60+ pound black dog" will screen out calls about lost Westies. If you respond to an ad, ask for information about the lost dog. Make the person claiming the dog identify him to your satisfaction. Certainly, the person should know the sex of the dog, whether he is neutered if a male (or spayed if a female, but that's harder for most laypeople to determine), and other identifying characteristics. Ask to see photos and veterinary records to prove ownership. In the final analysis, the dog will probably "tell" you whether this is its person, but preliminary questions will save you and the person looking for a lost dog a lot of time and disappointment.

If you cannot locate the dog's owner, you'll have to make a decision. If you like the dog and he seems to fit into your life, maybe destiny has found your dog for you. If not, then your best bet is to turn him over to a purebred rescue group, if he's purebred, or to a good shelter. You might try to place him privately. If you do, be sure to screen the adopters carefully.

The Least You Need to Know

- Many wonderful dogs of all breeds are available to good homes through purebred rescue programs.

- A shelter can also be an excellent place to find a great pet, purebred or mixed-breed.

- Private adoptions from people who want to place a dog can work out fine, but adopters need to be cautious.

- A stray dog may need your help to find his way home—or may wind up staying with you.

Chapter 8

Welcome Home!

In This Chapter

- 🏠 Preparing for your new dog
- 🏠 Shopping for Fido
- 🏠 Scheduling a check-up and training class
- 🏠 Introducing the new family member

You've done all the preliminaries. You're sure you really want a dog, and you've picked the right breed and the right source. Now it's time to get set—you'll soon hear the pitter-patter of paws around your place. Having your home and supplies ready ahead of time will enable you to focus on your new buddy, so let's get started!

Puppy-Proofing—for Adults, Too

Puppies, and many adult dogs, like to chew. Chewing serves to relieve stress. It's also a way to relieve the discomfort of teething, which pups do between four and six months of age. And chewing is just, well, enjoyable. The trouble is, your dog wasn't born knowing what he's allowed to chew and what's off limits. It's your job to teach him. It's your job to protect your belongings from canine teeth and to protect your pup (whatever his age) from things that could hurt him. Prevention is the best protection and can be accomplished in two ways: by puppy-proofing your home and yard, and by confining your dog when you can't supervise him.

Puppy-proofing is a lot like childproofing, except that puppies are smaller and are more active and mobile than babies and young toddlers. Puppies also have much sharper teeth than children.

First, get breakables out of reach. If you're adopting an older dog, think about tail height, too. A happy tail can clear a tabletop in no time. If you have tablecloths or runners, hanging ends may invite a canine tug, so remove the cloths until your pup learns house manners. Put attractive nuisances away. Shoes, floor-level decorations, plants, and other potential "playthings" don't belong at puppy level.

Next, remove potential hazards from reach. Puppies have died from swallowing pins, razor blades, cigarette butts, nylon stockings, and other unlikely objects, as well as chocolate, medicines, and other edibles. Toy cars and doll clothes are very bad for canine digestive systems. Having a pup or new adult dog in the house can be a great incentive for children to put toys away, too. Kids are usually more inspired by a puppy's well-being than by the virtues of good housekeeping. Still, it's up to the adults to ensure that hazards really are safely stowed away.

Get down on your hands and knees and look at things from your dog's perspective. Look under and behind furniture and in small spaces a pup might find inviting. Secure electrical and telephone wires in specially designed sheaths available in hardware and home stores or with PVC pipes cut to appropriate lengths.

Teach your pup from the start that some things are his to chew, and some things are not. If he picks up something he shouldn't, gently take it away and replace it with one of his toys. You don't need to yell or punish him—in fact, that's usually counterproductive. Just teach him gently, and he'll get the idea. Use good sense about the toys you give him. He won't know the difference between an old shoe you say is okay and a new one in your closet. Provide him with safe, chewy toys made for dogs his size.

Shopping for Rover

Shop for your new buddy before he comes home. That way you'll be able to devote yourself to getting to know each other instead of scurrying off to the store during those first few days. Let's see what you need.

A Crate Idea

First, you need a *crate*. Before you decide that it's mean to crate a dog, ask yourself this: Would you turn a toddler loose in your house without supervision? A puppy is a canine toddler. He will explore nooks and crannies, put anything portable in his mouth, and potty when the urge hits. He doesn't know what's right or wrong, and he doesn't know what's safe and unsafe.

Even if your new dog is past puppyhood, a crate is a good idea. A dog's first few days in a new home are stressful, and a crate provides a safe haven when you're gone. If you aren't sure that your new dog is completely housetrained, the crate will prevent accidents. All in all, a crate will keep your new friend *and* your belongings safe. And since you will supervise all free time, your dog will quickly learn what's allowed and what isn't.

Doggerel _____
A **crate** is like a den. Crates come in many forms—wire, plastic, aluminum, on wheels, with handles, and in various colors and sizes. For potty training, safe travel, and confinement if the dog is injured or ill, you can't beat a crate.

Crates cost from $25 to $200 and are available from pet supply stores, discount stores, and online (see Appendix C). The crate you purchase should be large enough to accommodate the adult dog your puppy will become, unless you're willing to buy a larger one when he outgrows a small one. Heavy-coated dogs often prefer well-ventilated wire crates because they stay cooler. Short-coated and tiny dogs, on the other hand, may prefer a plastic crate that retains more heat.

If you choose a wire crate, check that the bars are substantial enough to resist teeth and paws, and be sure the bars are spaced closely enough that your dog cannot get his head stuck between them if he gets too pushy. Make sure that the door fits tightly, and that the latch is secure. I've heard of puppies strangling when they forced their heads through bars or door frames and got stuck. Some dogs are escape artists, so check that the latch is out of reach of persistent paws and teeth.

Dogs are much safer traveling in a crate than they are loose in a car. Plastic, airline-approved crates offer the best protection in an accident, and if you expect to fly your dog, that's the kind of crate you'll need. If you choose wire, you may find that a folding crate is more convenient for the car than one that sets up with corner pins.

You may want to provide some padding for the bottom of the crate. If your pup likes to rip up his bedding, don't give him any for a while. Most dogs outgrow the need to tear their blankies, and adults tend to appreciate comfort more than pups do. Crate padding should be disposable or washable. One of the best crate pads I've found is a nonslip "furry" bathroom rug.

The Leash You Can Do

Your dog will need a *collar and leash*. Most places have laws that require all dogs to be under leash control. Besides, a leash will help keep your dog safe when he's outside your house and fenced yard. Don't underestimate the speed at which even a young puppy can get away from you and into danger.

An adjustable flat nylon collar with a quick-release closure works well for a growing puppy. Adjustable collars fold back on themselves so there's no dangling flap for a puppy to chew. Nylon collars come in a rainbow of colors and are inexpensive. Check the fit often and re-adjust or replace the collar when your puppy outgrows it. Provide your dog with an *identification tag* in case he gets lost. The tag should give at least your telephone number. You may want to look into having your puppy tattooed or microchipped for permanent identification.

Grrrrowls

A few simple precautions can mean the difference between life and death when it comes to dogs and collars. For safety ...

- Never leave two or more dogs together unsupervised with collars on—they can entangle their legs or jaws in one another's collars and be seriously injured or even killed.
- Check the fit often and readjust or replace the collar when your puppy outgrows it.
- Never use a slip collar (choke chain) on a young puppy—it can cause severe damage to the throat and spine.
- Never leave a slip collar on a dog in a crate or when you aren't present.

You need a *leash*—or two leashes, in case one gets lost or chewed. *Do not* buy a chain leash. It can injure your puppy or you, and is not effective as a training tool. I don't like nylon leashes either. They can chafe or cut your hands and legs if a whirling puppy wraps one around you. Leather leashes are strong, kinder to your skin, and much more effective for training. Choose a leash appropriate to your dog. A 10-pound adult can be controlled with a quarter-inch leash, but if your pup will mature to 70 pounds, you'll want a 1-inch leash. Check the snap that fastens the leash to the col-lar. A big, heavy snap can frighten or injure a small puppy or dog if it whacks him in the face or teeth. Check out the construction qual-ity. The hand loop and buckle should be stitched securely.

Grrrrowls

Never slip the loop on a leash over your wrist, unless your dog weighs less than 10 pounds. A sudden lunge of the dog could break your wrist. Teach children this rule and enforce it. Even a fairly small dog could pull a child over or drag a child into traffic. Safety first!

Leashes come in several lengths. Your choice depends on the size of your dog and your own preference. Some trainers like six-foot leashes, but I'm uncoordinated and find that much length a hazard except for specialized training. The best leash for controlling your dog on a walk is one that provides some slack, but not so much that the dog gets tangled up all the time.

Grooming Supplies

You'll also need to get some *grooming supplies*. What you need will depend on the type of coat your dog has, and whether you will do all the grooming or only some of it, leaving the rest to a professional groomer. (For more details, see Chapter 16.)

Play Time

Who doesn't like to shop for cute dog *toys*? There are plenty to choose from, so have fun shopping. Just remember that not all toys are safe. Puppies need to chew while they're teething, and many older dogs enjoy a good chewing session. Select good-quality chew toys, and throw them away when they develop sharp points or edges or become too small to be safe. Plastic eyes, synthetic stuffing, squeakers, and rawhides injure or even kill if swallowed. Select toys in sizes appropriate to your puppy so he can't swallow them. When in doubt about a toy's safety, ask your veterinarian.

Doggy Dinnerware

You'll need *food* and *dishes* for your dog. If you're getting your puppy or dog from a responsible source, they will send home a starter supply of whatever he's eating, along with feeding instructions, but you'll need to buy some food before or shortly after your puppy comes home. (See Chapter 12 for more information on foods and nutrition.)

(Photo by Close Encounters of the Furry Kind)

Teach your puppy to play with and chew his own toys, not your shoes or furniture.

Choose dishes that will suit your grown dog. As your puppy grows, his schnoz may become bigger than the bowl he could have slept in as a puppy. Some dogs have special needs when it comes to dinnerware, and special bowls are available to accommodate them. Tall dogs, or older dogs with arthritis, may be more comfortable eating from elevated bowls, for instance, and long-eared dogs like Bassett Hounds and Cocker Spaniels do better with bowls designed to let the ears fall outside. Plastic bowls cause allergic reactions and other problems in some dogs, and some ceramic bowls made outside the United States contain lead and other toxins. Stainless steel bowls are unbeatable—they're sturdy, easy to clean, resistant to chewing and breakage, and are available in a wide range of sizes. You need one for food and at least one for water.

Treats!

You'll want some *treats* for training and for the occasional reward for good behavior. Don't go overboard! Too many goodies will throw your pup's nutrition out of balance and can quickly lead to obesity. Buy healthy treats, and hand them out sparingly. Avoid products that are full of dyes—your dog doesn't care what color the cookie is. Ask your veterinarian's advice on treats. To control calories, try setting aside a portion of your puppy's daily ration to use as rewards. Somehow when kibble is doled out one bit at a time, it's special! Many dogs also enjoy carrots and small bits of fruits and other vegetables.

Schedule a Check-Up

Schedule a veterinary examination for your new puppy or dog soon after you bring him home. Most breeders and rescue groups require that you have the pup examined within a certain time frame to validate their health guarantees. The exam will also assure you that your dog is healthy and will establish some baselines for future reference.

Your vet will check your pup's general health and condition. She will weigh him, evaluate the condition of his skin and coat, and check his heart, lungs, ears, gums, bite, and external eye area. Many young puppies have roundworms, even when they come from careful breeders, so be sure to provide a fecal sample for your vet to check. Older dogs, too, should be tested for intestinal worms and for heartworms. Give your veterinarian whatever health-care records you received with your pet. If it's time for vaccinations, your vet will probably give them during this initial check-up. If you live in an area in which heartworms are a concern, start or continue your dog on heartworm prevention. The dosage of heartworm preventative is determined by the dog's weight, so you'll need to have your puppy reweighed every month to determine the right dosage until he is fully grown. (For more on health care, see Chapter 9.)

Register for Doggy School

No matter what age or size your dog is, a basic obedience class will help you form a bond based on trust and understanding, will give you better control of your dog, and will make her a better companion (see Chapter 18).

Many veterinarians advise against taking a puppy to class before he has finished his inoculations, and many training schools won't accept a puppy before that time. Enroll your pup as soon as he can be accepted into class. All the other things you buy for your pup will mean nothing if you can't live with her. So give her—and yourself—an education.

Bringing Doggy Home

Finally! Your new friend is coming home! Let's see what we can do to get him settled quickly and smoothly.

The Forty-Ninth-Day Myth

Some people believe that a puppy must come home at exactly seven weeks of age or he will never bond to his new family. Not true. That idea is based on research that showed that puppies need to have contact with people beginning no later than the seventh week or they will never be able to bond well with human beings. As long as the pup is handled and played with and socialized by his breeder and her family and friends, it doesn't matter if he is older than seven weeks when he comes home to his new family. He will have no problem bonding to you when he's a bit older.

Seven weeks is definitely the youngest a puppy should leave its littermates and mama. It's not necessarily the best time. From 8 to 10 weeks of age, puppies go through their first *fear imprint period*.

Doggerel _____
Puppies go through
several **fear imprint**
periods, usually at about 8
weeks, 5 to 6 months, and 18
months. It's important to keep
their experiences positive during those periods.

It's important to avoid exposing puppies to potentially frightening or painful experiences during this period, because the effects can be long-lasting. It's usually best not to move a puppy to a new home during this time, and some breeders keep their pups until they're at least 12 weeks old.

Ask the breeder how she handles the pups during the critical 7- to 12-week period. Ideally, she will spend time with each puppy every day, and each puppy will spend time away from his littermates. Potty training should begin during this time, if not sooner. Seven-week-old puppies can learn simple commands, such as Sit, Down, Stand, and Come, and they can begin to learn to walk politely on a leash. Socialization during this time is critical to your dog's social and emotional development. If you want a well-adjusted pup, *do not* get one that hasn't been handled during the seventh and eighth weeks, and don't take one home at this age if you can't spend lots of time with him.

Getting Settled

Your puppy is likely to cry during the first few nights in his new home. Remember, dogs are social animals. When they live in packs, they sleep close to one another. Your new baby probably slept with his siblings. Then suddenly here he is, alone in a strange place and a strange pack. He cries for attention and reassurance. If possible, make it a little easier on your puppy and your family by setting your puppy's crate up in your bedroom at night. Your puppy will be much more secure knowing you're close by. You'll be able to take him outside to potty when you hear him stirring in the middle of the night, and that will speed up the housebreaking process.

To get your puppy ready for bed, give him a good playtime and then a potty trip shortly before putting him to bed. If you let him sleep for three hours before bedtime, he'll be all rested and ready to play when you're ready to sleep. If your puppy whines or barks in his crate, and you're sure he doesn't need to potty (remember—puppies have small bladders and need to go often), try ignoring him. If he gets no response, he'll learn that noisy behavior gets him nowhere, and he'll quiet down. You want your pup to know he's safe and you're close by, but now it's time to sleep. If he wakes up in a few hours and cries, he probably needs to go. Carry him from his crate to his potty area—don't expect him to hold it and walk. Then put him back to bed. If he cries, ignore him again. Remember, he's a baby. Have you ever heard of a baby that didn't keep his parents up for a few nights?

BowWOW

How long can your puppy wait between potty breaks? A formula that works fairly well is to add one to your puppy's age in months. If he's three months old, he can probably wait four hours. But eight hours is about the limit. (Can you go all day without a potty break?)

If for some reason your puppy can't sleep in your bedroom, put an old sweatshirt that you haven't laundered since you last wore it in his crate. Your scent on the shirt will reassure him that you're nearby. A ticking clock near the crate or a radio on low may help soothe him as well. Expect some crying the first few nights, and if you aren't able to hear him when he wakes up, expect a few accidents in the crate as well.

Making Introductions

When dogs live in groups, they organize themselves into a *dominance hierarchy* in which an alpha dog or bitch is in charge, and every other dog in the group occupies a specific rank. This hierarchy helps reduce conflict within the pack. Dogs are also *territorial*. If you already have a dog, your home is his territory, and he may want to defend it against an intruder—your new puppy or dog. You can do several things, though, to reduce friction.

Doggerel _____

A **dominance hierarchy** is a social system in which an **alpha** is socially dominant, and each animal in the group occupies a specific rank. Among dogs, dominance, not age, sex, or even size, determines who is alpha. A **territorial** animal marks a certain area as his own. Among dogs, a pack will mark its territory by urinating around the perimeter, and members of the pack will defend their territory from intruders. When your dog barks at the mail carrier, he's protecting the territory you and he own.

Find a neutral location away from your house and yard for the first encounter so that territory won't be an issue. If you have more than one dog, introduce them to the new dog one at a time so the newcomer won't be intimidated. Don't choose a place that you often take your dog—he may view that as his territory, too. Both dogs should be on a leash. Have one person handle your resident dog and another handle the newcomer. Let the dogs sniff each other a bit, and talk to them quietly. Take the dogs for a walk and let them sniff and investigate each other at intervals. Continue with the "happy talk."

Pay attention to the dogs' body language. A play bow, in which a dog lowers her front end, keeps her rear in the air, and wags her tail, is an invitation to play. The other dog will probably be friendly in response. Hair standing up on a dog's back, bared teeth, growling, staring, stiff-legged walking, or attempts to mount the other dog are all aggressive behaviors. Don't let that sort of behavior continue. Distract the dogs. Call them away from one another, have them sit or lie down, and praise them or give them treats. Wait a few minutes and then try to let the dogs interact again. Keep these encounters short and controlled, and be alert so that things don't get out of hand. Don't give up right away—some dogs that start out disliking one another later become friends. But don't take any chances—dog fights are not pleasant, and it doesn't take long for two dogs to injure one another.

When the dogs stop intensively checking each other out—or better yet, start playing—take them home. Remain cautious for the first few weeks, especially if you already have two or more dogs or if there is a size difference between the old and new dogs. There's bound to be some jockeying for position in the pack, and there's no point taking a chance on a fight. When you can't supervise the dogs, it's probably best to separate them or crate them.

(Photo by Close Encounters of the Furry Kind)

With careful introductions and close supervision, your dog will soon be friends with all members of the family.

If you're bringing home a puppy, you still need to control the initial introduction and supervise all interaction for at least the first few days. Puppies are relentless little pests to older dogs. Well-socialized, kindly adult dogs will tolerate a lot from puppies. When things really get out of hand, a nice grown-up dog will growl and sometimes use his paw or mouth to put a puppy down and tell him to stop biting, leaping, pawing, or pulling. Puppies younger than four months aren't yet fluent in canine body language or manners, and they learn from encounters with good older dogs.

Be cautious with any adult dog that shows signs of aggressiveness or that hasn't been socialized properly. In fact, if you have a dog that is aggressive toward other dogs, be sure you know how you will protect a puppy before you bring one home. A puppy can be badly frightened and injured in a flash by an impatient canine disciplinarian. Never leave a puppy alone with an adult dog unless you're absolutely sure about the adult, and don't expect the older dog to baby-sit indefinitely. He needs some quiet time away from the puppy and some private attention from you. Be sure to give both dogs their own food bowls and toys, too, and don't let the pup annoy the older dog when he's eating.

Introducing a new dog to a resident cat should be done with control and caution. Don't allow the dog to chase or rough up the cat. If the cat bops or scratches the dog on the nose, just distract the dog with toys or petting. Don't punish the cat! She needs to tell the dog what the limits are. And don't allow the dog to retaliate—you don't want to teach the dog that it's okay to chase or harass the cat. If your cat has been with dogs before, chances are things will go smoothly once she sizes up this new dog. If she's not used to dogs, she may be stressed by the newcomer for a while. When we got married and I moved in with my Labrador Retriever, my husband's cat spent days on top of the refrigerator whenever the dog was in the house. A few weeks later they were sharing a big red dog bed.

To help the dog-cat relationship develop smoothly, set up "dog-free" areas where your cat can sleep, eat, play, and use the litter box without canine interference. Let the cat sniff areas of the house where the dog has already explored, but with the dog absent. Then bring the dog in, but confine him to a room or area of the house. If the cat wants to have a look, let her. If not, fine. Don't force a meeting. Let the cat determine how quickly the relationship will develop. Talk to both the dog and the cat. When they see that you talk to the other guy, too, they'll realize they're both part of the family.

Socialize, Socialize, Socialize

Your puppy will become a much better companion if you take the time to introduce him to many things while he is young. With some reasonable precautions, you can see to it that your pup is introduced to lots of people and things even while protecting him from disease before his vaccination series is complete. Avoid high-risk environments, such as places where other animals may leave disease-carrying feces and urine. But do get him out to see the world, even if you have to carry him part of the time. He can still meet lots of people and see and hear lots of things to help his confidence develop.

Once he has all his puppy shots, take your pup to lots of different places—obedience classes, parks, shopping centers, the sidewalk outside your local grocery store, and different neighborhoods. The idea is for him to see lots of people and lots of things. Your dog should always be on a leash in public places, partly for his own safety but also for the comfort of people you meet. Besides, in most places the law prohibits letting a dog run loose. Don't let your pup run up to any dog you don't know. Not all dogs like other dogs, and even those who do don't always like puppies. It only takes one encounter with the wrong dog for your pup to be seriously injured or badly frightened. A puppy kindergarten class is an excellent place to give your puppy a chance to interact with other puppies of different kinds as well as with more people who like dogs (see Chapter 19).

Welcoming Your Grown-Up Dog

An adult dog will require a little time to adjust when moving into a new home. How much time will depend on the dog, where he's coming from, and what your household is like. A well-socialized adult dog from a breeder or in some cases from rescues and shelters has the benefit of having lived with loving people with whom he felt secure. Depending on his breed and his individual personality, he may adjust in a matter of days, or it may take longer.

Animals from shelters may be considerably more stressed. The experience of being abandoned or lost, and then locked in a cage in a noisy place, is frightening. The dog may be grieving for his old home, people, and animal friends. He may have experienced several changes in a short period of time, going from his home to a shelter to a new home. With patience and guidance, he'll adjust.

Spend as much time as you can with your new dog. This will speed up the bonding process. If you already have another dog, and the two are getting along, then do things with both of them as well as with each individually. Go for walks, have short grooming sessions, and hang out together.

Provide your adult dog with a crate. It will give you a safe place to leave her when you can't be home (don't leave her loose in the house until she's well settled). If possible, have the crate in your bedroom at night, or near your other dog's sleeping area, so that she'll feel like part of the pack. She soon will.

The Least You Need to Know

- 🏠 Puppy-proof your house to protect your new doggy and your belongings.

- 🏠 Stock up on essentials before your new buddy comes home.

- 🏠 Schedule a check-up with your veterinarian.

- 🏠 Register for obedience class.

- 🏠 Take simple precautions to help your new dog and your existing pets become friends.

Part 3

Keeping Your Dog Healthy

If you want a healthy, happy dog, you have to do your part to keep him that way. We'll first take a look at the role your vet plays in your dog's life. Then I'll discuss routine preventive care that will help keep your dog in good health, from vaccinations to parasite prevention to spaying and neutering. We'll also look at some common health problems that afflict dogs, and what you can do to prevent or manage them. And since accidents do happen (my dog Rowdy broke his leg while I was writing this section!), I'll show you some basic canine first aid.

Of course, veterinary care isn't the only factor affecting your dog's health. We'll take a look at the basics of sound nutrition for your dog, and some of the advantages and disadvantages of commercial dog foods as well as homemade and raw diets. Finally, we'll see the importance of safe exercise for your dog's physical and mental well-being throughout his life.

Chapter **9**

Routine Health Care

In This Chapter

🏠 Your dog's second-best friend—his veterinarian

🏠 Protecting your dog from illness and injury

🏠 Keeping parasites at bay

🏠 Spaying and neutering

A healthy dog is a happy dog, and a terrific companion. Good regular veterinary care will prevent disease and detect potential problems early on. Spaying and neutering are also excellent ways to prevent some health problems as well as unwanted puppies. Your dog may or may not appreciate an apple a day, but he'll certainly appreciate the fun he has as a healthy canine companion.

Choosing a Veterinarian

Your dog's vet is an important person in his life, even if he doesn't much like going to see her. With your help, she'll give him regular examinations and provide vaccinations and preventive medications to keep him healthy. If he's sick or injured, she'll diagnose the problem and offer treatment options.

You should be comfortable with your dog's vet, and confident about the care she can provide. If you find you're uncomfortable with your vet, or you don't care for the atmosphere or policies of the practice, find a new one. It's to your dog's advantage to see the same vet most of the time. The veterinarian will keep a medical history of your dog, including a record of vaccinations, illnesses, injuries, treatments, and so forth. Your dog will also be more relaxed if he sees the same vet each time, especially if you both like her.

Finding the right veterinarian for your dog is a lot like finding the right doctor for yourself. If you already have a vet you feel comfortable with, great. If not, start looking as soon as you decide to get a dog and, if possible, select a vet before you bring your new canine buddy home.

If possible, choose a vet who has worked with dogs of your breed or who is open to input from you about peculiarities of the breed. Dogs of some breeds are sensitive to certain drugs, and it's important for vets working with those breeds to know that. If you are active in canine sports, look for a vet who is familiar with the stresses experienced by canine athletes.

How can you find such a terrific vet? If you're getting your dog from a local breeder or rescue program, ask who they recommend. Ask friends and neighbors who have dogs—particularly dogs like yours—about their vets. When you sign up for obedience or other training classes, ask for recommendations. Contact local kennel clubs and breed clubs for referrals. As a last resort, check the telephone book or Internet for local veterinarians.

Ask people what they like and don't like about their vets and about the practices in which their vets work. You might also ask whether they have used other clinics in the area and, if so, ask why they changed. Your approach to your dog's medical care may be different from someone else's, and what they don't like may be exactly what you do want. That's okay. Individual personalities are important in the vet-client-patient triangle. Some vets are better with big dogs, and others with toys. Some like input from well-informed clients, and some don't.

If possible, arrange to interview two or three veterinarians and ask for a tour of their facilities. Some will charge for an office call (usually around $25), but many will talk to you for a few minutes at no charge.

Vaccinating Against Common Diseases

Newborn puppies born to healthy, properly vaccinated mothers get some immunity to disease from the *colostrum* in their mother's milk. The protection given by the mother's colostrum wears off sometime between the puppy's fifth and tenth week of life, leaving him vulnerable to infectious diseases. To protect the puppy, a series of vaccinations is given, usually starting at about six weeks of age. Most veterinarians recommend a series of three or four sets of shots given at three- to four-week intervals. Most vaccinations are *subcutaneous* (under the skin) or *intramuscular* (into the muscle).

Doggerel

Colostrum is a highly concentrated mixture of antibodies, protein, vitamins, electrolytes, nutrients, and fluid produced by the mother's breasts during the first 36 to 48 hours after birth. Colostrum is very important to the newborn animal's chances of survival because it provides protection from infectious disease as well as fluids needed for the heart and circulatory system to work properly.

Over the past decade, many people have become concerned about health problems associated with overvaccinating pets. The American Veterinary Medical Association (AVMA) and a number of veterinary colleges are reviewing their recommended vaccination schedules, and many veterinarians are also modifying their approaches to vaccinations.

Despite the risks, proper vaccination is still the best line of defense against infectious disease. Talk to your vet about your circumstances.

Grrrrowls _____

Overvaccination has been linked to a number of long-term health problems in dogs, including auto-immune diseases in which the animal's own immune system attacks it.

The specific vaccines your dog should have, and the frequency with which he should have them, depend on where you live, your dog's potential exposure to specific diseases, and his age and overall health. Dogs are commonly vaccinated against some or all of the following diseases.

Rabies

Rabies can occur in any warm-blooded animal, including people. It is caused by a virus that attacks the animal's central nervous system. Rabies is spread in the saliva of an infected animal, usually by way of a bite. Wild animals, including skunks, foxes, raccoons, coyotes, and bats, are not uncommonly infected with rabies, and they can transmit the disease to domestic animals.

When we think of a rabid animal, we usually picture one frothing at the mouth and acting aggressively. These are symptoms of a form of the disease known as *furious* rabies. Most of us know instinctively to avoid such an animal and to get help if we or one of our pets is attacked by one. But rabies takes another form known as *dumb* rabies. Rather than becoming aggressive and foaming at the mouth, an animal with dumb rabies becomes paralyzed, usually beginning with the lower jaw and progressing through the limbs and vital organs until the animal dies. Once symptoms of a rabies infection appear, the disease is always fatal. That's why rabies shots are required by law in the United States and Canada.

Your puppy should have his initial rabies vaccination when he is three to four months old. After that, your dog must be revaccinated according to the laws of your state. Some states require rabies boosters for dogs and cats every year. Others require the boosters every three years.

Canine Distemper

Canine distemper is a highly contagious viral disease. Most puppies and about half of adult dogs who contract canine distemper die from it. If a dog lives through canine distemper, he is likely to suffer long-term damage. He may be partially or completely paralyzed. He may also lose some or all of his vision, hearing, and sense of smell. Respiratory problems, vomiting and diarrhea, and sometimes seizures are among the symptoms of distemper.

Canine distemper is easily spread from dog to dog, and is also carried and spread by raccoons, so it's very important to protect puppies. A series of three or four injections is used for puppies. Consult your veterinarian about the proper booster program for your adult dog.

Infectious Canine Hepatitis

Infectious canine hepatitis is another viral disease that attacks the liver and other tissues. The virus is spread in the urine of infected dogs—a good reason to keep your puppy away from places frequented by strange dogs until he has completed his puppy vaccinations. A series of three injections is normally used to protect puppies from hepatitis. Again, consult your veterinarian about the need for boosters for your adult dog.

Parvo

Say "parvo" to a breeder and you'll likely see the blood drain from her face. *Canine parvovirus (CPV)*, or parvo, is an extremely serious viral disease that can wipe out whole litters in no time. Parvo attacks the intestinal tract, heart muscle, and white blood cells. Symptoms of parvo include vomiting, severe diarrhea with a distinctive foul odor, depression, high fever, and loss of appetite. Affected dogs are usually dead within two to three days after symptoms appear. Puppies under three months of age who contract parvo often suffer *myocarditis* (inflammation of the heart). Puppies survive parvo only with intensive care, usually involving intravenous fluid replacement to fight against dehydration. Even with intensive care, many puppies who contract parvo die of the disease. Puppies who survive usually suffer permanent heart damage.

Parvo vaccines are given to puppies in a series of three shots, followed by boosters for adult dogs.

Kennel Cough

Canine Bordetellosis, also known as "Bordatella" or "kennel cough," is a bacterial disease of the respiratory tract much like a cold in humans. The primary symptom is a horrendous cough that makes your sweet little doggy sound like an elephant seal. The cough is sometimes accompanied by heavy nasal discharge.

If your adult dog is otherwise healthy, kennel cough isn't very serious. But in a puppy, an elderly dog, or a dog in poor health, kennel cough can be deadly.

Bordatella vaccines are usually given in a nasal spray, although injectable vaccines are also available. Vaccination schedules for Bordatella vary, so ask your veterinarian what's best for your dog.

Canine Parainfluenza

Canine parainfluenza is a viral disease that causes respiratory tract infection. Puppies are usually given a series of three vaccinations, and adults are given boosters as recommended for the area in which you live.

Lepto

Leptospirosis, or "lepto," affects the kidneys and can cause kidney failure. Symptoms of lepto include vomiting, convulsions, and vision problems. The bacteria that cause the disease are transmitted in the urine of infected animals. Lepto is not very common in most areas, but some evidence shows that it may be on the rise.

Grrrrowls

Many dangers lurk in places frequented by lots of dogs. For your puppy's health, wait until he has had his full series of puppy shots before you let him walk in parks, highway rest stops, or other places where lots of dogs may have left urine and feces. Remember, one or two shots won't protect him completely! Don't give viruses and bacteria a chance to hurt your pup!

Many breeders and owners choose not to vaccinate against lepto for several reasons. First, a relatively high number of puppies experience severe reactions to the vaccine. In addition, several strains of lepto exist, and unfortunately the vaccines that are available have minimal effect on the most common strain.

Discuss your puppy's risk of exposure and need for the vaccine with your veterinarian prior to vaccinating him. If vaccination for lepto is appropriate in your circumstances, consider having that vaccine given at a different time from the others to control a possible negative reaction.

Other Infectious Diseases

Other diseases occur in dogs in some areas. Talk to your veterinarian about the need to vaccinate your puppy or dog against Coronavirus, Lyme disease, and other diseases. There is no reason to vaccinate your dog against diseases that pose no risk for him, but at the same time you want to be sure he's protected against potential dangers.

Fleas and Mites and Ticks, Oh My!

External parasites can cause plenty of problems besides itching and scratching. Infections and allergic reactions to bites are common, and parasites carry disease.

Fleas

Fleas are small red, black, or brown insects. They are very mobile and hard to catch, and they have a hard covering that protects them. Adult fleas suck the blood of their hosts. Flea larvae feed on the adult fleas' feces, which is rich in blood.

Combing through his hair with a flea comb, which has closely spaced teeth, is an excellent way to check your dog for fleas. Even if you can't seem to find fleas on your dog, you may find flea "dirt" (feces), which looks like pepper on the dog's skin. You can confirm that it's flea dirt by moistening the black specks slightly. Flea dirt will turn red because it's made mostly of blood from the host animal.

Fleas reproduce by way of eggs. They sometimes lay their eggs on the host animal, but usually they lay them in a more favorable place, such as the dog's bedding. Flea eggs normally hatch in 4 to 21 days, depending on the temperature, but they can survive up to 18 months before hatching the *larva*, which look like tiny maggots. The larva molt twice before forming a *pupa*, which can survive long periods until the temperature, or the vibration of a nearby host, causes them to emerge as full-fledged fleas.

> **Doggerel** _____
> Larvae (plural of larva) are animals in a special feeding stage in their life cycle. In insects, the worm-like larva hatches from its egg and eats like crazy for a while. It then enters the **pupal** stage, during which it undergoes **metamorphosis**, or transformation, into the adult form.

Fleas are Pests with a capital P. Some dogs barely seem to notice when they have fleas, but others are allergic to flea saliva. When an allergic dog is bitten by a flea, he will scratch and bite his skin frantically to relieve the itching, opening sores that can become infected. Fleas also carry tapeworm larva and disease (see the following "Fishing for Intestinal Worms" section). A large infestation of fleas can cause anemia in the host animal, especially if it's a puppy or small dog.

Your veterinarian will be able to suggest the most effective strategy for flea control for your situation and area.

Ticks

Ticks are arthropods (relatives of spiders). Most ticks are round and flat until they gorge themselves on blood from a host animal. Then their bodies swell until they look like small beans with legs.

Dogs and people often pick up ticks in fields or woods. Your yard may also harbor ticks who arrive courtesy of wild animals, birds, or stray dogs and cats. Ticks, like fleas, are more than disgusting pests. They are also carriers of disease, including babesiosis, anaplasmosis, ehrlichia, East Coast fever, relapsing fever, Rocky Mountain spotted fever, and, most commonly, Lyme disease.

The deer tick is very, very small, but can be big trouble as it carries Lyme disease, which can be crippling in dogs as well as people. Their extremely small size makes deer ticks difficult to detect. By the time they swell up big enough to be noticed, they've often been feeding on the host for a few days—plenty of time to transmit Lyme disease.

Lyme disease is a problem, but only in certain places. Talk to your vet about the danger of Lyme disease in your area to determine whether a vaccination is a good idea for your dog's protection.

Always check your dog carefully after he's been in any area that harbors ticks. If deer ticks are a problem where you are, use a fine-toothed flea comb to search your dog's fur for the tiny pests. If you find a tick, remove it *carefully*. It's easy to pull the body off, leaving the tick's head in the host, and that can cause infection. Avoid squeezing a tick while removing it—that can force fluids from the tick into the host, increasing the risk of infection or disease. Dabbing a tick with a strong saline solution, iodine, or alcohol will make it loosen its grip. Then carefully pull the tick straight out with forceps, tweezers, or your fingers with a tissue over the tick. Special tick-removers are also available in some pet supply stores. After you remove the tick, you should see a small hole in the skin. (If you see a black spot, you have left the head. In any case, keep a close eye on the spot. If it reddens or swells, it may be infected, so see your veterinarian.) Clean the bite with alcohol, Betadine, or iodine. After about five minutes, apply antiseptic ointment. Then wash your hands and any tool you used.

If ticks are common in your area, talk to your vet about a preventive program.

(Photo by Close Encounters of the Furry Kind)

Regular veterinary check-ups are an important part of your dog's routine health care.

Ringworm

Ringworm is not a worm but a highly contagious fungal infection. Ringworm can be spread from one pet to another, and it's one of the few diseases that can be passed from dogs to people. It's extremely itchy, and can lead to open sores and infections.

Ringworm usually starts as a sore-looking bald circle, but if your puppy or dog develops any sort of bald spots, have your veterinarian take a look. Fungal infections are hard to treat and even harder to cure. Modern drugs are much more effective against ringworm than home remedies. If your dog has ringworm, ask your vet for guidelines to prevent its spread in your household.

Mange

Mange is caused by various species of mites that feed on skin debris, the hair follicles, and tissue. Symptoms of mange include hair loss often followed by a flaky crust on the skin. Often dogs will scratch themselves and worsen the original condition by opening lesions that make viral, fungal, or parasitic attack easy. Three types of mange occur in dogs.

Demodectic mange most often affects puppies from three months to one year of age. The demodex mite is found on the skin of many puppies and dogs and usually causes no symptoms. Occasionally, though, a puppy is less resistant, and the mites reproduce more rapidly than normal. Demodectic mange is characterized by patches of thinned hair around the eyes and mouth and on the front legs. Early diagnosis and treatment by your veterinarian is your best bet.

Sarcoptic mange, also known as *scabies*, develops when the microscopic mite that causes it burrows under the animal's skin to lay its eggs. The eggs hatch and the larvae develop into adult mites who begin to lay their own eggs, all in less than three weeks. Scabies causes intense itching, oozing sores, crusty ear tips, hair loss, and secondary infections when bacteria enter the injured skin. Hair loss occurs first on the ears, elbows, legs, and face, and then spreads throughout the body. Scabies can be passed from dogs to people and vice versa.

Cheyletiella mange, or "walking dandruff," is characterized by dandruff on the dog's head, neck, and back. It causes mild itching in puppies, and is highly contagious.

If you suspect that your dog has mange, have him examined by your vet. It's vital to determine the species of mite causing the problem in order to treat mange effectively.

Eczema

Eczema refers to many skin disorders with many causes. Sunburn, chemicals, food, drugs, plants, pollens, and even stress can all cause itching, hair loss, and open sores in susceptible dogs. With so many potential causes, eczema is often hard to treat or prevent. If your dog develops skin problems with no obvious cause, your best hope for a cure is to work closely with your veterinarian, be very observant, and keep a written record of your dog's activities and the ups and downs of his eczema so that you can identify the cause.

Fishing for Intestinal Worms

There are many species of worms, and a number of these live as parasites in dogs and other animals. Puppies should have fecal exams when they get their vaccinations, and adult dogs should have an annual fecal exam so that they can be treated if necessary. If you see evidence of worms in your dog's stool, take a specimen to your vet so that he can prescribe the appropriate wormer if worms are found in the feces. Your dog's best protection against worms is your attention to cleanliness and telltale symptoms.

Roundworms

Roundworms are common in puppies, and responsible breeders have their bitches and puppies checked for worms, and treat them as necessary. Roundworms can be transmitted to people, so it's important to practice good hygiene—especially washing hands after playing with the puppy—and to teach children to do the same.

Roundworms look like strings of spaghetti about 8 inches (20 cm) long. The worms eat the digesting food in the intestines of the host. In chronic cases, an infected puppy will develop a potbelly, diarrhea, and vomiting. At first, he will always seem to be hungry, but as the worms cause malnutrition, the pup will eventually become so ill that he will stop eating. Luckily, roundworms are easy to eliminate.

Tapeworms

Dogs get *tapeworms* primarily by ingesting fleas that carry the tapeworm larvae, although mice, rabbits, and other animals are also possible sources. Tapeworms are not as damaging to the health of the host animal as some other intestinal parasites, but it's still best to prevent and eliminate them.

Unlike other worms, tapeworms do not usually show up in feces. However, segments of the worm are often shed during bowel movements and may appear as small, white, rice-like bits clinging to the hair around the dog's anus. If you find such segments on your dog, see your veterinarian for medication to kill the worms. Keeping your dog free of fleas will help prevent tapeworms.

Doggerel
An intermediate host is an animal in which a parasite's larvae live until eaten by the final host. Once ingested by the final host, the adult parasites develop.

Other Worms

Hookworms, whipworms, and *threadworms* can cause problems including weight loss, anemia, respiratory infection, and diarrhea in puppies and dogs. They are three more good reasons to be sure a fecal exam is part of your dog's annual check-up.

Heartworm

Heartworm disease occurs when a mosquito carries heartworm larvae from an infected dog and injects them into another dog's blood stream. The larvae travel through the arteries to the new host's heart, where they develop into adult heartworms. Eventually, the worms fill the heart and cause congestive heart failure.

Daily, monthly, and now biannual preventive medications are available through your veterinarian. As an added bonus, many heartworm preventatives also prevent intestinal parasites. Heartworm is a serious problem in many places, but not everywhere, so ask your vet about the need for heartworm prevention where you live. If you plan to travel with your dog, check before you go—your dog may need protection during your travels. Before beginning heartworm prevention, and once a year thereafter, it's important to have your dog tested to be sure he hasn't been infected with heartworms despite the preventive medications. They are very effective, but no medication is 100 percent sure.

Grrrrowls

Ivermectin, a drug used to prevent or treat heartworm infection, sarcoptic mange, and some other parasites, causes seizures, coma, and death in some dogs of the Collie breeds (Collies, Border Collies, Shetland Sheepdogs, Australian Shepherds, and crosses containing one of those breeds). There is no way to know which individual is sensitive until symptoms appear. Use alternative drugs for these breeds.

Spaying and Neutering

If you spend any time at all with responsible dog breeders, rescue volunteers, shelter volunteers and workers, or other members of the "doggy community," you will hear that pets should be spayed or neutered. Shelters and rescue organizations require that adopted pets be sterilized, often before they go to their new homes. Most responsible breeders sell their pet puppies on contracts that require altering. Many also sell their pets on limited registration, which means that while the puppy itself is registered, if he becomes a parent his pups will not be eligible for registration. The national and local breed and kennel clubs that promote purebred dogs, the American Kennel Club (AKC), and most veterinarians will encourage you to spay or neuter your pet. So will I!

Why the emphasis on spaying and neutering? Pay a visit to your local animal shelter and you will get an idea of the shamefully high number of unwanted animals produced and discarded every year. You'll see mixed-breeds and purebreds of every size and shape. Most of them would be wonderful companions. Most don't deserve to be abandoned in a shelter. Many animals that enter shelters die there because no one wants them. Call your local breed rescue representative, or visit some rescue organizations on the World Wide Web, and look at the beautiful dogs in need of homes before you decide not to sterilize your pet.

BowWOW

Six to eight million unwanted pets are euthanized each year in the United States. That's 16,438 to 21,917 pets euthanized *every* day.

A person was involved in the breeding of nearly every one of those dogs, either by neglecting to prevent a pregnancy or by actively facilitating one. A responsible breeder knows that she remains responsible for every puppy she breeds *for its entire life*. If you would not be willing to take back a puppy at any age and take care of him properly for as long as necessary—perhaps for the rest of his life—then you should prevent your dog from reproducing.

Sterilization eliminates some health problems and reduces the chance of others. Not only does that spare your pet the pain of disease, it spares you and your family the emotional and financial cost of caring for a sick pet. Since spaying involves removal of the ovaries and uterus, it eliminates the chance of ovarian or uterine cancer. It also reduces the risk of breast cancer, especially if the surgery is done before the bitch's first estrous ("heat") cycle. A spayed bitch is also safe from the dangers of pregnancy and *whelping* (giving birth) (see Chapter 17).

Neutering of a male dog involves removal of the testicles, so there is no further risk of testicular cancer. Neutered males are also less likely to develop prostate disease.

Spayed and neutered dogs make for better companions. With a spayed bitch, you won't have the mess of bleeding during estrous, nor will you have boy dogs lined up from your front door to the end of the block for a month every time your bitch is in heat. Neutered males and spayed females tend to be less aggressive toward both dogs and people, and less likely to roam. Studies show that spayed and neutered pets are also less likely to bite.

What about the idea that having a litter will help a young bitch calm down? This may have great appeal if you have a young, rambunctious doggy girl. But it's not true. Maturity and training, not motherhood, lead to calmer behavior.

Contrary to popular belief, sterilization will not lead to obesity, either. Too much food and too little exercise make for fat dogs, whether they are altered or not. The problem is that many dogs are altered at around six months of age, at which time their metabolisms slow down because they aren't growing as fast as they were when younger. If your dog needs less food but you don't cut back the amount you give him, he'll get fat. Make sure your pet gets plenty of exercise, a proper diet, and not too many handouts, and he or she will stay slim.

The Least You Need to Know

- 🏠 Your dog's veterinarian is one of the most important people in his life.

- 🏠 Vaccinations are essential to maintaining your dog's good health.

- 🏠 Parasites can also be a serious threat to your dog's health.

- 🏠 Spaying or neutering will make your pet a better, healthier companion.

Chapter 10

Living with Health Problems

In This Chapter

- 🏠 Diagnosing chronic health problems
- 🏠 Understanding treatment options
- 🏠 Learning to manage ongoing canine health problems
- 🏠 Helping to reduce the incidence of chronic health problems in dogs

Despite the best efforts of conscientious owners and breeders, dogs do sometimes fall prey to serious acute or chronic health problems. Some are inherited, and some are acquired through disease or injury. With veterinary intervention, good nutrition, and careful management of exercise and other aspects of the dog's daily life, many dogs live long, active, happy lives despite their conditions.

Orthopedic Problems

A number of orthopedic problems affecting the bones and joints occur in dogs. Some are associated with injuries, some are inherited, and the causes of some are not fully understood. Some affect primarily large dogs; others affect mostly small dogs. The most common signs of orthopedic problems include stiffness, limping, favoring a leg, difficulty getting up, reluctance to jump or to climb stairs, and obvious pain. Let's look briefly at the most common forms of joint disease in dogs.

Grrrrowls

Don't give your dog regular aspirin, acetaminophen (Tylenol), or ibuprofen unless your vet recommends it. They can have serious side effects in dogs.

Degenerative joint disease (DJD) occurs when the smooth cartilage over the end of a bone in a synovial (movable) joint deteriorates. DJD is painful and progressive, meaning it will continue to get worse. Primary DJD results from normal wear and tear on an otherwise normal joint as the dog ages. Secondary DJD results from another condition.

Osteochondritis dissecans (OCD) is a disease in which cartilage in the joints grows abnormally or is damaged. OCD is primarily a disease of large and giant breed dogs. OCD is most common in the shoulder joint, but can affect the elbow or the hock (the second joint above the hind foot, where the long bones of the upper and lower leg meet). Symptoms usually appear between four and eight months of age.

Rheumatoid arthritis occurs mostly in small breeds. Symptoms, including swelling, stiffness, and tenderness, usually appear in several joints around five years of age. Rheumatoid arthritis is caused by overreaction of the immune system.

Elbow dysplasia is used to describe one or more of three conditions in the elbow joint: fragmentation of the coronoid process (FCP), ununited anconeal process (UAP), and osteochondritis dissecans (OCD). A dog with elbow dysplasia usually limps and may avoid walking on the affected leg. Symptoms of elbow dysplasia show up as early as four months.

Canine hip dysplasia (CHD) is a serious, potentially crippling inherited condition in which the bones of the hip joint do not fit together properly. This poor fit makes the dog prone to developing arthritis. CHD is most common in large and giant dogs, but can occur in any breed or mixture of breeds. Symptoms can appear as early as five months, but usually show up during the middle or later years of the dog's life. Dogs with CHD sometimes show no symptoms at all, so it's essential that dogs used for breeding be x-rayed prior to the breeding.

Panosteitis ("pano") is a bone disease most common in large-breed dogs between 6 and 18 months of age. Dogs with pano often have a "migrating limp"—first one leg, then another.

Ruptured anterior cruciate ligament is a knee injury in which the anterior cruciate ligament (which helps hold the bones of the knee together) is ruptured (torn), making the joint unstable.

Patellar luxation occurs when the patella (kneecap) slips out of place (luxates) and locks so that the leg can't bend. Patellar luxation is most common in small breeds, but can occur in larger dogs.

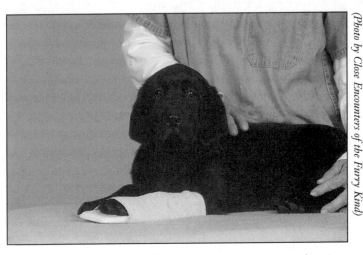

(Photo by Close Encounters of the Furry Kind)

Many dogs treated for orthopedic problems go on to live normal, active lives.

Orthopedic Treatments

A number of treatments are used for dogs with orthopedic problems. As always, ask your veterinarian before using any supplement or over-the-counter medications.

- *Biotin* and *fatty acid* supplements given in concert (but at different meals during the day) have reportedly helped some dogs with DJD.

- *Buffered aspirin* can be used safely as an anti-inflammatory and painkiller in most dogs. If your dog shows signs of an upset stomach, discontinue use of buffered aspirin pending a veterinary examination.

- *Carprofen* (Rimadyl) is a nonsteroidal anti-inflammatory painkiller. It is very effective, but can cause liver damage. Dogs on Rimadyl should be tested regularly for healthy functioning of the liver.

- *Corticosteroids* are used as anti-inflammatory painkillers. They have a number of short- and long-term side effects, and are usually used when other painkillers don't work.

- *Glucosamine* and *Chondroitin* are widely used to treat arthritis in animals and people. Glucosamine is a component of cartilage. Chondroitin promotes the formation of healthy cartilage and inhibits enzymes that break down cartilage.

- *Polysulfated Glycosaminoglycan* (Adequan) is given in a series of shots over several weeks. Adequan helps prevent breakdown of cartilage and may promote formation of new cartilage.

- *Surgery* is an effective treatment for some orthopedic problems.

- *Vitamin C* is sometimes recommended for preventing or treating orthopedic problems in dogs, but there is no scientific evidence that it works. Reasonable doses don't appear to have any harmful side effects.

Easing Your Dog's Discomfort

Here are some ideas that may ease your dog's discomfort if he develops an orthopedic problem:

- 🐾 Keep your dog at a healthy weight. Excess weight puts more stress on joints as well as internal organs.

- 🐾 Restrict your dog's exercise, but see that he gets enough *daily* exercise to maintain or increase his muscle tone and strength. *Don't let him jump.* Swimming will help maintain muscle mass without putting excessive stress on the joints.

- 🐾 Keep your dog warm. Arthritic joints ache more in cold, damp weather.

- 🐾 Provide a firm orthopedic bed made of "egg-crate" foam to evenly distribute your dog's weight and reduce pressure on joints.

- 🐾 If your dog has arthritis in his back or neck, elevate his food and water bowls so he won't have to bend down.

- 🐾 If your dog must negotiate steps to go in and out of the house, consider installing a ramp to make it easier for him.

Epilepsy

A dog with canine epilepsy will have seizures or "fits," but seizures don't necessarily mean a dog has epilepsy. A seizure occurs when nerves in the brain "fire" suddenly and without normal controls. This firing of the nerves causes muscles to contract repeatedly. Seizures can be caused by poisons, drugs, head injuries, or disease. If no clear cause can be found for seizures, the dog is then usually said to have idiopathic epilepsy, which is considered to be genetic. Dogs with idiopathic epilepsy usually have their first seizures between one and five years of age.

Seizures are rarely fatal, but they are terrifying to watch, and a seizuring dog can injure itself when thrashing around. In extreme cases, a dog may experience continuous, uncontrollable seizures that can lead to secondary problems including hyperthermia, hypoglycemia, exhaustion, brain damage, and even death.

Epilepsy can't be cured, but it usually can be controlled. Most epileptic dogs live fairly normal lives with medication. Idiopathic epilepsy is more prevalent in some breeds than in others, and in some families within those breeds. Ask breeders about epilepsy in their dogs' bloodlines. A dog with epilepsy should *never* be bred. Epilepsy occurs in all breeds, including mixed-breeds.

BowWOW

Not all seizures indicate epilepsy. Seizures can also be caused by physical trauma to the head, chemical agents, heatstroke, congenital defects, diabetes mellitus, hypoglycemia, kidney or liver disorders, infectious disease, tumors, toxins, fevers and hyperthermia, certain medications, and eclampsia (low calcium levels in a nursing female).

Phenobarbital, alone or with one of several other drugs, is the drug most commonly used to control epilepsy. Dilantin and Primidone are sometimes used. The drugs come in oral form and are given daily. Although the drugs are sedatives, once the proper dosage is determined you usually can't tell that the dog is on medication. If your veterinarian prescribes drugs to manage epilepsy, it's vital not to miss a dose or stop the medication suddenly, as that could cause severe seizures.

If your dog has a seizure, stay calm. *Never put any part of your body near the mouth of a seizuring dog*—he could bite you without even knowing it. If possible, clear the area of sharp or hard objects or furniture so your dog won't hurt himself by thrashing into something. If the seizure lasts more than 15 minutes, or if he has one seizure after another, call your vet. Then wrap your dog gently in a sheet or blanket (or towel if she's small) and take her to the vet. Long-lasting seizures and seizures in a series are potentially fatal.

If your dog has a single, mild seizure, record the date and time, and write down as accurately as possible what happened. Review the list of causes of seizures, and note any of those that may have triggered your dog's seizure. Call your vet as soon as possible.

Vision and Hearing Problems

Dogs can experience a loss of useful vision or hearing for many reasons. Some eye and ear problems are inherited. Environmental factors such as illness or injury can also cause a complete or partial loss of vision or hearing. The loss may be bilateral, meaning that both eyes or both ears are affected, or it may be unilateral, meaning the eye or ear on one side is affected, but the other remains normal. Many elderly dogs lose their vision to cataracts or other age-related causes, and many slowly lose some or all of their hearing.

Many breeds are plagued by eye problems and/or ear problems, and a mixed-breed dog whose heritage includes one of those breeds may also have the problem if the rest of the genes come together wrong. That doesn't mean that every dog of that breed will have a problem. It *does* mean that as a buyer you need to study your breed of choice, know what the potential problems are, and buy only from a breeder who tests her breeding dogs and, if appropriate, her pups (see Chapter 3). If your dog is a mixed-breed, you should read about the problems that are common in the breeds that you believe make up her ancestry so that you're alert to indications of a specific problem and so you know which tests may be appropriate for early diagnosis.

Know how to recognize a red flag in the breed. For example, in those breeds where merle (called "dapple" in some breeds) coloring occurs, the pairing of a merle sire and a merle dam sometimes results in a *homozygous* (or "double") merle puppy. Such a puppy will likely have a lot of white on its body and head—and that is a red flag in

Doggerel

Every puppy inherits one gene for each of his traits from each of his parents. Very simply put, if the two genes are the same, then the pup is **homozygous** for that trait. If the two genes are different, the pup is **heterozygous** for that trait.

those breeds. Homozygous merles are often deaf and often have serious eye defects. *Heterozygous* merles are not at risk for problems any more than nonmerle members of their breed.

We just don't have room here to cover all the ins and outs of living with a dog that has lost her vision or hearing. The important things to know are these:

🐾 Most dogs adjust well to partial or complete blindness or deafness and, with a few adjustments, live nearly normal lives.

🐾 Many excellent resources are available to help you adjust to your dog's special needs and to accept her new status (see Appendixes B and C).

🐾 Dogs with vision problems can be trained to follow specific voice commands that keep them safe when negotiating new terrain—Slow, Left, Right, Step Up, Step Down, and so on are useful.

🐾 Dogs with hearing problems can be trained to respond to visual commands to Come, Lie Down, Stay, and anything else you need to teach. Hand signals and light signals are commonly used to train deaf dogs.

Remember, your dog doesn't need to see you or hear you in order to love you, lick your face, appreciate doggy dinner or a belly rub, go for a walk, or be your best friend. And it's not his fault if he can't see or hear. If the situation were reversed, he'd still love you, and he'll still love you now. He sees you and hears you just fine with his heart.

Skin Conditions and Allergies

Dogs can be sensitive to many of the same *allergens*—things that cause allergies—as people: pollen, dust mites, mold, perfumes, dyes, insect bites (including flea bites), and food ingredients are among the leaders. Allergic dogs react to *inhalent* allergens (those that they inhale) by itching and scratching, chewing, licking, and biting at their skin. The skin becomes irritated, oily, and possibly raw and infected. Dogs with food allergies also itch. Other symptoms of food allergy include head shaking, inflamed ears, licking (especially of their front paws), diarrhea, flatulence, sneezing, difficulty breathing, behavioral changes, seizures, or sometimes vomiting. They may also rub their faces on carpets or grass. No fun for the dog, or the people who live with him.

It isn't always easy to determine the cause of an allergic reaction, so if your dog is doing a lot of scratching or licking at himself, see your vet right away. The sooner you find the cause, the sooner you can give your dog some relief, and the better your chances of preventing open sores on her skin. If you and your regular vet can't identify the allergen within a reasonable amount of time, consider taking your dog to a veterinary dermatologist for specialized testing. Testing isn't cheap, but in the long run it will cost you less than ineffective treatments that go on for years. And your dog will appreciate the relief!

Several treatments are available for a dog with allergies. The most obvious and basic is to remove the source. If your dog is allergic to corn or wheat, it makes no sense to keep feeding her dog food with corn or wheat. If she's allergic to flea bites, then it becomes even more important to keep her free of fleas. Other treatments for allergies include the following:

🏠 *Antihistamines* are fairly safe for dogs and are effective for some of them. Before giving your dog over-the-counter antihistamines, check with your veterinarian for the proper dosage, and be sure there's no risk of drug interaction with anything else your dog is taking. Antihistamines may make your dog sleep.

Corticosteroids such as cortiso prednisone are sometimes used on a short-term basis in extreme cases to reduce itching related to inflammation. The problem is that they can have serious side effects. In the short term, they may cause behavioral changes, increased thirst and appetite, and increased urination. If used long term, they can suppress the immune system (making your dog more susceptible to infection) and cause diabetes or seizures.

Fatty acids (Omega-3 and Omega-6) appear to relieve some dogs by preventing inflammations that lead to sores. They take three to four weeks to have an effect, and they don't stop the dog from itching. Omega-3 fatty acids come from fish oils, and Omega-6 fatty acids come from plants containing gamma-linolenic acid, such as oil from the evening primrose.

Immunotherapy (allergy shots) are safe and effective, but they're also slow to take effect—sometimes they take as long as a year. Your dog must be tested to determine the allergens causing her reaction in order to begin immunotherapy.

Heart Problems

Heart disease is as common in dogs as it is in people. Some dogs are born with *congenital heart disease,* which usually is found when a heart murmur is detected during a puppy exam. *Acquired heart disease* develops over time as a result of aging or other infections or diseases.

Common symptoms of heart disease in dogs include heavy panting, irregular or rapid breathing, coughing, an enlarged abdomen, lack of stamina, or weight loss. If your dog has any of these symptoms, see your vet. Dogs seldom have heart attacks and rarely experience coronary artery disease.

If your veterinarian suspects that your dog has a heart problem, she will probably suggest any of several diagnostic tests—electrocardiograms (EKGs), chest x-rays, and sonograms are commonly used.

Doggerel

A **congenital** disease or condition is one that is present at birth. It may or may not be inherited. An **acquired** disease or condition is one that develops as a result of aging, illness, or accident.

Canine heart disease can often be controlled with diet, controlled exercise, and medication. Some congenital defects are treatable with surgery.

You can help prevent canine heart disease. If you decide on a breed that is at risk of inherited heart defects, buy your puppy from a responsible breeder who tests her dogs' hearts annually (see Chapter 5). No matter what kind of dog you have, *don't let her get fat.* Excess weight puts extra stress on the heart. Keep your dog fit with exercise appropriate to her age and overall health and condition. Practice good doggy dental care—gum disease can contribute to heart disease (see Chapter 16).

Other Chronic Diseases

Dogs are prone to many more diseases than I can cover here. They can get nearly anything we can get, including cancer, diabetes, kidney disease, liver disease, pancreatitis—the list goes on. Some diseases are more common in certain breeds than in others, indicating that there is a genetic component to many diseases. This is one of the many good reasons to do your homework before you get your dog. If you buy a purebred, buy carefully and responsibly (see Chapter 5). If you adopt a purebred or mixed-breed with an unknown ancestry (see Chapter 7), be forewarned so that you know what is possible, what special preventive care may be useful, and what the early signs of disease may be.

The good news is that many of these diseases can be controlled if not cured, and new, more promising treatments are being developed every day. If you suspect that your dog has a particular condition or disease, see your vet. Try not to worry. Okay, try not to worry too much! It may be nothing.

If your dog is diagnosed with a serious or chronic problem, work with your vet or, in some cases, with a veterinary specialist. If you want to know more about the disease itself (see Appendix B), successful management of the disease, or alternative therapies, or if you just want to be in touch with someone who has been there with his dog, explore the Internet (see Appendix C). Bulletin boards, discussion lists, and informational websites exist for just about any canine malady you can think of.

> **Chew on This**
>
> If the unthinkable happens and the disease makes your dog's quality of life less than you think appropriate, be grateful that we have the ability to release our dogs from suffering with gentleness and love.

The Least You Need to Know

- 🏠 Dogs, like people, can suffer from long-term health problems.

- 🏠 Many long-term canine health problems are inherited—buy and breed responsibly.

- 🏠 Good health care goes a long way to preventing and controlling chronic health problems.

- 🏠 In many cases, your dog can live a happy, high-quality life despite a long-term health problem.

- 🏠 Remember that your dog loves you in sickness and in health— do the same for him, even if it means letting go.

Chapter 11

In Case of Emergency

In This Chapter

- 🏠 Assembling a first-aid kit for your dog
- 🏠 Planning for disasters
- 🏠 Keeping important supplies and documents handy
- 🏠 Knowing how to respond to sickness or injury

Few things in life are more upsetting than an emergency involving our family, friends, or pets. Emergencies can pop up in the wag of a tail—usually on the weekend or a holiday when your veterinarian's office has just closed—and natural or man-made disasters can force us to leave our homes at any time. Planning ahead allows us to respond more effectively. In fact, planning can save lives—including those of our pets.

Having basic first-aid supplies on hand, critical phone numbers and other information readily available, and supplies assembled in case you need to evacuate your home can make all the difference in an emergency. Your dog relies on you for his safety, and it's up to you to have the equipment and knowledge necessary to take care of him.

First Aid First

If you're like most people, you have some first-aid supplies in the medicine cabinet. But do you have everything you might need to handle your dog's emergency care? Consider assembling a canine first-aid kit. If you put your supplies in a portable box, you'll be able to pack it when you travel with your dog (or in an emergency evacuation). If you're out and about with your dog a lot, especially in the outdoors or at sporting events, you might want to keep canine first-aid kits in the car and at home.

Here are the essential ingredients of a good doggy first-aid kit:

- A muzzle. Even the sweetest, most reliable dog may bite when frightened or in pain. You can improvise a muzzle if you have to, but having one of the proper size readily available is easier, gentler, and often more secure. Soft muzzles are available from pet supply stores.

- Pepto-Bismol or a generic equivalent in case of diarrhea or stomach distress. Liquid works fast, but it's messy; pills are also effective. Ask your veterinarian for the proper dosage for your dog(s) and write the dosage on the container.

- A fresh bottle of 3 percent hydrogen peroxide (toss and replace after a year).

- Depending on the size(s) of your dog(s), a turkey baster, bulb syringe, or large medicine syringe for purging toxic substances when appropriate.

- The number for the National Animal Poison Control Center (NAPCC): 1-888-4ANI-HELP or 1-900-680-0000.

- A rectal thermometer.

- Lubricating jelly such as K-Y Jelly (*not* petroleum jelly).

- Sterile saline eye solution to flush eyes.

- A topical broad-spectrum antibiotic.

🏠 Mild detergent dishwashing liquid to remove oil or other contaminants from coat and skin.

🏠 Disposable gloves to protect your hands if you need to handle a contaminated dog.

🏠 Tweezers.

🏠 A basic veterinary first-aid manual (see Appendix B or ask your veterinarian or local Red Cross to recommend one).

🏠 Directions and telephone numbers for the nearest emergency veterinary clinic and your own veterinarian.

(Photo by Close Encounters of the Furry Kind)

A well-stocked canine first-aid kit can make emergency treatment easier and more effective.

Prepare to Evacuate

Emergencies can occur at any time, whether you're home or not. You can protect your dog and other pets in the event of a fire or other problems with a little advance planning.

First, no one can help your dog if they don't know he's there. Put stickers on the front and back doors to let neighbors and emergency personnel know that your dog is in the house. If he has a favorite hiding place, make a note of it. If you have an evacuation kit (see the following section), note where that is located—and make it easy to get. Keep your dog's leash, and collar if he doesn't routinely wear it, in a convenient spot, and note that on the sticker as well.

Also note the name and telephone number of your vet. Make arrangements with your vet so that, if necessary, someone could drop your dog off at the clinic. Sign a boarding and medical care authorization form, file one copy with the vet and one with your evacuation kit, and give copies to one or two trusted neighbors. If you live in an area prone to natural disasters (floods, tornadoes, hurricanes, earthquakes), make arrangements with a veterinarian and a boarding kennel at a distance as well, in case your own vet is affected by the emergency.

Pack a pet evacuation kit in an easy-to-carry waterproof container, and store it where it's easy to reach in an emergency. Include copies of important documents and telephone numbers in the kit (see the following section). Pack two meals worth of dry dog food in sealed bags or containers, one or two bottles of water, and a week's supply of any medication your dog needs. Replace the food, water, and medications once a month to keep them fresh. If your dog needs medication that requires refrigeration, make a note of that on top of the evacuation kit, and include a prescription from your vet with your important documents. Indicate, if needed, medications that are stored elsewhere due to temperature requirements, such as refrigeration. Include an envelope with enough cash or traveler's checks to get you through two days. Finally, tuck your doggy first-aid box on top of the evacuation kit.

Make sure your dog can be identified. A name tag, rabies tag, and license tag on his collar are useful. A tattoo or microchip is a good idea, too, in case his collar is lost.

Make a list of telephone numbers that will be useful in an emergency, and update it frequently. Again, make copies, and put one near your phone, one with your evacuation kit, one or two with neighbors, and one where you work.

It's a good idea to have a crate of the appropriate size for each of your pets. A crate provides a safe means of transporting or isolating a sick or injured animal. It is also a safe way to control a healthy animal while you deal with an emergency. Finally, a crate provides a safe method for transporting an animal in case of evacuation.

Chew on This _____

Keep copies of the following documents in your pet evacuation kit. Leave copies with a friend or relative in case the kit gets lost.

- 🏠 Your veterinarian's name, address, and telephone number.
- 🏠 Veterinary records, including vaccination records and rabies certificate.
- 🏠 Information about any medical condition your dog has and necessary treatment or medication. If your dog requires medication that needs refrigeration, include a prescription from your vet.
- 🏠 Proof of ownership—make copies of your dog's registration certificate, adoption papers, proof of purchase (contract or receipt), license tag number, and microchip or tattoo number.
- 🏠 A data sheet (updated each year) that includes your dog's name, breed, color, sex, and age. Attach a recent color photo of your dog—if your dog becomes lost and you can't get to your home, the photo will be useful for making flyers.

Basic Canine First Aid

Many, many things can happen to our dogs. Knowing how to respond if your dog becomes sick or injured will help you breathe easier and could make a life-and-death difference for your dog.

We have room here for only the basics, so consider purchasing a good veterinary first-aid book to keep on hand. You might also consider taking a pet first-aid or CPR class. They're offered from time to time by some college continuing education programs, veterinary schools, vet clinics, and the Red Cross.

Chew on This _____

Telephone numbers that may be useful in an emergency:

- 🐾 Your own numbers away from home—work, cell phone, and pager.
- 🐾 A friend or relative to contact if you aren't available.
- 🐾 Your dog's regular veterinarian.
- 🐾 An alternate veterinarian who can board your dog if necessary—25 to 50 miles away.
- 🐾 The local boarding kennel.
- 🐾 A boarding kennel 25 to 50 miles away.
- 🐾 The local animal shelter and animal control.
- 🐾 The local health department.
- 🐾 The local Red Cross chapter.

Poisons and Poisoning

A surprising number of things we keep around our homes are potentially toxic to dogs. Unfortunately, many of them are also attractive to dogs, so it's up to us to keep them out of reach of curious canines. Here are some of them, and some tips on how to respond if your dog gets past your precautions.

Medications, both prescription and nonprescription, can be deadly, especially in larger-than-normal quantities or in some combinations. Chocolate can kill a dog. More than 700 types of plants, many of them common garden and house plants, are poisonous. Garden chemicals, including fertilizers, herbicides, and insecticides, also pose hazards. Slug bait, ant poisons, and mouse or rat poisons are made to taste good to attract their intended prey, and they'll attract your dog. Some puppies and dogs eat the darndest things, and lead poisoning can occur in dogs who ingest lead paint chips or dust, toys, drapery weights, fishing weights, lead shot, some tiles, and some types of insulation. Lead poisoning can also occur in dogs that drink from improperly glazed ceramic bowls, or who drink water that's passed through lead pipes.

Grrrrowls

If you suspect or know that your dog has eaten or been exposed to a poison, contact your veterinarian, emergency clinic, or animal poison center immediately even if your dog doesn't show any symptoms. The effects of some poisons are slow, so don't assume that if you don't see symptoms your dog is okay. A quick response may save your dog's life.

Symptoms of poisoning include vomiting, diarrhea, loss of appetite, swelling of the tongue and other mouth tissues, excessive salivation, or seizures. If your dog has any of these symptoms, get him to the vet as quickly as possible. Effective treatment depends in part on promptness, and in part on knowing what he has ingested.

Some common garden dwellers can also be hazardous. Some dogs are allergic to bee stings—and to complicate matters, many dogs snap at the buzzing. I had a dog who liked to eat bees for the sweet nectar they carried! Some spider bites are poisonous, and in some parts of the country scorpions and snakes may be a threat. If you notice sudden swelling around your dog's face or body, get him to the vet.

Grrrrowls

Antifreeze is sweet and attractive to pets. It is also lethal. If you notice antifreeze on your garage floor or driveway, clean the area thoroughly. If your dog ingests antifreeze, get him to a veterinarian *immediately*.

Fractures

Four types of fractures are commonly seen in dogs: *closed*, *compound*, *epiphyseal*, and *greenstick*. All fractures should be treated immediately to prevent further damage and to control pain. Treatment depends on the type, location, and severity of the fracture and the dog's age. Just as in human medicine, splints, casts, pins, steel plates, and screws can be used to realign the bone and allow healing.

A dog usually will not step on a broken leg, although that's not always the case. If you know or suspect that your dog has a fracture, you need to keep him quiet so that he doesn't cause more damage to the bone or surrounding tissue, nerves, and blood vessels. If the fracture is in a leg, apply a splint if possible. Two straight pieces of wood or metal, one placed on each side of the leg, and wrapped with a bandage (not too tight—you don't want to cut off circulation), should do the job temporarily. If the fracture is on his body or head, slide or roll your dog onto a stretcher (a blanket or board will work), and use that to carry him to your car. If possible, have someone drive while you stroke and quiet your dog so that he doesn't move around too much or become more frightened.

Doggerel _____

A **closed fracture** is one in which the bone is fractured, but the skin over the break is unbroken. In a **compound fracture,** the broken bone protrudes through the skin, creating risk of infection. **Epiphyseal fractures** occur in the growth plates or epiphyseal plates of young dogs that are still growing (see Chapter 13). If the bone is cracked but not broken, the dog has a **greenstick fracture.**

Cuts, Bites, and Bleeding

If your dog is cut and bleeding, clean the wound with hydrogen peroxide or water and evaluate how serious it is. Some parts of the body, such as the nose and tongue, contain many blood vessels, and even a tiny nick will bleed profusely. In such a case, clean the area, and apply pressure with a clean towel or gauze pad until the bleeding slows or stops. Then apply a topical antibiotic ointment. Keep an eye on the area for a few days in case of infection.

If the wound is deep or long and is bleeding, apply pressure with a clean towel, cloth, or gauze pad and get your dog to your veterinarian. He may need stitches and an oral antibiotic.

If your dog is bitten by another dog (or any animal), clean the wound, stop the bleeding if necessary, and call your vet. Bite wounds are always at risk of infection because the mouth contains lots of bacteria. Your vet will likely prescribe an oral antibiotic, even if the wound itself doesn't require her attention.

Heatstroke (Hyperthermia)

Heatstroke occurs when the body temperature rises beyond a safe range. Because dogs don't sweat, they can't cool themselves as efficiently as we do. They can easily overheat. Symptoms of heatstroke include red or pale gums; a bright red tongue; sticky, thick saliva; rapid panting; and vomiting and/or diarrhea. The dog may act dizzy or weak, and may go into shock.

A dog with moderate heatstroke (body temperature from 104° to 106°F) will probably recover if given first aid immediately. If he displays any of the symptoms, take his temperature if possible. Use a hose, shower, or tub of cold water to wet and cool him. Check his temperature every 10 minutes and continue the cooling process until his temperature is down to 103°F. Give him a rehydration fluid (such as a sports drink with electrolytes) or water.

BowWOW
A dog's normal temperature is 99.5°F to 102.8°F. A dog's normal heart rate is 60 to 120 beats per minute. A dog normally takes 14 to 22 breaths per minute.

Severe heatstroke (body temperature over 106°F) can cause death or permanent damage, and it requires immediate first-aid and veterinary treatment. If your dog's temperature is 106°F or higher, he needs to get to a vet as quickly as possible. If you're more than 5 minutes from the vet and your dog is conscious, follow the cooling procedures outlined previously until his temperature is down to 106°F. Then wrap him in a cool, wet towel or blanket and proceed to the vet.

Dogs with moderate heatstroke usually recover fully. If your dog has had severe heatstroke, he may have suffered organ damage. Your vet will advise you about ongoing care. A dog that has had heatstroke once is at risk of getting it again, so take special care not to put him in risky situations.

Grrrrowls

Heatstroke is a potentially deadly condition. Never leave your dog in a car on a warm day, even for a few minutes. In hot weather, don't leave him outside without shade, or on concrete or asphalt. Make sure he always has access to clean, cool water. Restrict his exercise during the hot part of the day. If he has breathing problems, a history of heatstroke, or is elderly or ill, keep him indoors and cool.

Bloat

Bloat is the common term for *gastric dilatation and volvulus* (GDV), a potentially deadly condition in which the stomach fills with air (gastric dilatation), putting pressure on the other organs and the diaphragm. Once it's filled with air, the stomach may rotate on itself (volvulus). The rotation of the stomach cuts off the blood supply, causing the stomach tissue to die. Even with treatment (surgery), about a third of dogs with bloat don't survive. But knowing the symptoms of bloat and the need for immediate veterinary treatment will greatly increase your dog's chances if he does bloat.

Symptoms of bloat include restlessness, reluctance to lie down, pacing, rapid swelling of the abdomen, rapid and shallow breathing, and nonproductive vomiting and retching. As the pain increases, the dog may salivate heavily. The dog may go into shock, and the heart rate may become rapid and the pulse weak.

Although bloat can occur in many breeds, it's most common in large, deep-chested dogs, and males are more susceptible than females. Nervous dogs and underweight dogs are more at risk, as are those that eat only one meal a day and those that gulp their food.

These are just a few of the more common hazards that pet dogs may encounter. Other situations may also call for immediate first aid and prompt veterinary care. If you and your dog participate in athletic activities or spend a lot of time in the great outdoors, you both encounter dangers. That's just part of life. If you're alert to sudden changes in your dog's behavior or appearance, and prepared to respond, you can usually avert disaster.

The Least You Need to Know

- A good first-aid kit will enable you to care for your dog in an emergency.

- Having an evacuation plan in place may save your dog's life.

- Many things commonly found around the house and yard are dangerous to your dog.

- Knowing how to respond in case of injury, poisoning, or illness can mean the difference between a full recovery and death or permanent disability for your dog.

Chapter 12

Nutrition

In This Chapter

- 🏠 Feeding your dog well
- 🏠 Understanding commercial dog foods
- 🏠 Considering alternative diets
- 🏠 Controlling obesity

The available choice in doggy diets these days is mind boggling. No matter what you choose to feed your dog, someone will tell you what's wrong with that diet. So how can you be sure you're feeding your dog properly?

First, learn the basics of canine nutritional needs. Keep an eye on your dog's health and activity level, and understand that many problems, from itchy skin to flatulence to hyperactivity, are linked to nutritional problems and food allergies. The extra cost of a high-quality doggy diet will be balanced by lower vet bills.

Dogs Are What They Eat

Food is made up primarily of protein, fats, and carbohydrates. Food also contains vitamins, minerals, some other nutrients, and water. All foods provide some of the basic ingredients an animal needs, but

BowWOW

Cooking destroys some vitamins in food, so it's important to add vitamins back in after cooking. High-quality commercial dog foods have vitamins added after the heat process is completed. If you feed your dog a homemade diet or raw diet, a vitamin supplement is usually a good idea.

the value of a food to a particular type of animal depends on that animal's nutritional needs and on how well its digestive system processes that type of food.

Protein is found in meats and in plants. However, plants provide *incomplete proteins*, whereas meat proteins are complete. On the other hand, vegetables are a better source of most vitamins than meats. Vegetables are also rich in carbohydrates; meats are not.

Dogs are carnivores. In the wild, the bulk of their diet is meat, and their teeth are designed for shearing meat, not for chewing up vegetable matter. Dogs and their wild cousins eat vegetables and fruits, but the dog's digestive tract is designed to process meat proteins efficiently and doesn't break down the tough cellulose walls of vegetable matter. In the wild, canines eat the partially digested food in the stomachs of their prey. Domestic dogs need to have their veggies cooked to break down the cellulose so that they can utilize the nutrients.

Now let's look at the nutrients that make up food and provide for good health.

- *Proteins* are made up of amino acids. At least 10 of the amino acids are vital to good health. The richest sources of proteins are meat, fish, poultry, milk, cheese, yogurt, fishmeal, and eggs. Soybeans and dehydrated plant extracts also have a high protein content. How much protein your dog needs will depend on her activity level, her age, and the digestibility of the food. For most dogs, a dog food with about 28 percent protein is fine.

- *Fats* provide insulation against the cold and help cushion the internal organs. They provide energy and help carry vitamins and other nutrients to all the organs by way of the blood. Fat also makes food more palatable. Fat is essential for good health, but it shouldn't be excessive. A high-fat diet will provide for energy needs and make it seem that your dog is well nourished, but it may not fulfill your dog's need for protein, vitamins, and minerals. Deficiencies in those nutrients will eventually lead to health problems. Some lower-quality commercial dog foods are high in fat (which is cheaper than protein).

- *Vitamins* are chemical compounds that help the body in many ways. Fruits and the livers of most animals are rich sources of vitamins. Many vitamins are easily destroyed by light, heat, moisture, or rancidity. Some vitamins, especially A and D, are toxic in excessive doses. A good-quality diet will provide necessary vitamins in proper amounts.

- *Minerals* strengthen bones and cell tissue, and help organs function properly. If you feed your dog a good-quality diet, it's highly unlikely that he will suffer a mineral deficiency. Over-supplementation with minerals (and vitamins) is much more common than malnutrition in the United States, and excess minerals in the diet can cause serious problems, especially in growing puppies. *Never* add calcium or other minerals to a growing puppy's diet unless advised to do so by your veterinarian.

- *Water* is vital to life and good health. Dogs get water directly from drinking, and indirectly from the food they eat. A dog, like all animals, can tolerate a lack of food much longer than a lack of water. You may want to restrict late-night water intake when housebreaking your puppy, but otherwise your dog should have free access to clean water at all times.

A healthy dog should eat his meal in about five minutes. If your dog scarfs up his food and still seems to be hungry, and if he's very active and on the thin side, then he may need a bit more. If he eats readily but then picks at it or leaves some, you're probably giving him too much. If your dog starts to get fat or too thin, you need to adjust the amount you're feeding him. Run your fingers down the sides of your dog's spine, one on each side of the spinal ridge. You should be able to feel his ribs. If you're not sure his weight is good, ask your vet. If you feed him a commercial dog food, keep in mind that manufacturers nearly always recommend more food than the average dog needs per day. Use the amounts suggested on the bag or can as a starting point only, and adjust the amount according to your dog's needs.

The best way to determine whether the amount and content of your dog's diet are right is to observe his general health and physical appearance. If he is well covered with flesh but not overweight, shows good bone development and muscle, is active as appropriate for his age, is alert, and has healthy skin and coat, then his diet is probably fine. If not, then schedule a checkup with your vet, read the rest of this chapter, and consider altering his diet.

Feed your dog on a regular schedule. The specific times don't matter, but regular feeding times will help you monitor your dog's health and weight. You'll know right away if your dog's eating habits change suddenly—a common sign of a health problem. Free feeding, where you leave food out all the time, camouflages changes in eating habits and can lead to obesity. It's not a good idea.

Feeding Your Puppy

As with most things in the dog world, the subject of how to feed a puppy causes lots of debate among breeders, fanciers, veterinarians, and nutritionists. The best approach for your puppy will depend on his breed, age, size at maturity, and activity level. Some breeders require that their pups be fed a certain way to validate contractual health guarantees. If your breeder does not require your pup to be fed a particular food, then weigh the advice of the breeder, your veterinarian, and whatever articles or books you read on the subject, and make an informed decision.

Your breeder should give you information about feeding your pup. If not, ask the breeder how much the puppy has been eating and use this as a starting point. Keep close tabs on your pup's growth and weight gain. Her caloric needs will be less as her growth slows down, so you'll need to adjust her food intake accordingly. Don't let her get fat! Fat puppies are at risk for orthopedic and other health problems.

Puppies from 8 to 16 weeks old need 3 or 4 meals a day. Again, ask your breeder for her recommendation. Some small breeds need more frequent feeding to prevent hypoglycemia (low blood sugar), while some pups are fine with two to three meals a day. Older puppies and dogs should be fed twice daily. Feeding times should be regular, especially while you are housetraining a puppy.

If you have a puppy, feed her puppy food until she's four or five months old, and then switch to adult food. Too much protein and calcium can contribute to skeletal and joint problems. *Never* supplement your puppy's diet without consulting your veterinarian.

Grrrrowls
Never add calcium or other minerals to a growing puppy's diet unless advised to do so by your veterinarian.

Commercial Dog Foods

If you've ever walked down the dog food aisle of a store, you know that the dog food industry is thriving, and that it offers food in an incredible variety. There are foods for puppies, large-breed puppies, senior dogs, active dogs, dogs with tartar, overweight dogs .... There are foods that use beef, chicken, turkey, lamb, duck, venison, and fish. There are dry foods, frozen foods, and canned foods. Obviously, all dog foods are not created equal!

Good-quality commercial dog food sells for approximately $25 to $35 per 40-pound bag. At this price, you *should* be getting healthful ingredients, but the most expensive food isn't necessarily the best food for your dog. On the other hand, the 40-pound bag for $15 at your local discount store is not a bargain. Your dog may survive on it, but chances are that the money you save on food will go to your veterinarian for problems related to poor nutrition. Good food goes a long way toward preventing skin, coat, and other common long-term health problems, as well as some behavioral issues.

BowWOW

Most dog owners complain at one time or another about a gassy dog. And most people think you just have to live with it, or send the aromatic pooch to the backyard. You'll breathe easier knowing that there are some things you can do to ease your own canine gas crisis.

- Slow down his eating. Some dogs gulp air as they eat. If the air isn't belched out, it works its way into the intestines. There's only one way out from there. If you have only one dog and you feed dry food, try scattering it around the floor so that he gets only a few pieces at a time. If you have more than one dog, try feeding them in their crates or in separate rooms—sometimes a dog gulps his food for fear the other dog(s) will get it from him.

- Change foods. Poor-quality foods often contain fillers that cause flatulence. Some grains, as well as excess fat, also can give some dogs gas. Switch over gradually to give your dog's digestive system time to adapt to the new food.

- Watch what he eats besides meals. High-fat snacks, grass nibbled in the yard, and things he picks up in the yard or on walks can upset his system and cause gas.

- Control his portions. Too much food at one time can cause gas. If you feed only once a day, try splitting his food into two meals.

- Absorb the gas. Give him an activated charcoal pill (available from health-food and drug stores). We call them "fart pills" at our house!

The major advantage of commercial dog food is convenience. The major disadvantages are the use of questionable ingredients in some foods and the use of chemicals such as preservatives and dyes that have been linked to serious health problems. If you prefer to feed your dog a commercial dog food, choose a good-quality food with high-quality ingredients (see Appendixes B and C for more information on canine nutrition and dog foods).

(Photo by Close Encounters of the Furry Kind)

Proper nutrition makes for a healthy dog.

Homemade Diets

Some people prefer to make their dog's food. A carefully constructed homemade diet can provide excellent nutrition for your dog. If you like to cook and have the time to plan, shop, and prepare the food, and room to store the ingredients, then a homemade doggy diet may be to your liking.

The major advantage of a homemade diet is that you know what your dog is eating. You can

Chew on This

Better-quality dog foods cost more, but you make up for the extra expense with lower veterinary bills—not to mention a healthier dog.

use good-quality meat, poultry, and fish, as well as eggs and fresh cooked vegetables. If you choose to include grains, you can control what they are and how much of the diet they make up.

There are some disadvantages as well. On a practical level, shopping and preparing the food takes a fair amount of time. You also need room to store the ingredients, and for some people, adequate freezer space is a problem. On a more fundamental level, it's important to feed a diet that includes all the nutrients essential to your dog's good health. Although he doesn't have to have a completely balanced diet every day, over the course of a week or so he must get the proper balance of protein, essential fatty acids (found in fat/oils), minerals, and vitamins. If you don't get the overall balance right, your dog's health will suffer.

Another problem is that there's a lot of bad advice floating around about how to feed your dog. If you want to try a homemade diet, make sure you base it on reliable information from a qualified expert on canine nutrition (see Appendix B).

Raw Diets

Raw diets, sometimes known as Bones and Raw Food or Biologically Appropriate Raw Food (B.A.R.F.) diets, have gained popularity over the past couple of decades. Dr. Ian Billinghurst, an Australian veterinarian, summarizes the B.A.R.F. diet this way in his book *Give Your Dog a Bone:* "Feed your dog a diet consisting of about 60 percent raw meaty bones. The rest of the diet should consist of a wide variety of human food scraps. Most of them should also be raw."

Raw chicken and turkey bones usually make up the bulk of the raw, meaty bones in a B.A.R.F. diet. *Never give your dog cooked bones, especially cooked chicken bones!* They splinter easily and can perforate the intestines. Organ meat (liver, kidney, heart, brain, tongue, and tripe) is fed in moderation. Eggs are also fed for protein. Green leafy vegetables, crushed in a juicer or food processor, are also included in the B.A.R.F. diet, sometimes as is and sometimes with such additions as eggs, vegetable oil, brewer's yeast, kelp, or apple cider vinegar.

Some people also feed their dogs fresh and dried fruits and raw honey. Grains are kept to a minimum. Some dairy products are included in many B.A.R.F. diets—raw goat's milk, cottage cheese, and yogurt in particular.

Although some proponents of the B.A.R.F. diet are fanatical about its benefits (and correspondingly critical of commercial diets), many of the same disadvantages pertain to a raw diet as to a cooked homemade diet. In addition, raw meat, particularly raw poultry, contains bacteria, including salmonella and others that cause food poisoning. A healthy dog's intestines can deal with the bacteria and your dog won't become sick, but whoever handles the raw meat must be scrupulous about cleaning all counter space, cutting boards, knives, and plates that come in contact with it, and about washing her own hands. In fact, some B.A.R.F.ers wear disposable plastic gloves when handling raw meat.

Grrrrowls

Cooked bones splinter when they break and can perforate the intestines. Sometimes the damage can be repaired, but not always. Death from a perforated intestine is very painful. Never give your dog cooked bones, and keep garbage safely out of reach.

Obesity

For dogs, as for people, excess fat contributes to many serious health problems and shortens a dog's life span. How much food your puppy or dog needs will be influenced by several factors:

- **Activity level.** If your dog gets lots of running exercise, he'll need more food than if he's more sedate.

- **Quality of food.** The caloric and nutritional value of dog foods varies widely. The more nutritionally dense the food, the less the animal needs to eat.

- **Individual variation.** Your dog is an individual. Her genes will influence not only her looks and temperament, but also her nutritional needs. Two pups from the same litter may need different amounts of food even if their activity levels are similar.

The best approach to weight control is to keep your dog at a proper weight from puppyhood on. But sometimes the pudge creeps up slowly (believe me, I know!). If your dog is overweight, you can do a few simple things to help her lose the excess weight. One is to measure her regular meal, then soak half of it in water until it's soft, mix the wet and dry food together, and serve. The soaked pieces will expand and be more filling. Another approach is to add some low-calorie, high-fiber food to a reduced portion of her regular food—unsalted green beans, shredded or sliced carrots, canned pumpkin (just the vegetable, not pie filling), or air-popped, unsalted popcorn work well. Again, she'll feel satisfied with the amount of food, but won't be getting so many calories. If none of those options work, talk to your vet about a weight-loss diet or lower-calorie food.

The Least You Need to Know

- Good nutrition is essential to your dog's health and longevity.
- Commercial diets vary in quality, and you tend to get what you pay for.
- A good understanding of canine nutritional needs is necessary for success with a homemade or raw diet.
- A fat dog is *not* a healthy dog.

Chapter **13**

Run, Doggy, Run!

In This Chapter

- 🏠 Understanding the importance of exercise for your dog
- 🏠 Preventing injuries in your growing puppy
- 🏠 Avoiding injuries to your adult dog
- 🏠 Exercising safely year round

Exercise is essential if your dog is to live a healthy life. It's vital not just for his physical health, but for his mental and emotional health as well. Regular exercise will help your dog build strong bones, improve his cardiovascular system, and tone his muscles. It will help him sleep better, give him more energy, and help prevent boredom. Getting out with your dog will get you moving, too, and will enhance the bond between the two of you.

Some breeds need—and tolerate—a lot more exercise than others, so before you get a dog, be sure you know what to expect in terms of the breed (or combination of breeds) you choose (see Chapter 2).

As your dog ages, he probably won't need as much exercise as when he's young, but he still needs daily physical activity to keep his body and mind working. Speak to your vet about appropriate exercise—it can lengthen your dog's life. Whatever your dog's age, consult your vet before starting a vigorous exercise program, particularly if your dog is overweight, a puppy, elderly, or used to being a couch potato. The same goes for you! There's no point hurting yourselves by diving into an all-out fitness program.

But don't be too lazy, either. Sending your dog out to the backyard by himself doesn't count as exercise. A few young dogs will play by themselves, but most dogs don't self-exercise. For them, exercise is play, and it's something you do with a friend. That's you!

(Photo by Close Encounters of the Furry Kind)

Exercise is essential to your dog's physical and mental health.

The Hip Bone's Connected to the ...

Your dog's *conformation*—the way she is put together—is largely determined by her skeletal system, the framework on which all her other physical attributes rest. Conformation isn't important just for show dogs. A healthy structure gives your dog the ability to move comfortably and efficiently. Skeletal problems can limit your dog (see Chapter 10). Because the skeletal system is so important to a healthy, complete life, it's important to keep exercise "skeleton friendly." To do that, it's useful to know a little about how your dog's skeletal system is put together.

Bones

Dogs have about 318 bones (the number isn't exact because of variations in tail length). Bones are living organs made up of minerals (primarily calcium and phosphorous), blood vessels, and nerves.

Bones perform several functions. Some bones support the body and enable the animal to move—the leg bones, for instance. Some bones protect internal organs—the skull protects the eyes and brain, the vertebrae protect the spinal cord, and the ribs and sternum protect the lungs, heart, and other organs. The ear contains tiny bones that transmit sound so that your dog can hear. Oh, dem bones!

Joints

A *joint* is a place where two bones are joined by connective tissue. Joints are grouped into three kinds—synovial, fibrous, and cartilage—based on the type of tissues that connect the bones.

Synovial joints allow for movement and flexibility. The joints that connect the lower jaw to the skull, and the joints of the legs, are synovial joints. The ends of the bones are covered by *cartilage*. The area between the ends of the bones is called the *joint capsule*. It is made up of fibrous tissue and contains *synovial fluid* in a space called the *joint cavity*.

Not all joints move like synovial joints. *Fibrous joints*, such as those that join the 40-some bones of the skull, hold the bones together with tough, fibrous tissue and don't allow much movement. *Cartilage joints* join two or more bones together with cartilage. They allow a little movement. The joints between the vertebrae of the spine—also known as intervertebral discs—are cartilage joints.

Tendons attach muscle to bone. Ligaments connect bone to bone. Both are part of most joints.

Muscles

Muscles bring about movement. *Smooth muscles* work automatically—your dog can't control them. Internal organs such as the stomach, intestines, and bladder have smooth muscles. *Striated muscles*, most of which are attached to the skeleton, enable your dog to walk, roll over, cock her ears, catch a tennis ball .... In a healthy dog, the striated muscles are under conscious control.

Exercising Growing Puppies

It's important to remember that, although most puppies have lots of energy, their bodies are immature and not ready for exercise that causes sharp or repetitive impact during the first year. Large and giant breeds should be 18 months or older.

The leg bones grow from areas located near their ends. These soft areas of immature bone are called *growth plate*s (also *epiphyseal plates* or the epiphysis). At about 12 to 16 months, the growth plates "close" as calcium and minerals harden the soft area. When the hardening process is complete, most growth stops and the growth plates are said to be closed. Before they close, the growth plates can be injured or fractured more easily than mature bone. An injury to the growth plate can cause the bone to stop growing or to grow incorrectly.

To protect your pup against damage to the growth plates, postpone high-impact and leg-twisting activities until you're sure the growth plates are closed. Leaping after flying disks or over jumps, jogging (especially on hard surfaces), and similar activities should be avoided until the pup matures. If your puppy is going to mature at 25 pounds or less, she can begin to take part in "grown-up" exercise at 9 months. If she'll mature into a medium to large dog (25 to 95 pounds), wait until she's at least 14 months old. If she's going to be a really big girl of 100 pounds or more, wait until she's at least 18 months old. If you're really impatient, you can have your puppy x-rayed to determine whether the growth plates are open or closed.

Whether you do that or not, it's better to err on the side of safety—a few months of patience could make a lifetime of difference for your dog.

Preventing Injury in Mature Dogs

You can protect your adult dog from exercise-related injuries by taking a few precautions. Perhaps the most important is to keep your dog on leash whenever she's outdoors unless she's safely confined within a secure fence or is far from traffic in an area where off-leash dogs are allowed and where dangers are few. Off leash she's vulnerable to vehicles, wild animals, and many other dangers.

Next, be cautious when starting or upgrading an exercise program for your dog. Take your dog's age, general health, and current condition and activity level into account. If your dog has any health problems or is getting on in age, talk to your veterinarian before pushing too hard. If your dog seems to be tiring, slow down to a walk. Watch for signs of overexertion—very heavy panting, irregular breathing, stumbling, and wanting to slow down or stop. Most dogs will faithfully try to keep up with you, but pushing your dog past her limits could kill her, especially in warm weather.

Before you start a jogging or running program with your dog, be sure she's suited to your pace. If you run or jog with your dog, start with short distances and increase the length and difficulty of each workout gradually. Start with a 5- to 10-minute warm-up walk, and finish with a 5- to 10-minute cool-down walk.

Avoid hard or gravel surfaces when exercising your dog. In the summer, concrete or asphalt can become very hot and burn your dog's foot pads. Repetitive pounding on such surfaces is also very hard on your dog's joints. Gravel can be sharp. Large pieces can cut or scrape foot pads, and small chunks can get stuck in the hair between the pads, injuring your dog's foot. Try to find grass, dirt, or other soft surfaces on which to run your dog.

Swimming is an excellent form of exercise, especially for many dogs with orthopedic problems (see Chapter 10) because it's easier on their joints. As with any other type of exercise, start your dog out slowly. She'll be using different muscles and may tire quickly. Water also cools the body fairly quickly, so don't let your dog become chilled. Even a strong swimmer can become exhausted or be caught in a strong current and drown, so never leave your dog where she can get into water deeper than her chest unless someone is there who can pull her to safety if necessary.

> **Chew on This**
>
> If you want to jog or run with your dog, be sure your natural speeds are compatible. Forcing your dog to move for an extended period at too fast or too slow a pace compared to what is normal for her could cause muscle fatigue and possibly injury.

> **Grrrrowls**
>
> Don't exercise your dog hard right before or right after he eats.

Be sensible about how you exercise your dog. People get away with some incredibly stupid things, but sooner or later carelessness and poor judgment catch up with them. Our dogs can't keep us from doing dumb things, but they can be hurt or killed by our poor judgment. The person at the other end of the leash can be hurt as well. For everyone's safety …

- *Do* keep your dog on a leash. In most cities it's the law, and for good reason (see Chapter 4).

- *Don't* run your dog alongside your vehicle, whether on or off leash. You're teaching your dog to chase cars—a sport that is usually fatal in the long run—and your dog could easily be caught under the wheels of your own car.

- *Do* pay attention to how the weather affects your dog. Be cautious about exercising him when it's very warm or very cold.

- *Don't* ride a bicycle with your dog on a regular leash—it's too easy for the dog to pull you over or to run into the bike. If he's big enough, old enough, and healthy enough to join you without hurting growing bones, special devices are available through pet supply stores for attaching a dog to a bicycle safely via a strong spring (see Appendix C).

- *Do* take your dog in for regular checkups and keep his vaccinations up-to-date, especially if you take him to places frequented by other dogs that could carry—or catch—diseases or parasites.

- *Don't* push him hard on weekends and let him loaf all week. That's asking for injuries. A little exercise every day is much better than a lot of exercise once in a while.

- *Do* check him frequently for lumps, bumps, cuts, and other problems, especially on his feet, legs, ears, and eyes.

Seasonal Safety

It's important to consider the weather—especially the temperature—when exercising your dog. One dog's beautiful day is another dog's climatic nightmare. Consider your dog's size, the thickness and length of her coat, and how accustomed she is to heat or cold when deciding whether she should be out, or for how long, on hot or cold days. No matter what her breed, guard her from extremes of weather as well as from other hazards that accompany our changing seasons.

Warm Weather Safety

Spring and summer give us lots of opportunities to play outdoors with our dogs, but there are some hazards associated with warm, sunny days.

The dangers of overheating are very real for your dog in warm weather. Your dog can't cool his body as well as you can, and if his body temperature remains above normal for very long, he can die of heatstroke (see Chapter 11). Try to exercise your dog early in the morning or in the evening rather than during the heat of the day. Be extra cautious when the humidity is high—it makes it harder for your dog to cool off. If you plan to have him out in the heat for more than 20 minutes, carry cool water for both of you and offer it about every 20 minutes. Lightweight portable water dishes are available for carrying on walks. Try to walk in the shade, and watch for signs of overheating. If necessary, stop and rest in a shady spot and let your dog cool off a bit before heading home.

Grrrrowls

Heatstroke can kill your dog or cause him permanent brain damage. Don't exercise him during the heat of the day, and always watch for symptoms of overheating during warm weather (see Chapter 11).

Besides the heat, spring and summer bring a few other dangers for dogs. Here are a few more tips for keeping your best friend safe during those hazy, crazy days:

- Risk of exposure to rabies, distemper, parvovirus, Lyme disease, and other infectious diseases increases in warm weather. Be sure your dog is protected (see Chapter 9).

- Mosquitoes are out and spreading heartworm in some parts of the country. If you live (or travel) in a heartworm area, have your dog tested for heartworm once a year, and protect him with heartworm preventative (see Chapter 9).

- Spiders, bees, wasps, and other insects also bite and sting dogs. If your dog has a reaction to a bite or sting, or is bitten or stung several times, see a veterinarian immediately (see Chapter 11).

- More bugs! Warm weather also brings out the fleas and ticks. Check your dog frequently for the little pests, and if you find any, take appropriate action (see Chapter 9).

- Poisons are within easy reach in warm weather—insecticides, weed killers, mouse and rat poisons, fertilizers, and poisonous plants all pose dangers to your dog. Even if you don't use them, chances are some of your neighbors do. If you think your dog has walked through grass treated with chemicals, wash his feet with soap and warm water when you get home. If you think he's ingested a poison, get him to a vet (see Chapter 11).

🐾 Care for your dog's feet. Hot surfaces will burn him just as quickly as they'll burn you. Don't keep your dog on hot concrete, asphalt, or sand for any length of time, or if you must, put booties on him for protection.

🐾 Swimming is great fun, but keep your dog safe. Even good swimmers can drown (see Chapter 22).

(Photo by Close Encounters of the Furry Kind)

Most dogs enjoy swimming, but it's up to their owners to be sure they're safe in the water.

Cold Weather Safety

Colder weather poses its own dangers. Many dogs enjoy romping in the snow and are invigorated by chilly weather. Others—particularly small dogs and dogs with very short coats—would just as soon stay indoors when Jack Frost shows up. Be sensible about what you ask— or allow—your dog to do when the thermometer drops. Let's look at some of the hazards and how to manage them:

- Your dog's feet, ears, and, depending on his size and coat, other body parts are susceptible to frostbite. Frostbite occurs when a part of the body freezes. If not treated immediately, frostbitten areas die and may fall off or have to be amputated. Frostbitten skin is pale and cool to the touch. It may look burned after thawing. If you think your dog has frostbite, warm the affected body parts slowly and get him to a veterinarian as quickly as possible.

- Jagged ice, frozen plant stems, and sidewalk salt are common in yards and on walkways in winter. They're sharp and can cut your dog's foot pads. Snow can also collect on the hair between the pads, sometimes forming icy balls that can cause pain and injury to the foot. Trimming the long hair from the bottoms of the feet may help prevent problems with snowballs. Always check your dog's feet after he's been out in snow. If you go for walks in the snow, check your dog's feet frequently, or consider getting him some booties to protect his feet in bad weather.

- Icy surfaces, especially stairs and steps, are as dangerous for your dog as they are for you. Dogs with arthritis or other problems that limit their mobility are particularly in danger of falling on slippery surfaces. Try to provide an ice-free path from your door to your dog's potty area to prevent injury.

- Salt and other chemicals used to melt ice from streets and sidewalks can irritate your dog's paws. They are also toxic if ingested. If such chemicals are used where you walk, wash your dog's paws when you get home, or have him wear booties for walks. Consider using a nontoxic ice melter on your own walks.

- Pools, ponds, and other bodies of water present special risks in cold weather. Swimming in very cold water on cold days can cause *hypothermia*, or dangerous chilling of the body. Only very fit dogs that are built for and conditioned to cold-weather swimming should be in the water. Once the water freezes over, thin ice can be extremely hazardous. *Do not* allow your dog (or anyone else) to run on the icy surface of frozen water unless you know *for certain* that the ice is solid all the way across. If your dog falls through, he may not be able to find the hole again, or if he does, he may not be able to climb out. He could drown.

🏠 If you walk or hike near snowmobile trails in winter, keep your dog on leash and off the trails. Snowmobiles can kill dogs.

Outdoor Dogs

I'm not a fan of keeping dogs outdoors, especially alone (see also Chapter 4). Dogs are social animals and need companionship. They're intelligent animals and need mental stimulation. They're athletic animals and need physical exercise. A few breeds do fine living outdoors, as long as their social, mental, and physical needs are satisfied, but most dogs do much better indoors with their human families. Some dogs simply can't make it outdoors—or they may "survive," but they live miserably.

Before you decide to have an outdoor dog, be sure that you will be able to give him daily attention. That doesn't mean just tossing him some food and water. It means spending time with him playing or working, seeing that he gets proper exercise, and checking his physical condition. It also means providing him with decent living conditions. What are decent living conditions for an outdoor dog?

🏠 Your dog needs proper *shelter* in all seasons. In warm weather, he needs well-ventilated shade. In winter, he needs a properly insulated doghouse that's the right size for him. A doghouse should be large enough for the dog to lie down comfortably. A house that's too big won't keep your dog warm, and in severe weather could expose him to hypothermia and frostbite. He needs clean bedding in his shelter year round.

🏠 Dogs need clean, fresh *water* year round. In summer, the water should be freshened at least twice a day, and the water bowl must be cleaned frequently to prevent algae. In winter, your dog needs water, not ice, at all times. Avoid metal bowls in winter (they get too cold and freeze quickly) and avoid plastic or ceramic bowls (they crack when the water freezes). Use heated buckets or bowls with chew-safe cords designed for use with animals.

🏠 Your dog needs good-quality *food* in proper amounts. He needs to be fed regular meals, and food bowls should be picked up and washed after every meal. Food left out attracts rodents and insects, and can go bad. In cold weather, an outdoor dog will need a quarter to a third more food than he needs in warm weather in order to generate enough body heat.

🏠 An outdoor dog deserves a properly fenced area that will keep him safe from the dangers of wandering, from other animals, and from possible thieves or abusers. *No dog deserves to live his life on a chain.*

If your dog lives outdoors, he still needs all the routine care of an indoor dog—training, grooming, play, and outings that get him beyond the confines of his living space. He needs regular veterinary and home health care. Above all, he needs the love that he feels in your voice, your hands, and your eyes. Don't get a dog if he'll live alone and lonely out back.

The Least You Need to Know

🏠 Proper exercise is essential to your dog's health and happiness.

🏠 Puppies need controlled exercise while their bones are growing.

🏠 Simple precautions can protect your dog from injuries.

🏠 Hot and cold weather present special hazards for dogs.

Part 4

Living with Your Dog

Dogs are social animals, like we are, but their society has different rules than ours. In this section, we'll take a look at how canine societies are set up, and how that affects your dog's relationship to the members of your household, human and nonhuman. Then we'll see what you need to do to teach your puppy the basics of good manners so that you get off to a good start to a successful lifetime together.

Of course, good behavior isn't enough to make your dog a pleasant companion. He also needs to be clean and tidy for his health and for your viewing—and sniffing—pleasure. I'll tell you how to keep your dog properly groomed, from his bright, shiny eyes to the tip of his tail, and how to make grooming sessions pleasant for both of you. Finally, we'll take a look at the realities of breeding a litter. There's a lot more to it than the sweet little puppies we all picture.

Chapter 14

Dogs Being Dogs

In This Chapter

- 🏠 Seeing the social side of dogs
- 🏠 Understanding a dominance hierarchy
- 🏠 Living with more than one dog
- 🏠 Establishing a peaceable kingdom with other pets

Dogs are social animals—like you. Most dogs enjoy the company of other dogs. They form friendships. They play together. Some dogs sleep cuddled up together or side by side. They touch one another in various ways that show dominance, concern, and affection. Anyone who doesn't think that dogs live a rich emotional life hasn't watched interaction among dogs very carefully.

If you have just one dog and no other pets with which he can interact, then you and your family become the dog's pack. He relies on you not just for his basic needs—shelter, food, health care, and exercise—but also for his emotional needs. Dogs need to be loved and they need to love. If you have other pets, they also help satisfy your dog's need for social interaction.

But don't make the mistake that too many people make of thinking your dog is just a little person in a furry coat. He's not.

He's a dog, with a long genetic heritage that has given him the traits that make us love him and live with him—his looks, his abilities, and the friendship he willingly gives us. If we pretend that he's human, "just like us," we not only demean what it is to be a dog, but we miss out on the rewards of seeing a member of another species for what he really is. It's unfair to your dog and to you.

The Role of the Alpha

As we saw in Chapter 8, dogs that live together normally organize themselves into a *dominance hierarchy* in which each individual has a specific rank or status compared to each other animal. The "top dog" in the hierarchy is called the *alpha*, and in mixed-sex packs there will be an alpha dog (male) and an alpha bitch (female).

The alpha controls the resources. In the wild, the alpha will eat first and take many of the choicest parts of a kill. The alpha sleeps in the best sleeping place. In your house, the alpha "owns" the toys, although he may let the other dogs play with them. He goes through doors first if he wants to (although this "rule" tends to be fairly relaxed in most household packs) and leads the way on family outings.

Doggerel
The **alpha** is the socially dominant animal in a dominance hierarchy.

In the overall scheme of things, the human members of your family "pack" should hold positions of higher rank than any of the dogs. This sometimes becomes a problem when a puppy or dog lives with children. The dog may challenge a child's position in the pack. If your dog shows any sign of trying to control the child, get help immediately from a qualified trainer or behaviorist to prevent a dangerous situation from developing. (See Appendixes B and C for more information on childproofing your dog.)

You can't "appoint" an alpha for your pack. Even if you think that Rex the Big Dog should be alpha and Bingo the Little Dog should be subordinate to him, Rex and Bingo may have different ideas. Dogs aren't democratic, and they don't vote for alpha. They establish their relative ranking through ongoing interaction. Each dog's breed traits and individual personality play a part. In some breeds, most dogs get along well with other dogs and establishing pack order is a relatively uneventful process. In other breeds, members of the same sex may not do well together, and establishing and maintaining the pack order may be more difficult. A few breeds are generally antisocial with other dogs of either sex.

Dogs usually establish and reinforce the dominance hierarchy through the use of ritualized behaviors. A dog that places one or both front paws on another dog's neck or shoulder, or that attempts to mount another dog outside a normal mating context, is expressing dominance. A dog that stares at another dog may be doing the same thing. If the dog displaying the dominant behavior has a stronger personality than the other dog, the second dog will submit through other ritualized behaviors. Lying down, rolling belly up, urinating, and looking away from a stare are all ways by which dogs "say uncle."

 Grrrrowls _____

A dog with certain inherited temperament traits, or one that is poorly socialized, or one that has had a bad experience with an aggressive dog may respond aggressively to dominant behaviors in other dogs. Be cautious about letting your dog socialize with a strange dog unless you know that both will behave appropriately.

So how can you tell who the alpha is, and how the other dogs in your household rank in relation to one another? The dog that wants to be first for everything—dinner, a treat, a walk, out the door—is probably the dominant dog. The subordinate dogs will normally honor his position. Rankings are somewhat fluid, though—one dog may be more dominant in the house and another dog outdoors—and individual rankings sometimes change over time. If you introduce a new dog into the pack, whether it originally consisted of 1 or 10 members, there will probably be some jockeying for position as the new dog finds his place and the others reestablish theirs.

(Photo by Close Encounters of the Furry Kind)

Dogs are by nature social animals, and most dogs enjoy the company of their own kind.

Living with More Than One Dog

When the members of the pack are clear about their status—Rover is #1, Fluffy is #2, and Spot is #3—then the dominance hierarchy system keeps things running smoothly among them. Problems come up when the hierarchy is unstable or unclear. Instability may occur when, for instance, the alpha gets too old to be in charge, or when a young dog with a more dominant personality gets old enough to challenge the alpha's position. The dogs often sort things out with some posturing and possibly a growl or snap. However, if the two dogs are evenly matched in terms of dominance and neither one will back down, then the situation can escalate into a fight. Dogfights are fast and violent, and one or both dogs could be seriously injured in the blink of an eye.

Conflicts also occur when individual pack members are unsure of their status. In a large pack, the status of individuals at both ends of the hierarchy is often stable and unquestioned. Individuals in the middle, though, may not be so sure of where they stand and may have minor conflicts or full-blown fights as they sort things out.

Unfortunately, owners of multiple dogs often create problems where the dogs on their own would have none. If you try to apply human ideas about equality and fairness to your family of dogs, you create confusion. For instance, if you try to treat the dogs equally and you alternate who gets a treat first "to be fair," you undermine the dominant or alpha dog's position. In a pack, the alpha eats first, gets the best bed, and controls the resources. If your alpha dog is hogging the chewy toys and you take them from him and divvy them up, you again undermine his position.

BowWOW

Sexually intact animals are more likely than altered animals to quarrel with others. Reduce conflict among your dogs by spaying and neutering them.

Make sure all the humans of your household rank high in the dominance hierarchy, including children. Obedience train your dog and have each family member practice some of the training with him—making sure that an adult is *always* present when a child interacts with the dog (see Chapter 19 and Appendix B for more on child-proofing your dog). Make your dog earn everything that he wants—his dinner, a ball game, a treat—by obeying a command that he has learned or is learning. If your dog is in your way, don't step over or around him—make him move for you. That's the privilege of rank. He won't be insulted—he'll respect you more for being sure of your dominant position. An added bonus is that if your dogs know that they all rank below all the human beings in the "pack," they'll be more likely to sort out and maintain their own rankings with little fuss.

Observe your dogs carefully and figure out who ranks where in the pair or pack. Then play by their rules. When you hand out treats, give the first, biggest, and best treat to the alpha, then proceed in order of rank. If you only have enough for one, give it to the alpha. If the alpha takes over the comfy dog bed or gathers all the toys into a pile, don't take them away from him and give them to the others, but do occasionally take them for yourself. If the alpha takes things away from the subordinate dogs, let him. If he butts in when you're petting someone else, pet him. You can always find a way to give your subordinate dog or dogs the attention they need when the alpha is outdoors or chewing a bone in his crate. But don't undermine his position. Don't interfere in ritualized behaviors unless neither dog is willing to back down. If that's the case, get help from an experienced dog trainer or behaviorist before the situation escalates to fighting (see Chapters 18 and 20).

The dominance hierarchy already established among your dogs may be upset by any of several events, particularly the loss or addition of a dog, or changes related to age. Don't interfere as long as there's no fighting, but don't let a situation get out of hand if someone might be injured. Be particularly cautious when there's a big size difference between dogs—a small dominant dog who goes after a much bigger dog is asking to be killed or seriously hurt.

If your dogs get into a fight, *do not* reach into the fight to pull them apart, and don't grab them by their collars. Chances are good that you'll be bitten, possibly by both of them, and they probably won't even know it was you they bit. If you're indoors or within reach of a chair, and the dogs are medium to large, set a chair down feet first over one of the dogs to pin him, then pull the other dog off by the hind legs. If you have someone to help you, and the dogs aren't too big, you can usually separate them by grabbing both of them by both hind legs and pulling them apart—but believe me, that's a lot harder than it sounds. You can stop some fights by spraying both dogs with a hose or squirting them in the face with a vinegar-and-water mixture, if you happen to have some handy for clean-ups (see Chapter 15).

Once you get the dogs apart, make sure they can't get back at each other until tempers cool down. Put one outdoors, in a crate, or in another room. Then check each one for bites and other injuries. Check carefully—punctures are difficult to find under hair, and they don't always bleed. If you suspect that one or both dogs did get bitten, ask your vet about antibiotics, even if the bites themselves aren't serious. Bite wounds become infected easily because the mouth is full of bacteria.

Don't try to punish your dogs for fighting. They won't understand, and you won't solve the problem that way. If fighting is an ongoing problem between your dogs, get professional help. Start with your veterinarian to be sure there are no medical problems contributing to the situation. Then see a competent behaviorist who can help you get control of the situation.

Grrrrowls

Dogs are well equipped to tear flesh and break bones with their teeth and jaws. Never reach into a dogfight—you could be badly injured.

Dogs with Other Pets

Dogs can and do live peacefully with all sorts of other pets, from white mice and bunny rabbits to parrots and ferrets, as well as with cats and farmyard critters. The secrets to a peaceable kingdom are patience and caution—give them time and keep them safe.

Introduce your puppy or dog to your other pets carefully. The last thing you want is for anyone to be frightened or hurt. Be sure that a responsible adult is in a position to intervene immediately whenever your pup or dog interacts with the other animal until you're certain they're safe together. Remember, when different species meet, they have to learn how to communicate with one another.

Be reasonable about what you ask. Your dog may love and cherish your child's hamster, but if your dog was bred to hunt and your hamster skitters across the floor, the instinct to chase and kill could cause a family tragedy. If you have a puppy, teach him from the start to be gentle with other animals, particularly those who have no way to escape or fight back (see also Chapter 8). If you have an adult dog and want to introduce a new animal to the household, be cautious. Give your dog time to get used to the idea of another animal in his space. If he's never met an animal of this kind before, let him sniff and watch while you hold the newcomer, or while it's in a cage.

(Photo by Close Encounters of the Furry Kind)

The belly-up position demonstrates submission—and this Golden Retriever's hope for a good belly rub!

Remember, too, that even if he's a lot bigger than the other animal, your dog could be hurt in an encounter gone wrong. More than one puppy has lost an eye to a feline swat, and I recently heard of a dog who lost part of his nose to a parrot. So watch both animals, and be alert to signs of fear or unhappiness that could lead to aggression.

Happily, once the introductory period is over, most dogs get along well with other pets, and together they enrich our lives.

The Least You Need to Know

- 🏠 Dogs are social animals with their own "governmental" rules.
- 🏠 The top dog rules the roost.
- 🏠 Human members of the household should always be the "top dogs."
- 🏠 Your dog can live peaceably with other pets with a little help from you.

Chapter 15

Basic Puppy Manners

In This Chapter

- Setting the scene for effective puppy training
- Using a crate for puppy training
- Training your puppy to potty where he should
- Teaching your puppy not to jump up, nip, or beg

Everything in your puppy's life affects his ability to learn what you want him to learn. If you plan ahead and set the stage to encourage good behavior all the time (well, okay, nearly all the time) and to prevent or discourage unwanted behavior, you'll make things a lot easier on your puppy and on yourself.

Training is essentially the process of encouraging your puppy to form new habits—habits you want him to have. Your puppy is always learning, and anything he does more than two or three times will become a habit, whether you like it or not. It's easier and faster to prevent bad habits and encourage good ones than to try to eliminate bad ones once they're established.

Preparing Your Puppy to Learn

Your puppy wants to please you. If he learns that learning is fun, he'll learn quickly and you'll enjoy each other more. Your goal in the beginning should be to forge a bond of trust, mutual respect, and understanding with your puppy. That bond will see you both through your dog's adolescence (something like the "terrible twos" that children go through) and beyond.

Never hit your puppy, not with your hand, not with a rolled-up newspaper or flyswatter, not with anything. There's no reason to hit a dog, and hitting him won't teach him anything you want him to learn. Some dogs will react to being hit by becoming afraid of people and of people's hands coming toward them. Frightened dogs often become shy, nervous, and withdrawn, and some bite out of fear. Other dogs will react to being hit by trying to fight back. Either way, you will end up with a very unhappy (and possibly dangerous) dog, and you probably won't be very happy, either.

Doggerel
Positive reinforcement is the process of rewarding your dog with something she likes for doing what you want her to do. Praise and a treat (see Chapter 19) for sitting on command provide positive reinforcement.

Positive reinforcement is the most effective and fair approach to training a puppy. Some people use purely positive reinforcement, meaning that they don't use corrections in training. Others use a combination of positive reinforcement for correct behaviors and fair, gentle corrections for unwanted behaviors (see training resources in Appendixes B and C).

Training should start as soon as you bring your puppy home. That cute little roly-poly guy is going to grow into a dog, and he needs to learn what you want from him. The number one reason people get rid of their dogs is that the dogs have bad manners—and that's nearly always the owner's fault. Your puppy wasn't born knowing what you want. He's a dog, and his instincts tell him how to live with dogs, not people. Luckily, with your help your puppy can learn what he needs to know to make you the happiest dog owner around.

Remember that puppies have short little attention spans. Make your training sessions short, fun, and frequent. Focus on one behavior— "Sit" or "Down" or "Come"—during each session (see Chapter 19 for specific training techniques). If your puppy does what you ask two or three times, then quit for a bit and just play with him. You can do a few more minutes of training a little later.

Be sure all your human family members understand and apply the same "puppy rules." You need to be consistent to help your puppy learn. If you tell the puppy to stay off the couch but your spouse invites him up, he'll end up confused and you'll end up frustrated. (Be aware, though, that family members are much harder to train than puppies are!)

Most of us have to work for a living. If you have to be gone all day, plan for your puppy before you bring him home. Remember, he's a baby. It's unfair to ask a puppy to spend eight or nine hours alone, and more than unfair to ask him to wait that long to potty. If you can't come home at lunch time to let him out, play with him, and check on him, consider hiring a pet sitter or other reliable person to come in once or twice during the day to walk him, play with him, and feed him if necessary. He'll be happier, and you won't have quite so much pent-up energy to contend with.

Grrrrowls

Don't let problem behaviors start. Let your puppy explore your home and yard—*his* home and yard—but only when a responsible person can supervise him. If you can't watch him, confine him. It's easier to prevent mistakes than to correct them.

Make sure the pup has plenty of toys, but don't give him everything at once. I've seen puppies chew on shoes and furniture despite having puppy toys all over the floor. If all the toys are there all the time, your puppy may lose interest. So give him two or three toys at a time—maybe a hard chew toy and a soft puppy toy or rope that he can shake and "kill." Put everything else away. Every day or two, switch the toys—take those away and give him a different two or three toys. If he sees each toy only sometimes, it will be a lot more interesting.

You'll do most of your puppy's training at home or out and about, but it's still a good idea to take him to a good class. Your best bet for a young puppy is a puppy kindergarten class with a qualified instructor who can answer your questions, help you get your pup off to a good start, and encourage socialization. If your puppy is older than six months, look for a basic obedience class. (See Chapter 18 for more on choosing a training class.)

If you plan to go on to compete in obedience, agility, conformation, or other sports, try to find an instructor who understands where you and your pup are headed. The groundwork for advanced training can be laid very early with good puppy training. Consider taking more than one class, possibly from more than one instructor so that you get more than one point of view. No dog is fully trained in six or eight weeks, and even if he's doing very well, it's good for your adolescent puppy to continue to have contact with lots of dogs and people.

Beware of any school or trainer who claims to be able to train your dog completely in just a few weeks. Training takes time, and if the claims seem too good to be true, they are.

If you plan to compete eventually, you may be able to find puppy "competition" obedience or agility classes. Young dogs shouldn't jump until their bones mature (see Chapters 10 and 13), but they can start on low obstacles and learn to follow directions.

Start teaching the behaviors you'll want in your grown-up dog while he's still a baby. If you don't want your dog to jump on you or lie on the couch when he's grown up, don't let him do it as a pup. It's not fair to change the rules after your puppy gets well into the game of living with you. Of course, if he's doing something you can't allow, then you do need to "change the rules" and retrain him. But it'll be a lot easier on both of you if you think ahead and train for the future.

Crate Training

A crate (see Chapter 8) is a puppy owner's second-best friend. Properly used, a crate will help with potty training your puppy, prevent chewing and other destructive behaviors, provide a familiar refuge at home or away, and keep your puppy safe. If you use the crate as it's meant to be used, your dog will consider it his den. Some dogs choose to lie in their crates even when the doors are open.

When you're potty training a puppy, his crate should be big enough for him to stand up, turn around, and lie down. It should not be bigger than that. Most dogs don't like to sleep where they eliminate, so you don't want to give your puppy room to potty at one end of his crate and go sleep at the other end.

BowWOW _____

How long should a puppy stay in a crate? A general guideline is that a puppy should be crated for no longer than his age plus one. So if your puppy is two months old, don't crate him for more than three hours. If he's four months old, no longer than five hours.

How long should a puppy stay in a crate? The rule of thumb is that a puppy should be crated for no longer than his age plus one. So if your puppy is two months old, don't crate him for more than three hours. If he's six months old, no longer than seven hours. But keep in mind that that's a general guideline—puppies vary. If your four-month old pup does fine in the crate for four hours, but piddles at four and a half hours, then don't leave him longer than four hours without a break. An adult dog can occasionally tolerate crating for eight or nine hours, but that's hard on a dog physically and mentally. How would you like to stay in one small room with no toilet for eight hours?

Remember, you're using the crate in part to teach your puppy not to potty in there, so don't put paper or weewee pads on the bottom. Use a blanket for bedding if your puppy doesn't potty on it or rip it up. If he does, don't give him any bedding until he outgrows the urge to shred it or dirty it.

Don't use the crate for punishment. It should be a good place, a safe place. Feed your puppy in the crate. When you're training him to get into his crate, toss a toy or treat in and say "Crate!" When he hops in, praise him, close the door, and give him another small treat. If possible, put the crate in your bedroom at night (see Chapter 8 on getting your puppy settled).

Potty Training

Potty training is, to most owners, the first and most important kind of training a puppy needs. When it comes to potty training, all pups are not created equal. Some breeds are known for being easy to potty train while others are more difficult—this should be one of the things you look into as you explore different breeds (see Chapter 2).

(Photo by Close Encounters of the Furry Kind)

With patience and persistence, you can teach your dog to be a well-mannered companion who is a pleasure to be with.

Individual puppies also vary. Be patient. A puppy is a baby, and babies need time to master acceptable potty procedures. Young puppies don't have complete control of their bladders or bowels, and sometimes by the time they realize they have to go, they simply can't hold it any longer. It's your job to keep your puppy off your carpets until he's reliably trained, to teach him where he should go, and to be patient when he has an accident. At least your puppy doesn't wear diapers!

Here are some guidelines to help you potty train your puppy. These procedures will work whether you're training your puppy to go outdoors or to go in a litter box indoors (which many toy dogs are trained to do). I don't advocate paper training, especially with a dog that you will eventually want to potty outdoors. If you paper train him to go indoors, you'll just have to retrain him later to go outdoors. Why not start by training for what you really want?

- If you buy a puppy, buy from a responsible breeder (see Chapter 5) who has already started potty training.

- Crate or confine your puppy when you can't watch him— *always*. Train other family members to do the same.

- If you feed your puppy a commercial dog food, feed dry food. It will keep his stools more solid.

- Confine your puppy to rooms with tile or other washable flooring so mistakes don't ruin carpets.

- Keep your puppy on a schedule. Feed him at the same time every day, and try to get up and go to bed close to the same time every day while he's being potty trained.

- Puppies need lots of water, especially if they eat dry dog food. However, while you're potty training, feed your pup at least four hours before bedtime, and remove his water two hours before bedtime.

- Take your puppy to potty after every meal as well as the first thing in the morning, the last thing at night, every time he wakes up from a nap, after an active play session, and in the wee hours of the morning if you hear him moving around. Take him on a leash to the place you want him to use—that will teach him to use that spot, and also teach him that he can go even on leash with you standing right there. That can be important if you're away from home.

🏠 When you take your puppy to potty, don't play with him until after he does his business. If he doesn't go within 10 minutes, put him in his crate for 10 to 15 minutes, then take him to potty again. When he potties, praise him and reward him with a treat or short playtime. Wait a few minutes before you take him in— sometimes puppies don't finish on the first try, so give him time to be sure he won't have to go again in three minutes.

🏠 Keep your puppy's potty place clean—pick up feces every day. You don't like to step in it, and neither does he.

🏠 If you don't have the time or patience to potty train a puppy, then adopt or buy an older puppy or adult dog that is already potty trained.

Puppies do have accidents. It's very important to remove all trace of odor from any place your pup potties. Regular cleansers won't do it—you may not smell urine or feces after washing the area with soap and water, but your pup has a much more sensitive nose than you have. If he smells waste odors, he'll think he's found the toilet. Pet supply stores sell several types of special cleansers designed to eliminate odors. An inexpensive alternative for urine odors (but not feces) is a 50-50 mixture of white vinegar and water. I keep a spray bottle full when I expect puppy messes to clean up.

If you see your puppy start to go in the house, say "No" or "Anh!" pick him up, and take him out. When he's finished, put him somewhere safe and clean up the mess. Don't yell at your puppy or punish him for accidents. Don't rub his nose in it. If you don't see him start to go but find an accident later (a minute later is later), just clean it up and scold yourself for giving him the opportunity to make a mistake. Puppies don't go in the house to be mean or to "get you." They do it because they haven't learned where they should go. Remember, he's a puppy, not a child. You can talk until you're blue in the face and he still won't understand why you're upset about the peepee on the rug.

BowWOW

Most puppies will signal that they're about to potty. When your pup is loose in the house, *keep a close eye on him*. If he starts to turn in circles, sniff the floor, or arch his back while walking, *pick him up and take him out*. Once a baby starts to go, he can't stop if he's on his own feet. Help him get to the right place; then praise and reward him with play or a treat when he finishes.

If your puppy is still having regular accidents in the house at four months or older, talk to your veterinarian. Some medical problems can interfere with housebreaking.

Don't Jump on Gramma!

If you won't want your dog to jump up on people when he's bigger, don't let him do it as a little puppy. A small dog that jumps up can be a big problem for children, and a major annoyance for adults. A medium or large dog that jumps up is downright dangerous.

When your puppy jumps up on you, he wants attention. If you touch him, push him down, yell at him, or otherwise interact with him, he gets what he wants. If you ignore your puppy's antics, though, he'll soon figure out that jumping up doesn't get him what he wants at all.

Many puppies will stop the jumping nonsense very quickly if you fold your arms, look up at the sky, and completely ignore the behavior. If you do this, you need to do it consistently and never respond to the puppy any other way while he's jumping. Then as soon as he gets off you and has all four feet on the ground, quietly tell him he's a

good puppy and pet him gently. Stay low key—the last thing you
want to do with a pup that likes to jump up is get him excited again.
If he does react to your attention by jumping up again, ignore him
until he stops.

Grrrrowls _____

Never knee a puppy in the chest, kick him, or step on him in
an attempt to keep him from jumping on you. If you don't connect, your pup will probably see your maneuvers as a fun
game. If you do connect, you could severely injure your puppy.
Teach him that jumping up doesn't get him what he wants, but
that calm, polite behavior does.

If you use this method, you need to be sure that while he's learning not to jump, you never put yourself within reach of your puppy
unless you're willing to be jumped on. He won't know the difference
between your grubby puppy clothes and your work clothes, so don't
go near him unless you're wearing puppy duds until you're confident
that he won't jump on you. If that means you have to get up a little
earlier, do your puppy duties, and then crate him before you get
dressed for work, so be it. Same thing when you come home—go
change before you let the puppy out. If you stick to this regimen,
your puppy will learn not to jump. But if sometimes you ignore him,
and sometimes you react by pushing him off, hollering, and otherwise getting all excited, he'll figure that sometimes jumping starts a
good game and he might as well give it a try!

See Chapter 20 for more on teaching your puppy not to jump on
people.

Mouthing and Biting

When your puppy played with her siblings and her mama, she used
her mouth. When she plays with you, she'll probably want to use her
mouth until you teach her not to. Most puppies don't mean to hurt
you, but those puppy teeth are very sharp and you don't have fur
to protect your skin like her canine playmates had. Your puppy is

motivated to mouth and bite not because she wants to hurt you, but because she thinks it will get you to play—after all, it works with other dogs! I'll suggest two effective ways to teach your puppy not to mouth and bite.

First, use the same method we just discussed to stop jumping up. If your puppy nips you, say "Ouch!" and then stand up and ignore her. If she jumps up, keep ignoring her—you can teach her not to bite and not to jump at the same time! If she bites your ankles or pulls on your pants, leave the room, ignore her until she calms down, then come back, sit down with her, play gently, and try the second method.

Second, give your puppy something else to put in her mouth besides your hand. When you pet her or play with her and she takes your hand in her mouth, gently offer her a chew toy and continue to pet her. She'll learn that hands are not for chewing, but they're great for ear scratches and belly rubs. If she insists on mouthing and biting you instead of the toy, go back to method number one.

A word about tired puppies: Puppies are like young children. Sometimes they get so tired that they're completely out of control. They're not smart enough to just go to bed, so they keep playing and getting sillier and sillier from fatigue. If your puppy has been out playing for a while and is getting more and more out of control, put her in her crate, give her a treat, and let her rest. Very often a tired puppy will protest for, oh, two minutes and then fall fast asleep.

If you're having a problem with mouthing and nipping, make sure that no one plays tug-of-war or other rough games with your pup. The last thing you want to do is encourage your puppy to grab for things or compete with people for possession of things. Teach her instead to give you toys, which you can then throw for her to retrieve. The no-roughhousing rule applies especially to children.

Interaction between children and puppies should always be supervised by a responsible adult who is close enough to intervene immediately if play gets out of hand. Don't expect a child younger than 12 or 13 to be able to apply any of the training methods I've outlined. An adult needs to be in a position to help. Children tend to react to nips by screeching, pushing the puppy away, and generally acting excited. Your puppy will think the child is playing and will probably keep jumping and nipping. The child will get more excited, things will quickly get out of hand, and someone could end up injured, frightened, or both. (See also Chapter 18 on kids and dogs.)

Begging

If you're like most people, you'd prefer to eat without a dog staring at you. Dogs don't have to beg, but many people teach them to do it. If you reward your puppy for staring at you by giving him a bit of what you're eating, he'll quickly learn that his "feed the dog" look works. That's true whether he stares at you at the dinner table or when you're munching chips on the couch. And if the technique works on you, he'll try it on everyone who ever eats in his presence. So if you don't want an obnoxious beggar for a buddy, don't feed your dog when you're eating.

Okay, I confess, I'm not that tough. I do sometimes share with my dogs—a little bit of bread or fruit, a corn chip, or pizza "bones." But not while I'm eating, and not where I eat. If you want to share a little (after all, he *is* your best friend!), that's okay, but let your pooch earn the treat. Have him lie down and stay while you eat. When you've finished, take him to another area away from where you eat, have him do something (sit, lie down, perform a trick), and give him just a teensy taste. You won't feel so stingy, and your dog won't become pushy or pudgy.

The Least You Need to Know

- 🏠 Consistency and rewards make puppy training fun and effective.

- 🏠 Potty training and basic obedience training should start when your puppy comes home.

- 🏠 You can use your puppy's love of play to teach him good canine manners.

- 🏠 Don't expect children to train puppies—an adult needs to be in charge.

Chapter 16

The Well-Groomed Canine

In This Chapter

- 🏠 Understanding the need for grooming
- 🏠 Choosing your grooming tools
- 🏠 Caring for your dog's coat, skin, teeth, eyes, and nails
- 🏠 Choosing a professional groomer when necessary

If you want to enhance your relationship with your dog as well as his health and good looks, start a regular grooming routine as soon as you bring him home, and continue it throughout his life. Your dog will enjoy your hands on him as much as you will enjoy the feeling of warm fur against your skin. (If you'd like to carry this pleasure of touching your dog a bit further, see Appendix B for resources on canine massage.)

Grooming is also vital to your dog's health. It helps keep him clean and free of mats, and gives you a chance to check your dog for bumps, cuts, and other abnormalities that may be early signs of health problems.

Regular grooming will help keep the added housework that comes with dog ownership under control. Most house dogs shed year-round, and regular brushing will remove a lot of dead, loose hair from the dog before it can find your furniture, floors, carpets, and clothes.

Tools of the Trade

Choosing the right brushes and combs can be mind-boggling if you don't know what will work best for your dog's coat. *Bristle brushes* can be used on any type of coat. Widely spaced, long bristles work well on a longer coat, while short, closely spaced bristles work better on short, coarse coats. *Wire pin brushes* work well on curly and medium to long hair. *Slicker brushes* normally have a flat back set with fine wire bristles. Slickers are good for taking out mats and tangles, for smoothing the coat after brushing with a pin brush, and for removing dead hair. *Combs* are good for combing out long hair once tangles are removed. *Flea combs*, which have closely spaced teeth, are used to check the coat periodically for fleas and other pests and debris. *Undercoat rakes* are useful for pulling out dead undercoat, especially during the heavy shedding seasons of spring and fall.

Caring for Your Dog's Coat and Skin

Take your time when brushing your dog, and be gentle when removing tangles or mats. If you pull his hair as you fight through tangles, your dog won't stay keen on grooming for very long, and neither will you. Frequent, preferably daily, brushing will keep tangles and mats from forming.

If your dog has a thick coat, begin at the front and use a pin brush to brush small sections of hair forward, against the direction of growth, working your way from head to tail on one side, then the other. Be sure to separate the hair down to the skin to prevent mats from forming in the undercoat. This will also remove dirt and debris from the hair, and help the hair stand slightly away from the skin. When you have brushed all the coat forward, begin at the rear and brush the hair back into place in the direction of growth.

If your dog has long hair, he may get mats from time to time. Mats start as small tangles. If you catch a tangle or mat while it's small, you can usually tease it out with a comb or pin brush. It doesn't take long, though, for small tangles to grow into sizeable mats, reinforced with shed hair and sometimes plant matter and dirt. As mats grow bigger, they can pull the dog's skin and create warm, moist pockets that promote growth of bacteria and yeast, which can cause infections, hot spots, and open sores. Soon the poor dog is a miserable mess.

Small mats can be removed with a slicker brush. Place your hand between the mat and the dog's skin so that you don't jab him with the wires. Press the pins into the mat, and move it gently from side to side. Repeat three or four times, then brush the mat gently, and see if it will come apart. If that doesn't loosen the mat enough to brush it out, you can try cutting through the mat. Be careful not to cut the skin (blunt-tipped scissors are good for this). Make three or four cuts lengthwise through the mat. Then gently try to brush through the mat with your pin brush. If you still can't, you may need to cut the mat out. Be careful not to cut the dog's skin. If your dog has large mats, or if the mats are tight to the skin, causing a lot of discomfort or possibly sores, you may want to pay a professional groomer to remove them. Once they're out, you can set up a regular grooming schedule to keep the coat mat-free.

Dogs don't have to smell bad. Unpleasant odors can usually be traced to one or more of several causes: oil, bacteria, or yeast on the skin; ear infections (see "Keeping Ears Healthy" in this chapter); impacted or infected anal glands (see "Anal Glands [Sacs]" later in this chapter); gum disease (see "Doggy Dental Hygiene"); intestinal or stomach gas (see Chapter 12); or a foreign substance on the coat and/or skin.

Some breeds have oily coats to protect the dog in cold and wet working conditions. Unfortunately, oily coats smell a bit, especially when wet. Regular brushing will help remove some of the oil and reduce odor. Bathing will remove the oil temporarily, although bathing too often will stimulate the oil glands to make even more oil. Some shampoos are made to help control odor, so if it's a problem, ask your breeder, veterinarian, or groomer for guidance for your breed.

Bacterial and yeast infections of the skin can cause odor and lead to itching, "hot spots" (open, itchy sores), and hair loss. If you suspect an infection, you'll need your veterinarian to diagnose the problem to treat it effectively. Using an antibacterial shampoo on a dog with a yeast problem will probably make the problem worse, and a product for yeast won't help with bacteria at all.

Bath Time

Dogs love to roll in any stinky thing they can find, from animal droppings to dead fish. When that happens, it's definitely bath time!

Bath time doesn't have to be a wrestling match. Teach your dog that the bath site—probably the bath tub for medium and large dogs, maybe the kitchen sink for small dogs—isn't a scary place.

Put the dog in the tub or sink, give him a treat, praise him, and cuddle him gently. When he relaxes a little, take him out of the tub. Don't make a fuss about him or give him a treat after he's out—you want him to associate the goodies with the tub, not with escaping from it. Do this once or twice a day for a while, slowly increasing the time he has to stay in the tub. Pretty soon he'll look forward to tub time. Next, put a little lukewarm water in the tub so he gets his feet wet when he gets in, and reward him again with treats, praise, and petting. When he accepts that routine, wet him a little with lukewarm water from a sprayer or by pouring water onto him from an unbreakable container. Follow the same routine—begin with a short time, reward him, and slowly increase the time. Soon you'll have a dog that likes to get into the tub. This approach takes a little time up front, but it sure beats having to wrestle a dog into a bath for the rest of his life.

Now your dog is ready for a real bath. Assemble everything you'll need. Brush your dog to remove loose hair, tangles, and mats.

Get your dog into the tub—and don't forget to reward him. Consider fastening a grooming loop (available from pet supply stores—see Appendix C) in the tub so that you can tie your dog. You don't need a sudsy, wet dog making a break for it! Insert a cotton ball shallowly into each ear to protect the ear canal against water. Apply an ophthalmic ointment (available from your vet or a pet supply company) to the eyes to protect them from soap burns.

Don't use shampoos meant for people on your dog. The pH balance is wrong and will damage the dog's skin and coat. If your dog has a skin condition, your veterinarian may recommend a medicated shampoo. If you're concerned about killing fleas, wet and lather the dog thoroughly, beginning with a "collar" of lather high around the neck to prevent fleas from moving forward to hide in the ears. Leave the lather on for about 10 minutes (be sure the bathroom is warm so your dog doesn't get chilled) and then rinse. The wet lather will drown any passengers without exposing you and your dog to toxic chemicals. (See also Chapter 9 on parasite control.)

Wet your dog thoroughly using lukewarm water. Cold water can chill your dog, and shampoo won't work as well in cold water. On the other hand, most dogs don't care for a hot bath. Apply shampoo and work it in with your fingers, or apply shampoo to a net bath sponge and use that to wash the dog, working over the body in the direction of hair growth. Begin at the neck and work to the tail. Don't forget the belly and up under the hind legs. Use a washcloth for more control when washing the face, and be careful not to get shampoo in your dog's eyes.

Rinse your dog thoroughly. Don't forget between his toes, his armpits, groin, and belly (there is a groove between the ribs on the bellies of dogs in proper weight, and soap loves to hide in there). Go over his body with your hands after rinsing to be sure you got all the soap. If you hit a slimy, slippery spot, that's soap, so rinse again. Soap residue can cause serious skin irritations, so be sure you get it all. Gently squeeze excess water from his coat. Then towel. If your dog has a short coat, rub vigorously with the towel, finishing up by smoothing it in the direction of growth. If he has longer hair, pat dry or press sections of his coat with the towel to avoid creating tangles.

Before you let your dog out of the tub, praise him and give him another treat for being so good. Now *carefully* release. Don't let him leap wildly—he could slip and scare or injure himself. You may want to put a leash on him—most dogs have "crazy dog attacks" after their baths, and they like to run and roll and rub themselves on things (carpets, couches, bedspreads ...).

You can blow dry your dog if you like, but don't use a hot setting—it will dry out his skin and coat. Otherwise, crate your dog or confine him to a specific room until he's dry. If he needs to go out, take him on a leash—dogs love to roll on the ground when wet, and they're regular dirt magnets. Be sure to keep your dog warm and out of drafts until he's dry.

Doggy Dental Hygiene

More than three quarters of dogs over three years of age have gum (periodontal) disease. It's the number-one health problem in pet dogs. Gum disease is one source of "doggy breath." It can also lead to tooth loss and, just as with people, contribute to heart and kidney disease. So preventive dental care is important to your dog's overall health and well-being throughout his life.

Ideally, you should brush your dog's teeth daily, but realistically, every few days will do. Have your vet show you how to brush your dog's teeth properly, and have her recommend tooth-care products. Toothbrushes for dogs are smaller, softer, and shaped differently than ours. If your dog is too tiny for a small toothbrush, try a dental sponge (a small, disposable sponge on a flexible handle). If your dog has sensitive gums, or if you have trouble holding his toothbrush, try dental cleaning pads or surgical gauze wrapped around your fingers, dampened with water, and dipped in a little baking soda or canine toothpaste. Don't use toothpaste meant for people on your dog—it can cause an upset stomach when swallowed, and it's hard to teach a dog to rinse and spit!

Your dog should have regular dental checkups by your vet, with a thorough cleaning and polishing as often as necessary. If your dog shows signs of gum disease—bad breath, visible tartar along the gum line, bleeding gums—or other mouth problems, be sure to see your vet.

Feeding dry, hard kibble helps somewhat to slow the formation of plaque. Some dog food companies now offer foods designed to help keep your dog's teeth free of plaque. Some chew toys and large raw or sterilized beef bones may also help. Ask your veterinarian for recommendations.

If you have a puppy, keep an eye on his mouth and teeth as he grows. Puppies, like babies, are born toothless. At about four weeks, they begin to get their *deciduous*, or baby, teeth. Between three and five months of age, the deciduous teeth are replaced by the bigger and stronger permanent teeth. Once in a while a permanent tooth fails to push the baby tooth out. This is most common with the incisors and upper canine teeth. The baby tooth that doesn't come out on schedule is called a *retained deciduous tooth*.

If deciduous teeth are retained, your puppy will end up with too many teeth crowded into his jaw. His permanent teeth will be out of normal alignment, which can prevent normal growth and development of the jaw bone. A badly placed tooth can cause your dog severe pain as he bites into his own soft flesh, and can contribute to oral infections. Check for normal exchange of baby teeth for permanent teeth, and if you suspect that your pup has a retained tooth, see your vet.

Keeping Ears Healthy

Ear problems are common in dogs. *Bacteria* and *yeast* both like the warm, moist environment of the ear canal, but are controlled in the normal ear. *Allergies, hormonal problems,* and *excess moisture* can all promote abnormal growth of yeast or bacteria. *Ear mites* are not as

common in dogs as they are in cats, but some dogs are hypersensitive to mite saliva and may injure their own ears scratching at the itchy bites. *Foreign matter,* such as dirt and plant matter, can enter and irritate the ear canal, causing the dog to scratch and injure the ear. A few breeds are prone to inherited diseases that affect the ears.

If your dog develops an ear problem, don't try to treat it without consulting your veterinarian. The wrong treatment won't help and can make things worse. Ear infections are painful and can spread deep into the ear, causing permanent damage, including hearing loss, so don't delay diagnosis and treatment.

The best way to prevent ear problems is to keep your dog's ears clean. Check his ears at least once a week. The skin inside the ear should be pink or flesh-colored. There may be a little wax, but not excessive amounts, nor dirty-looking discharge. The ear should be free of strong, nasty odors. If the ear looks inflamed, seems sensitive to the touch, or has a foul smell or gunky discharge, see your vet.

 Chew on This

Common signs of ear infection include the following:

- 🐾 Foul odor
- 🐾 Discharge
- 🐾 Swelling or redness in or around the ear canal
- 🐾 Rubbing or scratching at the ears or head
- 🐾 Head shaking
- 🐾 Tilting of the head
- 🐾 Crying or pulling away when touched near the ears

If your dog's ear is dirty but doesn't seem to be inflamed or sensitive, clean it with a commercial or home-made cleaner (see accompanying "Chew on This" sidebar). After having his ears cleaned, your dog will shake his head, so stand back! (Ear cleaning is best done outdoors or in a bathroom where you can clean up easily.) When your dog has finished shaking, gently wipe his ears out with a cotton ball or tissue. Do *not* push Q-tips into your dog's ears—they can pack the wax in tight and damage the ear drum. If your dog's ears seem to be particularly waxy, or if he swims a lot, clean his ears once a week. If his ears are clean and healthy, cleaning once a month will help keep them that way.

Chew on This

You can save money by using one of the following ear-cleaning solutions in place of expensive commercial cleaners. The rubbing alcohol helps to dry out the ear, and both solutions help to make the environment of the ear inhospitable to bacteria and yeast. Use one or the other—*not both at the same time*.

Note: These solutions are not meant to clear up an existing infection. If your dog has an ear infection, see your veterinarian.

Solution 1

- 🐾 1 part rubbing alcohol
- 🐾 1 part white vinegar

Shake well in a squirt bottle. Fill the ear canal, massage, and let the dog shake. Use once a month, or more often if needed.

Solution 2

- 🐾 2 tablespoons boric acid
- 🐾 4 oz. rubbing alcohol
- 🐾 1 tablespoon glycerine

Shake well. Fill an eyedropper with solution and empty it into one ear. Massage, and then let the dog shake. Repeat with the other ear.

Bright, Shiny Eyes

Healthy canine eyes are clear and moist. Redness, swelling, excess tearing or mucous, and squinting are not normal and may indicate an eye infection, abrasion, or other problem. If you notice any of these symptoms, take your dog to the vet.

As your dog ages, the lenses of his eyes may take on a cloudy appearance. Sometimes this is simply *nuclear sclerosis*, which is

associated with aging and does not affect vision. However, clouding may also indicate a cataract, which can affect vision. If you notice a change in your dog's eyes, consult your veterinarian.

Routine eye care is simple for most dogs. If you notice mucous in the corners of your dog's eyes, gently wipe them clean with a moist washcloth or tissue. Your dog will look better, and bacteria that can cause an eye infection will be controlled. If your dog has long facial hair, keep it out of his eyes. Hair can scratch the *cornea*. Breeds with protruding eyes and wrinkly skin around the eyes are susceptible to eye injury from their own hair. You can pull long hair into an elastic band or barrette, or trim the hair so that it doesn't fall into the eyes. If you trim, *be careful*. Use blunt-end scissors and keep them pointed away from the eye as you cut the hair.

 Grrrrowls

We've all seen dogs enjoying the rush of the wind as they hang their heads out car windows. But if you value your dog's eyes, keep his head inside the car. Many dogs suffer eye injuries or lose their eyes to wind-borne debris.

White or light-colored hair around the eyes is prone to staining by proteins in the normal tears that cleanse the surface of the eye. Ask your breeder or a breed rescue representative, your veterinarian, or a groomer about products to clean and control tear staining. Commercial products are available, but they seem to work more or less successfully on different breeds. They also need to be used regularly to be effective.

Before bathing your dog or using any insecticides or other chemicals on his face, apply ophthalmic ointment to protect the eyes. Ask your vet to recommend a suitable product.

If your dog's breed is prone to inherited eye problems, consider having his eyes checked every one to three years by a veterinary ophthalmologist. Early diagnosis may provide time to control a problem, or at least give you a chance to plan for what is to come. Please let your breeder know the results of your dog's eye exams.

Responsible breeders want to know about all inherited problems in their pups—and they're delighted to hear about the healthy ones.

Keeping Feet and Nails Healthy

Examine your dog's feet frequently. Check between his toes and pads, especially if he spends time in places where he may pick up burrs, stones, small sticks, and other debris. Remove foreign matter carefully with your fingers or tweezers. If necessary, trim the long hair between his toes, especially on the bottom, so that it doesn't form mats or collect debris that can hurt him, and so that he will have better traction on smooth surfaces.

Keep your dog's nails trimmed. Long nails hit the ground, forcing the dog's toes out of their normal position. Long nails can distort the foot, especially in a puppy, and cause lameness and permanent deformity. They may curl into the foot or, in the case of the *dew claw*, into the leg. When your dog walks on a hard surface, you shouldn't hear the click of nails. If you do, it's time to trim.

Doggerel

The **dew claw** is the small toe located above the foot on the inside of the leg. Some breeds have dew claws on the front legs only, while others have them on front and back. In many breeds, the dew claws are customarily removed, but the breed standards of a few breeds require front and back dew claws, and a few even require double back dew claws.

Clipping your dog's nails isn't difficult. Doing it regularly will get you both used to the process, and at each session you'll need to trim only a tiny bit.

As with bathing, you can take certain steps to make nail trimming much easier. If the only time you touch your dog's feet is when you're going to clip his nails, he's likely to object. Teach him that having you fiddle with his feet is no big deal. When you're snuggling your dog, hold and gently massage each of his feet. If you start this with a young puppy, he'll get used to it quickly. If he doesn't like it, start with short sessions and slowly extend the time. If he fights having his feet held, keep some treats nearby. Gently take a foot in your hand, and give him a treat with the other *while still holding the foot.* If he pulls his foot away, don't give him a treat until you're holding his foot again. You want to reward him for having his foot held, not for getting it away from you. When you can hold your dog's foot for at least 30 seconds without a struggle, you can begin trimming his nails. If necessary, do just one nail, give him a treat while still holding his foot, and quit. Do another nail later. Eventually, you'll be able to do all his nails without a fight. If your dog is relaxed, then go ahead and do all the trimming in one session.

(Photo by Close Encounters of the Furry Kind)

Nail-trimming sessions don't have to be wrestling matches if you take your time and teach your dog that it won't hurt.

Use good, sharp dog nail clippers. A dull blade will not cut cleanly and may cause pressure and pinching, hurting or scaring your dog. You may want something handy to stop any bleeding if you cut into the quick. Pet supply stores carry styptic powders to stop bleeding, as do the shaving sections of drug stores. An inexpensive and effective alternative to commercial products is corn starch. If you accidentally cut the quick, put a little styptic powder or corn starch into a shallow dish and dip the nail into it. The powder will stick to the nail and seal the blood vessel.

When you're ready to trim, find a comfortable position. If your dog is small, have him lie on your lap or on a towel on a table at a comfortable height in front of you. If he's bigger, have him stand, sit, or lie on the floor or on a grooming table. Hold his paw gently but firmly. Press on the bottom of the pad—that will extend the nail and make it easier to get at. Trim the nail below the quick. If the nail is light colored, you'll be able to see where the quick ends (the quick appears pink from the blood it contains). If the nail is dark, look for the place where the nail curves downward and narrows. Cut a little and then check by looking at the nail end-on. When you see a black dot near the center of the nail, you're at the start of the quick and it's time to stop trimming.

Anal Glands (Sacs)

Dogs, like other predators, have anal glands. When the animal passes stool, pressure is placed on the sac, which *expresses*, or secretes, a substance onto the surface of the stool. The odor of each dog's secretions is distinct. This is why dogs greet one another by "tail sniffing"—the distinctive odor of each individual's anal gland secretions is one way they have to identify one another. If you look at the dog from behind, you'll see the anal glands located on both sides of and slightly below the anus.

Anal glands sometimes become impacted. Impacted anal glands must be expressed, or cleaned out. You can learn from your vet or groomer to do this yourself if you're brave (people tend to find the odor from the anal glands much less pleasant than dogs seem to), or you can have your veterinarian or groomer do it when needed. Impacted glands are not in themselves a health hazard, but the dog can injure the delicate tissue around the anus by scooting and biting at it. If an infection or abscess sets in, your dog will be in considerable pain and will need to have veterinary and home care. Dogs with chronically impacted anal glands are often put on high-fiber diets to make their stools bulkier, hopefully causing the glands to express themselves when a stool is passed. In serious cases, the anal glands may be surgically removed.

BowWOW

Scooting along the floor, which people often think means the dog has worms, is usually an attempt to express the anal glands. A dog with impacted anal glands may also lick at his anal area, and he may have problems defecating.

Choosing a Professional Groomer

If you don't have time to groom your dog regularly, or if he has a coat that requires special skills, a professional groomer is your best option. Even if you do most of your dog's grooming at home, you may occasionally want to take him to a groomer for a serious "do."

Not all groomers are created equal, so choose carefully. Some groomers are excellent with certain breeds or types of coats and cuts, but not so great with others. Most groomers are kind and gentle with dogs, but, as in any business, there's the occasional bad apple. You don't want your Bichon to come home trimmed like a Poodle, and you certainly don't want your dog handled roughly or injured.

To find a good, reliable groomer, ask your veterinarian, family, and friends for recommendations. You can do some preliminary screening on the telephone. Here are some questions to ask:

🐾 What sort of training do the groomers in the shop have?

🐾 How long have they been grooming dogs?

🐾 Do they specialize in any particular breed(s)? If they do your breed, do they offer different styles of cuts?

🐾 Do they use a handheld drier or cage drier? If a cage drier, how often do they check your dog? Is someone always present when the dog is exposed to the drier?

🐾 Do they clean the ears and, if appropriate to your breed, pluck the hair from the ear canals?

🐾 Do they check the anal glands and express them if necessary?

🐾 Do they use sedatives for grooming? If so, who sedates and monitors the pet, and what training do they have in the proper use of sedatives and in first aid? Who will they call and what will they do if something goes wrong?

🐾 How long does it usually take to get an appointment?

🐾 How long will your dog need to be there on his appointment day? Where will he be kept when he's not being groomed? Where will he be taken to potty? Is the area fenced?

🐾 What are the normal fees for your breed? What's included in that fee?

When you find a place that sounds suitable, stop by for a visit before setting up an appointment for your dog. The facilities should be tidy and clean. Dogs that are not being groomed should be housed in reasonably comfortable cages or crates, and should have access to drinking water. The grooming stations should be much like your hairdresser's—scissors, combs, brushes, clippers, and grooming tables should be disinfected between dogs. You should feel comfortable with the groomer, who should pay attention to what you want. And above all, your groomer should like dogs and relate well to them. You wouldn't leave your child with a barber or hairdresser you didn't trust. Your dog deserves no less.

The Least You Need to Know

- 🏠 Regular grooming contributes to your dog's health and to your relationship with your dog.

- 🏠 The right tools make grooming easier for you and your dog.

- 🏠 Bathing and nail-trimming sessions don't have to be wrestling matches if you teach your dog to accept them.

- 🏠 A carefully selected professional groomer may be worth the price if you lack the time or skills to groom your dog well.

Chapter 17

Canine Birds and Bees

In This Chapter

- 🏠 Deciding to breed your dog—or not
- 🏠 Understanding the risks of breeding dogs
- 🏠 Living with sexually intact dogs
- 🏠 Facing the sad side of breeding
- 🏠 Adding up the numbers

You love your dog and have several friends who want one of her puppies. You think it would be fun to have a litter, and maybe you could even make some money. Besides, what better way for the kids to learn about "the miracle of birth"?

But *please*, before you take the plunge and breed your dog, please, please, *please* (yes, I'm begging you) carefully consider the points covered in this chapter, and reread Chapters 2 and 3. Then, if you still want to breed dogs, learn as much as you can about your breed, about genetics, and about the proper handling of newborn and young puppies. Contact an experienced breeder or two, get some guidance, and please breed and place your puppies responsibly.

(Photo courtesy of the author)

These one-day-old puppies are completely dependent on their dam and their breeder.

What's So Hard About Breeding Dogs?

The road the responsible breeder travels is filled with hazards and heartbreaks, as well as pleasure and joy. Dedicated breeders find breeding quality dogs to be very rewarding, but most of the rewards are intangible. It's the fortunate rare breeder who breaks even on a responsibly bred litter. Breeding dogs is hard work mentally and physically. Puppies are messy and time-consuming. Breeding isn't just cute, roly-poly puppies. It's also long nights and days nursing sickly puppies who, despite your loving care, still die. It's stillborn puppies. It's emergency Caesarian sections at 2 A.M. It's watching a beloved bitch die from any of a number of risks inherent in pregnancy and whelping.

The goal of breeding shouldn't be to make more puppies. There are already more than enough puppies in the world, many of whom live short, miserable lives because too little thought went into planning for them before they were conceived. The goal of breeding should be to produce puppies who are just a bit better than their parents, just a bit closer to the ideal for their breed in terms of physical traits, temperament, instinct, ability, and individual and genetic health. Serious breeders often spend years preparing to breed a litter.

Meeting such lofty goals requires tremendous investments of time and money. The responsible breeder starts with the best possible bitch and breeds her to the stud dog who best complements her, but only after both are tested for those inherited health problems that can be discovered only through testing (see Chapter 3). Not all inherited diseases are discoverable with tests, so the responsible breeder researches the health history, temperament, longevity, strengths, and weaknesses of as many relatives of the potential parents as possible.

Time, Time, Time

First-time breeders nearly always underestimate the amount of time required to do right by a litter of puppies. Most of the pregnancy is a waiting game, but when the due date approaches, the time-consuming work begins. First, you need to spend some time with your mama-to-be. She needs emotional support as her body changes. She'll appreciate cuddles and gentle belly rubs (a good chance for you to feel the puppies moving). If she has long hair you'll need to trim around her nipples and vulva for cleanliness. During the last week, you need to take her temperature twice a day to anticipate the beginning of labor.

Once your girl's temperature drops (assuming it does), you can anticipate labor within 24 to 36 hours. Most breeders don't like to leave a bitch alone at this time, especially if it's her first litter. So the waiting game begins, and it can be long and tedious. If all goes well, the puppies will arrive with a minimum of fuss over the next 24 to 48 hours. Some normal labors, though, are long and drawn out. Some bitches take their sweet time, with two or three hours between puppies. At that rate, a

BowWOW

You can expect your bitch's temperature to drop from her normal 100° to 101.5°F to around 98° to 99°F about 24 hours before she goes into labor.

litter of 8 could take 24 hours to be born. That's a long time to sit up and monitor—and if you're doing this for the kids, they aren't likely to stick around for that extended a miracle of birth.

Some deliveries are difficult and you find yourself at an emergency veterinary hospital for a C-section at 3 A.M. Chances are your new mother and the pups will come through surgery just fine, but the fact is that she and some or all of her puppies could also die. If your bitch dies, you'll need to hand-feed her litter every two hours, around the clock, for at least four weeks. You'll also need to stimulate the puppies to urinate and defecate every two to three hours for the first couple of weeks, because they can't do so on their own.

Some deliveries are very quick. I had a puppy born on the couch (the *brand-new* couch) a couple years ago. I had just checked and didn't think my bitch was anywhere near ready. Five minutes later, I heard squeaking in the other room and it just didn't sound like a squeaky toy. There were Magic and her brand-new son on the couch, with three very curious canine spectators crowding around. We barely had time to move mother and son to the whelping box before the next puppy came, and the third arrived about five minutes after that. Eventually, I had a chance to clean the couch.

Labor and delivery are just the first in a two-month marathon of time-consuming activities. You need to consider the puppies' need for socialization and exercise during the 7 to 12 (or more) weeks they are with you. Young puppies should be accustomed to living with people and our noises, smells, and activities from the beginning. Puppies should be handled gently two or three times a day from birth onward. Since their surroundings will need to be cleaned three or four times a day, that's a good time to handle each puppy. From the third week onward, puppies should be given a variety of toys to play with. They should spend a few minutes outside the whelping area each day, together at first, and then each one individually. At five weeks, they can spend a little time outdoors each day if weather permits. When I have a litter, I spend a minimum of three hours a day, every day, handling the puppies, cleaning and disinfecting their environment, doing laundry, and, starting at four weeks, mixing their baby food and feeding them four times a day. Having written this, I remember why I'm taking a year or two off from breeding!

Did I mention that most bitches develop a roaring case of diarrhea 24 to 48 hours after whelping? It's brought on partly by hormonal shifts and partly by the placentas, which most bitches eat and which puts considerable blood into the feces. You may be able to limit your bitch's intake of placentas, but good luck. It's hard to grab the placenta away from a bitch who's determined to eat it while you're trying to clamp off an umbilical cord on a slippery newborn. Trust me, you do not want your doggy girl having an attack of postpartum diarrhea on your carpets, so you'll need to monitor her closely and confine her securely until you know her system is back to normal.

Another thing that first-time breeders often don't know is that not all bitches are good mothers. Some are neglectful, refusing to clean or nurse their puppies. Some are careless and injure or even kill puppies by accidentally stepping or lying on them. The occasional bitch intentionally kills one or more of her puppies. Although mothering skills do seem to be inherited to some extent, there's no way to know for sure that your bitch will be a good mom until she has her puppies. Chances are she'll do fine, but if she doesn't, you can count on spending even more of your time feeding, cleaning, and caring for the puppies.

If you're like most breeders, you can't keep all the puppies forever even if you want to, so you'll need to spend time finding homes. If you're new to breeding, you'll need to advertise the puppies. Even if you're an established breeder with a waiting list of buyers, if you care about your pups, you'll spend a lot of time screening potential buyers, asking them questions, checking their references, and answering their questions.

Doggerel

A female canine is properly known as a **bitch**, and a male as a **dog**. When a bitch becomes a mother, she is **dam** to the puppies, and the dog to whom she was bred is the **sire**.

You'll spend many hours on the phone and/or the Internet communicating with people, not all of whom will want your pups and not all of whom you will want to have your pups. You'll spend hours putting together information packets for the puppies' buyers, with puppies' pedigrees; copies of registration papers and health clearances on their parents and, where appropriate, on the puppies; and information on puppy care, nutrition, training, your breed, and lots of other useful things.

Most breeders don't allow visitors to the pups until they're around six weeks old, but after that you'll need to spend more time with your buyers. Some will want to visit before the puppies are old enough to leave, and you can count on each visit lasting at least an hour. When the pups are ready to leave for their new homes (not before at least seven weeks of age—see Chapter 8), you'll need to plan at least an hour for each puppy's "adoption party" so that you can go over the paperwork, potty training, feeding, early training, and other puppy matters once again.

Is that it? The puppies leave and you can resume your old life and schedule? If you're a responsible breeder, you'll remain available to your buyers for the life of their dogs. During the first few months, you'll probably spend several hours a week on the phone or computer answering questions—and, of course, enjoying stories of the puppies' antics in their new homes. Then things will probably quiet down, but the occasional question may still come up. If an unanticipated hereditary problem pops up, you'll spend time again answering questions, doing your own further research, and probably crying a bit. If one of your buyers finds she can't keep the pup she got from you three years ago, you'll need to make time to either help her find him a suitable new home or take him in yourself, temporarily or for good.

Some of these time eaters are, of course, pleasurable—who wouldn't love to hear how well those little guys have turned out and how much joy they bring to people's lives? But some of the things that take up a breeder's time are anything but fun. Most breeders spend all too many hours wrestling with disappointment, concern, sorrow, anger, and even fear for their pups. Only you can decide whether you're up to the downside of breeding dogs.

What Will the Parents Give to the Puppies?

Before you breed her, you should have your bitch evaluated by a knowledgeable person who can assess her strengths and weaknesses in terms of the breed standard, including both her physical traits and her temperament. This will help you select a stud dog who will complement the bitch—he should be strong where she is weak so that you hopefully don't reproduce the weaknesses of either parent. No dog is perfect, but responsible breeders try very hard to come closer and closer to perfection.

Responsible breeders want all their puppies to be healthy, good-looking dogs their owners can live with and be proud of. The physical traits called for in a breed standard are not purely cosmetic. A dog with poor skeletal structure or badly placed eyes will be much more likely to suffer from painful injuries and an inability to move and enjoy life as he was meant to. Why would anyone breed dogs without trying to give them healthy, happy lives?

Before she's considered for breeding, a bitch needs to pass the health tests recommended for her breed to decrease the chances that she will pass along inherited disease to her puppies. Even if your bitch has never limped a day in her life, if she carries the genes for dysplasia, some or all of her puppies could be crippled as adults—not a nice thing for the dog or the person who gets him from you. The same goes for many inherited health problems. Responsible breeders use the tools of science to produce puppies with the best possible health.

Grrrrowls
Failure to use screening tests to reduce the chances of producing puppies with serious inherited problems is irresponsible to the puppies, to their breed, and to the people who buy them.

Testing for genetic disease is expensive and it's not foolproof, but it dramatically improves the odds. Besides, responsible, well-informed buyers who would give your puppies the kind of homes they deserve will be reluctant to buy from a breeder who doesn't do the proper tests (see Chapters 3 and 5).

Sex and the Single Canine

We've already talked about the health advantages of altering your dog in Chapter 9. But suppose you really think you'd like to have a litter from your bitch or use your dog at stud. You think you have a realistic idea of the resources required to breed and raise healthy puppies. You're willing to accept the risks involved with breeding. You're proceeding responsibly and will have your dog's strengths and weaknesses evaluated by a knowledgeable person. You'll be sure that both the sire and dam have passed the health-screening tests recommended for the breed, and you'll research the health and temperament histories of their bloodlines. Now let's look at the reality of living with a sexually mature and intact canine.

Let's be clear about one important point first: Your dog does not need to have "children" to be fulfilled. Nor does your dog need a healthy sex life to be happy. Your dog does not dream of seeing his pups graduate from obedience school or of having grandpuppies. If he or she is honored and cared for as a companion dog should be, then you and your family are your dog's fulfillment and dreams come true.

The Unspayed Female

Now let's consider what it's like to live with an unspayed bitch. Some of the behaviors and traits I'll mention vary from one animal to another, but they're all possible and most will be present to some degree. In brief, you can look forward to messy heat cycles, risky fertile periods, mood and behavioral changes, false pregnancies, unwanted all-too-real pregnancies, uterine infections, and visits from all manner of suitor. What fun!

Most worrisome to most people is an intact bitch's heat cycle, during which she first bleeds and then is fertile. Most bitches bleed for 10 to 21 days. Some are very messy and need to be confined to prevent them from leaving blood on carpets, bedding, and upholstery. It is possible to have a bitch wear panties with sanitary pads, but some won't keep the darn things on. If your bitch will wear panties and a pad, you'll have to remove them whenever she needs to potty and change the pad frequently.

Occasionally, a bitch has a *silent heat* in which she doesn't bleed at all. That may sound like a blessing, but it means that unless you have a male dog around, you may not know she's in heat. If you planned to breed her, you'll probably miss the fertile period. But she won't, and neither will any intact male that can get to her. Even experienced breeders often fail to notice when a bitch is having a silent heat, so it's highly unlikely that a beginner will know until a bulging tummy tells the tale a month or so later.

Doggerel

A **silent heat** is a heat cycle in which the bitch doesn't bleed or bleeds so little that the owner never knows. Many a silent heat results in a litter of puppies if there's a male dog within striking distance. A **standing heat** is the period, usually after the bleeding stops, when the bitch is fertile and receptive to males. The standing heat may last from one to two weeks.

The hormones that control your bitch's fertility, sex drive, and heat cycle can also play havoc with her emotions and her body. She may be moody while she's in heat and between heats because her hormone levels are rising and falling throughout the entire cycle. She may become aggressive to other bitches and even to male dogs who show too much interest when she's not in a *standing heat*. She may mount other bitches. She may refuse to eat during her heat cycles and lose considerable weight. After her heat, she'll shed most of her coat. Other bitches, both intact and spayed, may become aggressive toward your bitch when she's in heat. Your bitch may not pay much attention to you while she's in heat. She has other things on her mind.

You'll need to keep your bitch safely confined indoors and away from male dogs while she's in heat. To be absolutely safe, that means you must let her out only on a leash. If you leave her in your fenced backyard, there's a very good chance some neighborhood Romeo will impregnate her. Believe me, two determined canines can get the job done in bare minutes. You'll need to be sure that all members of your family are well trained so that they don't let your bitch out when you aren't around. That goes for visitors as well. I know many a breeder who has discovered six weeks after the fact that her husband, kid, or brother-in-law let a bitch out "by mistake" and now they have a litter on the way.

You will need to prevent access by any intact male dog to your bitch. Make no mistake—dogs and bitches will breed in spite of unbelievable obstacles. I know of bitches who have been bred through chain link and picket fences and through wire crates. I know of male dogs who have chewed through a wall and opened or broken doors to get to bitches. Dogs from miles away will know that your bitch is breedable and will come calling if they can. You and your neighbors probably won't be thrilled about a gang of canine Don Juans hanging out around your house in hopes of passing on their genes.

BowWOW

The average length of gestation for a litter of puppies is 63 days. Some normal litters come as early as the fifty-seventh day, and some as late as the sixty-seventh day.

The Intact Male

Now, what about those would-be daddy dogs? Aside from being motivated to move heaven and earth to get to a sexually receptive bitch, what are they like? To some extent, that depends on the breed, the fundamental temperament of the individual dog, and the training and socialization he gets. Intact males don't all go around humping people's legs and urine-marking all over the house. On the other hand, they do generally exhibit some or all of a number of traits that are directly attributable to the presence of testosterone that wouldn't be there if they had been neutered at about six months.

Intact male dogs are always ready to breed. Some don't wait for a bitch in heat, but try to mount just about anything or anyone, including other male dogs, many of whom don't appreciate the gesture and respond accordingly. If that happens, you may be faced with the formidable, frightening, and dangerous task of breaking up a dog-fight. A dog with a runaway libido may also try to mount bitches who are not in heat, spayed bitches, children, or your Aunt Tilly's leg. He won't be the least bit embarrassed, but what about you?

This is all bad enough. Introduce a bitch in heat, and the fun of managing an intact male dog really begins. Bear in mind, this doesn't have to be a bitch that you plan to have him breed. This may be a bitch you own but don't plan to breed, at least not now or not to him. It may be a neighbor's bitch—dogs can detect the scent of a receptive bitch for miles. If he does, he'll do anything within his power to get to her—dig, climb, break out of the fence you thought secure, break a chain or leash, you name it.

Aside from your responsibility of preventing your dog from siring unplanned litters, you also need to keep him safe. Your dog's urge to escape and go courting puts him at risk. I know a dog who lost a hind leg when he tried to climb out of a 10-foot-high kennel run to get to a bitch. His foot got caught and he hung that way for hours before he was found, destroying the muscles, nerves, and blood vessels in his leg. I know of dogs who have been hit by cars and killed trying to get to a bitch. You may have your hands full just controlling your dog's sex drive if you don't neuter him before he reaches sexual maturity.

Let's assume you can keep him safe at home. If you have more than one male dog, you will probably need to keep them separated while your bitch is in heat to prevent fights, even if the other boy is neutered. (Some intact males are aggressive toward other males all the time.) Some males become so focused on trying to satisfy their lust that they just don't think straight. I know experienced breeders who have been bitten by their own normally well-mannered and even-tempered stud dogs when around a bitch in heat.

Even if your guy doesn't become aggressive, he's liable to display some annoying behaviors. Many dogs refuse to eat whenever they smell a bitch in heat. If he lives near the bitch, this may mean that he goes a week or more eating little or no food. He'll lose weight and may make himself sick. He may do things he'd never do at other times. I have seen my normally reliably housebroken stud dogs urinate on crates and, even more delightful, once on the wood railing and carpet in my family room. I'm not sure who was more surprised, me as I hollered or my dog as he realized what he'd done, but the fact is that like many males bent on procreation, he'd simply lost his mind.

Most stud dogs pace the floor and whine and howl the whole time they're around a bitch in heat—the whining will eventually drive you bonkers, and you'll likely lose some sleep to mournful howling in the wee hours of the morning. If your dog happens to live outside, or your windows are open, your neighbors may benefit as well from his serenades, and they probably won't be pleased. Your dog will drool and get a runny nose. All in all, the average intact male dog is a mess when he's near a bitch in heat.

Living with an intact canine of either sex has serious and annoying drawbacks. It can even be dangerous to the dogs themselves, to other dogs, and to people. Finally, but most importantly, owning an intact dog gives you a serious moral burden. Whether you own the sire or the dam, *you*—not your dog or bitch—are responsible for the life and death of every puppy you allow your dog to produce.

The Sad Side of Breeding

Okay, you're willing to take on the responsibilities, and you're doing everything you can to produce healthy puppies with sound temperaments. You have a good mentor and a good veterinarian. Now you need to face the fact that no matter how well you plan, no matter how good and healthy your bitch, no matter how careful you are, things sometimes go terribly wrong.

Birth Complications

Most bitches have their puppies naturally without complications. Many do not. Sometimes a puppy is too big for the birth canal. Are you prepared to take your bitch to an emergency vet at 2 A.M. for a costly C-section? If you don't, you could lose them all—the stuck pup, the other puppies, and your bitch. You could lose them anyway. I know an experienced breeder of very nice, healthy dogs who lost a whole litter of nine puppies. He nearly lost his beloved champion bitch and had to have her spayed during the emergency surgery. I know another breeder whose bitch hemorrhaged and died shortly after whelping a litter of seven, which then had to be hand-raised. I could fill a book with such stories. Although most whelpings are problem-free and most bitches and puppies (and breeders!) survive them, that really doesn't matter if it's *your* beloved friend and her puppies you watch die.

Puppies can be born with serious birth defects—in fact, with all the same birth defects as human babies, ranging from cleft palates that prevent them from nursing properly to hydrocephalus (water on the brain) to missing or deformed organs to autoimmune diseases. They can be severely injured during whelping, sometimes suffering damage that will prevent them from living happy lives. Are you prepared to have deformed puppies euthanized, or to keep them and care for them throughout their lives?

Sometimes even puppies who appear to be fine at birth don't make it. They can succumb to viral and bacterial infections. If the environment is too cold, they can die of hypothermia. They can waste away from "fading puppy syndrome," which happens for no discernable cause and is devastating to experience. We lost four puppies from a litter of eight within the first five days. One puppy had uncontrollable seizures beginning shortly after birth, probably caused by a head injury during birth, and we had to euthanize her. On the third day, a little boy simply died, and a postmortem examination didn't tell us why. Despite veterinary care and around-the-clock care, two more little boys died in my hands over the next two days. We were lucky to have four beautiful survivors, but I can still feel those tiny bodies in my hands as their lives slipped away, and I still mourn them.

Ask yourself and your family before you venture into dog breeding whether you are willing to accept that nothing is certain. Ask yourself whether you can handle the sorrows as well as the joys. Most important, ask yourself if the quality of the puppies you will produce, and the quality of their lives as you pass the responsibility for them to other people, will be high enough to risk the life of your loving companion bitch.

The Cost of Breeding

Breeding isn't cheap. At least not if you do it responsibly. Let's take a look at some of the costs.

You'll want to be sure that your bitch has been found clear of those hereditary diseases for which we can test. For most breeds, that means at least Orthopedic Foundation for Animals (OFA) or Pennsylvania Hip Improvement Program (PennHIP) x-rays and evaluations. Count on $30 to $50 for the x-rays, $60 to $100 for anesthesia, and $20 for certification. Elbow (two x-rays), shoulder (two x-rays), and spinal examinations are also recommended for some breeds. If your breed is prone to hereditary heart disease, then plan on $150 to $200 for heart certification by a board-certified cardiologist. Eye certifications by board-certified veterinary ophthalmologists run $25 to $50, plus $10 if you want the Canine Eye Registry Foundation (CERF) certificate (see Chapter 3). Additional tests are recommended for certain breeds, many of them involving blood work. Costs vary depending on the test to be performed, so check with your veterinarian or the appropriate specialist.

In bitches, *canine brucellosis* causes abortion or the early death of infected puppies. Infected bitches may have no other clinical signs. In male dogs, brucellosis leads to infertility, enlargement of the testes and scrotum, and infection of scrotal skin. In both sexes, brucellosis causes eye inflammation and infection of spinal discs, resulting in back pain, rear leg weakness, and paralysis. Brucellosis is difficult to treat successfully and may be passed from an infected dog to human beings. It's well worth the cost of testing both parents before breeding a litter.

Doggerel

Canine brucellosis is a bacterial disease spread primarily through sexual contact with an infected animal. It can also be acquired through contact with aborted fetuses, through milk from an infected bitch, and occasionally by airborne transmission. The bacteria enter the body through mucous membranes and spread to lymph nodes, spleen, uterus, placenta, prostate gland, and other internal organs.

Your bitch should have a prebreeding exam to be sure she's free of parasites, vaginal or urinary infections, and brucellosis. She should be brought up-to-date on her vaccinations. Any stud dog owner worth dealing with will require a brucellosis test on your bitch within about 10 days prior to breeding, and a health certificate. All told, the prebreeding exam will probably run $150 to $200. Some stud dog owners will require you to have progesterone tests done to determine when your bitch is fertile so that they don't waste time trying to breed her when she's not ready. You may have to run those tests daily for several days, so add $30 to $210. Don't forget the cost of trips to the vet.

If you don't own the stud dog, you'll have to pay a stud fee, which usually equals the price of a puppy. Some stud dog owners will take the first-pick puppy instead, but that will depend on the quality and pedigree of your bitch and the stud owner's situation. Either way, it will cost you one puppy sale. Don't forget to add in the cost of transporting your bitch to and from the stud dog at least once, usually two or three times. If you need to leave her there instead, you may be charged board.

(Photo courtesy of the author)

Good food for a good start in life is just one of the costs of breeding puppies responsibly.

During the prenatal and nursing periods, your bitch will need extra food and vitamins, so figure on increasing her food bill about 50 percent for the second month of her pregnancy, and 100 percent for the first month postpartum.

You need equipment for whelping and raising the pups. A whelping box that can be easy cleaned and disinfected will be $20 to $200, depending on the size of your bitch and the size of a normal litter in her breed. It also depends on whether you go on the cheap with a plastic swimming pool (which exposes the puppies to more risk of injury by their dam, although many people use pools successfully), or whether you want a box with pig rails to protect the puppies, a gate for the bitch, and other features. You'll need a heat source to keep the puppies warm during the first two weeks—add $25 to $100 depending on whether you use a heat lamp or a more reliable whelping box heating pad. You'll need an indoor puppy pen from about the fourth week onward—that's about $50 to $100. You'll need a scale so that you can weigh the puppies daily for the first two weeks—$20 to $50.

You'll need to assemble a whelping kit before the big day. Include a hemostat, scissors, iodine, alcohol, cotton swabs, disposable bedding for the whelping, washable bedding for after the pups are born, and cleaning supplies—$100 should get you started, barring emergencies. An emergency C-section can easily cost $800 to $1,500.

Your bitch should have a post-partum veterinary exam within 24 hours of whelping to be sure she has passed all the placentas and is in good condition. The pups should be checked by a vet—for a litter of eight that will be anywhere from $50 to $100. If they need their dew claws removed (most breeds do), that's $5 to $10 per puppy. Tail docking, if called for, is about $8 to $15 per puppy.

Chew on This

It's important to have your bitch checked by your veterinarian soon after her litter is born. A retained placenta can make her very ill or even kill her. Occasionally, a dead puppy is retained, and again, the results can be life-threatening.

If you send the pups home at seven weeks (the minimum age for well-adjusted puppies), they'll need one set of vaccinations before they leave, so plan on $25 to $40 per puppy. They should have at least two fecal exams and be wormed if necessary—add another $50 to $100. And you'll have to feed them from about four weeks onward, so add in at least one bag of the appropriate size of puppy food for your breed—let's say $30 to $60 for a litter of eight of a medium-size breed. By now you're probably ready to send these guys to their new homes, but you'll probably need to advertise the litter, so there goes another $50 to $150.

Even being very conservative, you've now spent over $1,000. Then add toys, collars, leashes, and crates for puppies; laundry expenses (you'll be amazed at how many sets of clothes you go through in a day); extra electricity for the whelping room; and the cost of repairing the lawn, woodwork, or whatever pups may damage.

Okay, so your bitch gave you a nice litter of eight. The average neonatal loss rate is 25 percent, which means you could expect to lose two. But let's be generous and say you lose only one puppy. You still have seven to sell. Subtract one more for the cost of the stud fee. Ah, you say, but I own the stud dog. If you've done this right, you've also spent money having him tested for inherited health problems, you've fed him, and hopefully you've trained and proven him in competition .... Owning the stud dog is usually far more expensive in the long run than paying for stud service, so subtract one more puppy's price. You have six to sell at $500 apiece. Wow! You'll take in $3,000! Ah, but you've spent over $1,000, and remember, that's a very conservative figure. But okay, you've been lucky, had no emergency veterinary expenses, lost just one pup, and have kept your other expenses down. You have $2,000. But wait! Your family has fallen in love with little Splotch, so he's staying. You now have $1,500.

Your time has value, and the time you spend taking care of the puppies is time you don't give to your other interests, your family, your children, or yourself. Breeders go very short on sleep when they have puppies. You will undoubtedly spend at least 20 hours planning the litter (serious breeders spend hundreds of hours, but let's say you're a quick study). You'll either spend time managing your bitch and stud dog while she is in standing heat, or you'll transport your bitch to the stud dog for breeding. If he lives nearby, let's say the whole business of getting mom and dad together or managing their courtship at home took 10 hours (it probably took 2 or 3 times that).

You do get a couple months of normal time, aside from possibly a trip to the vet to find out if indeed there are puppies on the way (add $70 to $150 for an ultrasound or x-ray). We won't count that time, though. Now the pups are due, so you spend four hours setting up the whelping area. The big day arrives, and you spend 24 hours monitoring the labor and birth. (You have to take off work, so subtract a day's pay from your balance sheet at the end.)

Let's say you spend three hours a day (you work faster than I do) cleaning up, taking care of your bitch, and handling the puppies. And suppose they all go home on their forty-ninth day. That's 21 hours a week for 7 weeks—147 hours. You've taken mother and puppies to the vet twice, once for their postpartum examinations and once for the first round of puppy shots—let's say six hours for travel and time in the vet's office. You've had lots of response to your ad, so you've spent at least an hour a day on the phone for 2 weeks—there go another 14 hours. That's 225 total hours—and if you manage the whole thing in that little time, *please* write and tell me how you did it!

(Photo by Close Encounters of the Furry Kind)

No responsible dog lover wants a puppy she has bred to end its life in the euthanasia room of an animal shelter

How much did you make? If everything really went as smoothly as I've described (ha!), you made about $5 an hour after taxes if you count only the hours I mentioned. And we didn't even count the cost to buy your bitch in the first place, because you got her as a pet, not a money machine. Your home life and social life haven't been nor-mal for two months, you've done two or three extra loads of laundry a day, the puppies have chewed here and piddled there, they've dug up your pansies and pulled your clematis off the trellis, and you've cried yourself a headache every time one of them went home. If you're breeding for the money, you'd do better with a part-time job.

The Least You Need to Know

- The responsible breeder performs a labor of love, with an emphasis on the labor.
- Breeding healthy dogs with good temperaments is expensive.
- Sexually intact dogs of both sexes are not always easy to live with.
- Sorrow is as much a part of dog breeding as joy.
- You'll make more money with a part-time job than you will breeding dogs.

Part 5

Educating Fido

Every dog deserves to be trained. Training prevents most serious behavior problems and makes for a much happier canine-human relationship. Whether your dog is big or small, old or young, male or female, you'll both be a lot happier if you give your dog at least a basic doggy education. You can do it—really! I'll show you how to teach a few things that your dog needs to know (and you need your dog to know!). I'll also suggest some effective ways to deal with common behavior problems. We'll take a look at the advantages of taking your dog to a good puppy kindergarten or basic obedience class, and what you should expect from a training class and from an instructor.

Chapter 18

How to Approach Dog Training

In This Chapter

- 🏠 Training your dog for everyone's well-being
- 🏠 Choosing the right training equipment
- 🏠 Deciding how you want to train
- 🏠 Going to doggy school
- 🏠 Training at home

Nobody likes to live with a brat, human or canine. Contrary to what many Hollywood movies suggest, though, your dog wasn't born knowing what you want her to do, and you weren't born knowing how to train your dog. Your dog needs to learn what you want, and you need to learn to understand her perspective and to communicate what you want effectively. If you approach dog training with patience, a sense of humor, and willingness to learn from your dog as well as from knowledgeable trainers and instructors, you'll be effective and your dog will be a well-behaved friend and companion. Clear, consistent training will build a bond of trust and understanding that will enhance the love between you and your dog.

Good obedience training is simply the process of training your dog to do what you tell her to do. For most dogs, that means basic manners and maybe a few cute tricks. For others, it may mean following directions for competitive and noncompetitive sports, police and detection work, or service work for disabled owners. Anything that a dog is trained to do on command involves obedience training of some sort.

Chew on This
If you love your dog, train your dog.

There's lots of information available on effective, humane methods of dog training, and there are good instructors in most parts of the country. In this chapter I'll get you started and then point you toward more help and information.

Training Tools

Having the right equipment can make all the difference in training your dog. The tough part is deciding what's right! Ask three obedience instructors or dog trainers about what kind of collar or leash is "best" and you'll probably get three opinions. Honestly, the best piece of equipment for your dog is the one that works best for you and the dog at a particular time for a particular purpose. You need at least one collar (possibly more, depending on your dog) and at least one leash. Let's look at what's available.

Grrrrowls
More dogs are turned over to shelters and put to sleep for poor behavior than for any other reason. Poor behavior is nearly always caused by lack of training and socialization. Don't let your dog die because you failed to train her.

I use different collars on my dogs depending on the dog's age, level of training, individual personality, and type of activity. Several types of collars are commonly used for basic and more advanced training:

🐾 A *flat collar* is fastened with a buckle or a quick-release clasp. Flat collars come in leather, nylon, and fabric. This is the collar that should carry your dog's name, license, and rabies tags. A flat collar should be neither tight nor loose—you should be able to slide two fingers between the collar and your dog's neck. Flat collars don't provide much control, and an excited dog can slip out of one. *A flat collar is the only collar that should be used on a young puppy.*

🐾 A *martingale* collar slips over your dog's head. If the martingale fits properly, when you pull against it with your leash the collar will tighten enough to keep your dog from slipping out of the collar but not enough to choke him. Martingales are commonly used in agility, flyball, and some other dog sports.

🐾 The *choke chain* (also called a slip chain or slip collar) is usually made of metal chain, although they are also available in nylon and leather. Although many good dog trainers use choke chains without being cruel to their dogs, it is extremely easy to misuse a choke chain. Used improperly, a choke chain at best will be ineffective—many dogs learn to ignore the collar, and many people never learn to fit the collar to the dog or to put the collar on correctly. Either way, its value as a training tool is about zero. At its worst, a choke chain can cause permanent injury to your dog's throat and the organs it contains.

BowWOW

A choke chain that is put on wrong or fits poorly is ineffective as a training tool and potentially dangerous for your dog. When you stand with your dog on your left, both of you facing the same direction, the "live ring" (the ring that moves the chain through the other ring) should pull across the top of the dog's neck. If the live ring pulls the chain under the dog's neck, the collar is on backwards. A choke chain should fit your dog so that when you pull the live ring and chain through the "dead ring" (the one that the chain slides through), two to three inches of chain are free. (If your dog has a very large head, you may have to allow a little more chain for putting on and taking off the collar.)

🐾 The *halter* (also known as a head collar) looks rather like a horse halter. It gives you control of your dog's head on the principle that where the head leads, the body must follow. Halters are so effective as control devices that people often neglect to actually train their dogs. If you do that, you wind up with a dog that's under control with his halter on, but not obedient with it off. See Appendix C for resources on proper use of a halter for training.

🏠 The *prong collar* (or pinch collar) might look like a medieval torture device, and many people are opposed to using them, but I feel that used properly the prong collar is an effective training tool for large, strong dogs and for many dogs that become overexcited. The prong collar works by applying pressure from the prongs to points around the dog's neck. You can adjust the collar so that it uses no prongs, only a few prongs, or all the prongs. Prong collars are less likely to cause damage to the dog's neck and throat than are choke chains, and they usually give better control with less force. Before using a prong collar on your dog, have a knowledgeable obedience instructor (not a salesperson in a pet supply store!) show you how to fit the collar and use it properly.

🏠 Electronic collars (shock collars) are seen by some people as a quick and easy way to train a dog. Most people use shock collars to punish the dog for doing something rather than to teach him what to do. In the hands of a very experienced dog trainer, a shock collar *may* be effective and no more cruel than any other method of correction, but I do not recommend a shock collar for most dog owners or dogs. A shock collar can cause more problems than you started with. Shock collars should never be used on an aggressive dog.

Common Approaches to Training

You can train your dog at home by yourself, at class, with friends, or with a private instructor. Wherever you train, the process should be fun. Of course, there are frustrating moments—things don't always go smoothly. When your dog has trouble learning something, keep in mind how hard it is for you to learn something new. Then imagine that the new thing you want to learn is being taught to you by an alien who communicates with beeps and clucks. That will give you some idea of what you're asking your dog to do. Remember to be patient, and if you lose your patience, quit for a while. Come back to the lesson when you're relaxed again.

Chew on This

There are nearly as many ways to train dogs as there are dog trainers. No matter which method you choose for training your dog, someone will tell you it's wrong, ineffective, or bad for the dog. If you feel comfortable about what you're doing and it works for you and your dog without hurting either one of you, then chances are it's a good method for you and this dog at this time.

Many methods of dog training exist. Some of them are very similar but others are very different from one another. Some trainers use food rewards while others don't. Some trainers use pinch collars and choke chains, while others use only a flat collar—or no collar at all. Some trainers use clickers (plastic devices that "mark" a correct behavior for a dog trained in their use), while others see clickers as a gimmick.

Trying to decide on the "best" way to train can be confusing, and the truth is that there is no single best method. Some methods work for some dogs but not for others. Some people do well training their dogs with one method but not another. The bottom line is that training should be fun for both of you and it should get you the results *you* want in what you see as a reasonable amount of time. Personally, I use a mishmash of training techniques that I've found work for me and my dogs. It's well worthwhile to learn a little about different approaches to dog training, and to find an approach that appeals to you and that you can apply (see Appendixes B and C).

Whatever method you decide to use, keep training sessions short so your dog doesn't get bored, and keep them fun. When your dog does something right, praise her and play with her for a minute or two. You want her to be thrilled when she sees the training leash come out.

Going to School

A good dog training class is well worth the time, money, and effort you spend on it. A class provides a chance for your dog to learn to behave and to obey you even in the presence of exciting distractions. The instructor is there to help when something just isn't working in your training. She's also there to tell you when you're doing something silly that you didn't even know you were doing to undermine your dog's training.

Grrrrowls

Never leave a choke chain or pinch collar on your dog when you aren't with him or when he's in a crate, and never let dogs play together with choke chains or pinch collars on. Choke chains and pinch collars can get caught and strangle your dog or cause severe injury.

For a puppy, the socialization provided by going to class is important. Even if you have other dogs at home, your pup needs to get out and meet strangers. Classes give him weekly exposure to lots of other dogs and people, which will help him grow up to be socially well adjusted, confident, and polite.

Doggerel

An **obedience instructor** teaches you to train your dog. A **dog trainer** works directly with your dog, teaching him various commands and then teaching you how to use them with your dog.

When you're choosing an obedience instructor, here are some questions to explore. The answer to most of these should be *yes*. If you don't feel comfortable about the instructor's knowledge, attitude, or methods, go somewhere else.

🐾 Does the instructor have *experience* training dogs and teaching classes? Long experience isn't necessarily a sign of knowledge or good teaching skills, but your instructor should have some experience. Even if she's teaching a class for the first time, she should have training experience with her own dogs, and experience assisting another instructor with some classes.

🐾 Does the instructor have some serious *education about dogs and dog training?* Has she attended seminars, workshops, or advanced classes? Has she kept up-to-date with the ever-growing body of knowledge about how dogs (and people) learn? Don't be shy about asking what her credentials are.

🐾 Does the instructor hold *professional membership* in the National Association of Dog Obedience Instructors (NADOI), the Association of Pet Dog Trainers (APDT), or another professional organization?

🐾 Does the instructor *communicate well* with her students? Does she listen carefully and respond clearly? Does she seem to be able to get her own dog and the dogs in her class to do what she wants without resorting to extreme measures?

🐾 Does the instructor seem to *really like dogs?* Does she seem to *enjoy teaching?* Does she reward her students with praise and encourage them to do the same with their dogs?

🐾 Does the instructor appear to be *effective as a trainer and as a guide to training?* If you want to train your dog to behave around other people and dogs, but the instructor's dog is poorly behaved, the instructor probably can't help you accomplish your goals.

🐾 Is the instructor *flexible?* Dogs don't all respond the same way to training. Some dogs will do anything for a bit of food; others will ignore it. A good dog trainer adapts to the needs of the individual dog, and a good instructor will help you find a method that works with your dog.

Always remember, your dog is *your* dog—she relies on you for her safety and well-being. Never do anything you're uncomfortable about just because an instructor told you to, and never allow anyone else to do anything you don't like to your dog.

Training Classes

Whatever you want to do with your dog, there's probably a class for you somewhere. Here are some of the more common types of dog-training classes. The details vary from place to place and instructor to instructor, but the following types of classes are offered in many areas:

- *Puppy kindergarten classes* are usually for puppies from about two to five months old. A good puppy kindergarten class provides controlled socialization—your puppy should have a chance to play with other puppies. All free play should be closely supervised to prevent problems that can come up from size and age differences, or from the occasional pushier pup. The puppies should also interact with people during puppy kindergarten. You'll learn how to teach your puppy to sit, lie down, and come on command, and walk on leash without pulling. Most puppy kindergarten classes also cover potty training, socialization outside of class, problem behaviors, grooming, and basic health care.

- *Basic obedience classes* are usually for dogs five months or older. A good basic obedience class will teach you how to train your dog, building on puppy kindergarten if your pup attended or starting with the basics if necessary. Most basic classes focus on basic commands—Sit, Down, Stay, Come, and walking politely on leash. Some basic classes aim at preparing your dog to pass the American Kennel Club (AKC) Canine Good Citizen® (CGC) test (see Chapter 19).

- *Competition obedience classes* are designed to teach people how to train their dogs for competition in obedience trials. They focus on handling skills as well as techniques for teaching the dog the advanced exercises (see Chapter 23).

🏠 *Conformation classes* are usually designed to prepare dogs to show in conformation (see Chapter 19). Some of these classes provide training for the handler, but many focus on simply practicing with the dog. If you want to learn how to show your dog, look for a handling class.

🏠 *Handling classes* teach you how to show your dog in conformation dog shows.

🏠 *Agility classes* teach you how to train your dog to negotiate the jumps, tunnels, A-frames, dog-walks, and other obstacles used in the sport of agility (see Chapter 19). Your dog should be finished growing before you enroll him in a regular agility course (refer to Chapter 15), but some clubs and training schools offer puppy agility classes that don't include work that stresses immature bones and joints.

🏠 *Therapy dog training* is offered by some training clubs as well as some hospitals and other institutions. Therapy dogs visit residents or patients in nursing homes, hospitals, schools, and other facilities, bringing them love, joy, and real "warm fuzzies."

🏠 *Specialized* training classes are available for training your dog for hunting, herding, coursing, pulling, and other activities (see Chapter 23). These classes are often offered by local breed clubs or clubs devoted to a particular activity. If you're interested in trying or pursuing a specialized sport, ask your breeder, veterinarian, or other people with your breed or similar breeds about classes or private instruction in your area.

Training schools and clubs vary considerably in what they offer in terms of facilities, classes, private instruction, and quality of instruction. In addition to checking out the instructor for any class you might take, here are some things to check out as you choose a school or class:

🏠 **How big is the class?** If there are more than 10 people and dogs, will the instructor have an assistant? How qualified is the assistant? Will you get individual help when you need it?

🏠 **Are the facilities adequate?** Is there room for all class members to take part safely without being jammed together? Is the floor reasonably clean? Is the footing good so you and your dog won't slip? Is the outdoor potty area kept reasonably clean?

🏠 **Are policies in place to protect your dog's health?** Are all dogs required to show proof of vaccination for common infectious diseases? If you prefer not to vaccinate annually, are titers acceptable (see Chapter 9)? Are dogs expected to be reasonably clean and free of fleas?

🏠 **Are procedures in place to keep you and your dog safe?** What happens if a dog in your class is aggressive toward other dogs or people?

(Photo by Close Encounters of the Furry Kind)

Training will make your dog a happier, better-behaved companion.

Training at Home

Most of your training will be done at home. That doesn't mean you shouldn't take a class or two or three. But you need to practice and reinforce what you learn in class once a week with daily practice at home. Several short sessions from 10 to 20 minutes during the day are more effective than one long one, which can lead to boredom and resistance from both your dog and you.

Take advantage of training opportunities as they come up. If you're teaching your dog to sit on command, have her sit for her dinner, to get her leash on for a walk, at the door before he goes out, and at the corners when you're out for a walk. Have her practice Stays while you dust the furniture, eat your dinner, or shine your shoes. Have her lie down or stand before you'll throw her ball. Practicing commands in different situations will help her understand that Sit means "put your fanny on the floor" whether she's outdoors, in the basement, a block from home on a walk, or at training class.

If you can't find a good training class, then read as much as you can. The next chapter gives you some basic training methods for commands that most people want to teach. Chapter 20 addresses some common behavior problems and suggests ways to correct them. I've also listed some excellent books, videos, and Internet training resources in the appendixes of this book. Work with your dog. She'll be a better companion for you, and the better you understand her, the more you'll appreciate her for her wonderful canine self.

The Least You Need to Know

- 🏠 Training is for both you and your dog.
- 🏠 The right collar is a basic training tool.
- 🏠 The best training method is the one that works well for you and your dog.
- 🏠 It's worth the effort to find a good training school and instructor.
- 🏠 Many resources are available to teach you more about dogs and dog training.

Chapter 19

What Every Dog Should Know

In This Chapter

- 🏠 Applying a few basic "rules" for dog training
- 🏠 Teaching five commands every dog should know
- 🏠 Making your dog an official Canine Good Citizen® (CGC)
- 🏠 Teaching kids and dogs to get along

Every dog deserves to be taught good manners that will make him more pleasant to be around. You'll enjoy your dog more if you teach him a few simple behaviors—Sit, Down, Stay, Come, and Leave It. In this chapter I'll tell you how to teach your dog to be a good citizen whose company you and your neighbors will enjoy.

Five Essential Commands

Who wants to stand in the yard calling a dog that ignores you until he's good and ready to obey? Who wants a dog that won't lie down and stay where you tell him? We've probably all known dogs like that, and they're no fun to live with. The sad fact is that dogs are trained to ignore their owners—by their owners! Happily, any reasonably healthy dog of any breed can be trained to respond to basic commands.

Come, Sit, Down, Stay, and Leave It—these five basic commands can make a huge difference in your relationship with your dog. I'm going to give you a few simple "rules" for training in general, and then a basic method for training your dog to respond to each of the five fundamental commands. You should still take your dog at least to a basic obedience class (refer to Chapter 18) for socialization, training under the eye of an instructor, and fun, and I suggest you read at least one good training book (see Appendix B).

Before we get to the individual commands, here are some training basics that apply to dog training:

- **Be consistent.** Always use the same word to mean the same thing. Remember, human language is not natural to your dog—he has to learn that words have specific meanings. He'll learn "Sit," but he'll have a lot of trouble with "Aww, baby, pweeze sit here by me" or "You better sit right now, dammit!" or "Sit ... sit down! ... sitsitsit ..." So play fair and use one word consistently.

- **Be concise.** Give your command once and once only. If you repeat a command three, four, or five times, your dog learns that he doesn't have to do it until you say "down ... down ... down ... down" or until you yell really loud or until you say the word and wave your arm at him or some other silly thing.

- **Be generous.** Reward your dog for doing what you tell him to do. When you begin teaching a new command, reward him every single time he gets it right. A reward is something your dog likes—that might be a treat, a toy, or a butt scratch, as long as it obviously makes your dog happy. Use a word of praise— "good dog" or "pretty!" or whatever you like—along with the reward, and eventually the word itself will become a reward.

🏠 **Be smart.** If you're not in a position to enforce a command, don't give the command unless you know for certain your dog will obey. If you're in the bathtub, don't tell your dog "Down" unless you're willing to get out of the tub, drip through the house, put your dog where you want him, and have him lie down. If you give a command that you can't enforce, your dog learns that he has to do it if you're standing there holding the leash, but he doesn't have to do it if you're all wet or otherwise unable to make sure he does it. The point of training is to teach the dog that he must do what you say when you say it— and if you're consistent and smart when you're training him, you'll end up with a reliable dog.

🏠 **Be prepared.** If you're going to need a leash to manage your dog while teaching him to sit, then have the leash on him or close at hand. If your dog doesn't yet come reliably when called, then keep a long line near the backdoor and put it on him when he goes out at night to potty. Then if you say "Come" and he doesn't, you can reel him in.

🏠 **Be happy.** Your dog is your friend, and he really does want to please you. Use a happy voice when you give commands, and a very happy voice when you praise him. Put yourself in his place—if two people called you, one in a tone that said, "Oh, I'm so happy to see you; come and be here where I am!" and the other in a growling tone that said, "You get over here right now," which one would you go see? Use your voice to tell your dog how delighted you'd be to have him do what you tell him.

I recommend that you use treats for training rewards. Most dogs are motivated by food. (If your dog truly isn't interested in food, then find a toy, a certain ear scratch, or something that does tickle him.) Remember, you're using treats to reward your dog for a job well done, not to feed him. Once your dog knows the command and does it reliably, you won't need the food reward—although you should still reward him with a praise word most of the time.

Use small bits of foods that are soft, tasty, and easily chewed. You want your dog to gobble the treat and get back to training, not stop to munch. Treats are more interesting if you make a sort of "training trail mix" of goodies your dog likes—then he's never sure just which taste sensation he's about to encounter. Ideas for treats include plain unsweetened cereal, string cheese, plain air-popped popcorn, thinly sliced hot dogs (you can cook the slices in the microwave to reduce the greasiness—usually three to five minutes will do), tiny or soft dog treats, a little dry cat food, tiny bits of apple—whatever turns your dog on. My dog Rowdy will do anything for a bit of carrot! Many trainers use a small pouch on a belt to hold their training treats to avoid messy pockets.

You also need two special training words. First, you need a *praise word*. This is something you say when your dog does something right. At first, you need to say the word as you give your dog a treat. He'll learn that your praise word is a good thing, and you'll be able to phase out the treats and reward him with the word by itself most of the time. Try to find a word that you don't use all the time with your dog. If you're in the habit (like I am) of telling your dog he's a "good boy" even when he hasn't done anything except be your wonderful dog, then don't use "good boy" for praise in training. I use "pretty!" or "very nice" for praise.

Second, you need a *release word*. When you give a command, such as Sit, you should expect your dog to sit and remain sitting until you tell him he doesn't have to anymore. Your release word tells him he's finished with that command for now. Many people use "Okay" for a release word, but I don't recommend it. Most of us say okay a lot, and you don't want to release your dog by accident just because you say okay to someone. I use "free!" for my release word. The word itself doesn't matter, but it should be one you can remember but that you don't use frequently in other circumstances.

(Photo by Close Encounters of the Furry Kind)

Puppies and children both need to learn how to be good citizens.

Come

One of the most important commands you can teach your dog is Come. A dog who comes reliably is safer than one who doesn't, and the owner of a dog that comes reliably is less frustrated. Here's my way of training a dog to come reliably.

Start with your puppy or dog on leash, or in a *very* small room or fenced area where he can't go far. Have a toy or a small treat. Say "Fido, Come!" in a happy, playful voice. Say it only once! Then do anything necessary to encourage your dog to come to you—act silly, walk or run the other way, crouch down, anything to make him curious enough to come to you. Then reward him— use your praise word and play with

Chew on This

Wherever you are should be the safest, most fun place your dog knows. If you call your dog to you, always reward him for coming with at least your praise word and sometimes with petting, a treat, a toy, or play time. Never call your dog to you to lock him up or do something he doesn't like—go get him instead.

him, give him a treat, or give him a toy. Then let him go back to what he was doing. Repeat the process two or three times; then quit for this session. Do this several times a day if possible.

If your dog doesn't come despite your best efforts, then gently pull him in your direction. If you're training in a small space with no leash, then start over with the leash on. If he starts to come on his own, don't pull anymore, but encourage him with happy talk, and reward him when he gets to you. Keep the leash on for every Come command until you no longer have to get him started with a pull on the leash.

If you're not the only human in the family, then make a game of teaching Come with other family members. You can call your dog back and forth or from one person to another in a circle. Just make sure that only one person calls at a time, and make sure each person rewards the dog for coming.

Remember the basic training rules as they apply to Come:

- *Always* use the same word—don't use "Come," "Come here," "Here," "Get over here," "Get your butt over here ..."

- *Never* call more than once—you'll be teaching your dog to ignore you. If he doesn't come the first time, go get him, put the leash on, then call him, and start him or pull him in with the leash. Then *praise and reward him for coming*!

- *Always* reward your dog for coming—a reward may be a treat one time, a cuddle the next, and your praise word every time.

- *Never* call your dog if you can't enforce the command. If you can't trust him to come when you call, then put him on a leash or a long line so that you can get him back from the cold, wet yard. And *never, ever* let your dog off leash in an unfenced area if he doesn't come reliably. Coming reliably means coming immediately on the first command every single time he's called, even when he'd rather investigate another dog, a squirrel, or something else of interest.

Sit

"Sit" is a very useful command. It can be used to control a rambunctious dog, and to give him something positive to do in place of leaping on you or otherwise being a pest. Sit gives you control over your dog on walks, at the vet, and at home.

To teach your puppy or dog to sit on command, begin with him on leash or confined in a small space. Hold a small treat in front of his nose, but don't let him take it. When he shows interest in the treat, *slowly* raise the treat and move it back over his head toward his tail. As his head comes up to follow the treat, his butt has to go down. When he starts to fold his hind legs into the sit, tell him Sit. Keep moving the treat slowly backward. The instant he sits completely, give him the treat and use your praise word. Then release him with your release word. Do not release him before you give the treat—you'll be rewarding him for no longer sitting! If he gets up before you release him, have him sit again before rewarding him. Repeat three or four times. Then quit for a while. If you do several sessions a day, your dog should sit on command in no time. When he gets pretty good at sitting on command, start to lengthen the time he has to stay sitting before he gets the treat. Start with a few seconds, gradually increasing to half a minute, and then a minute. He should remain sitting until you release him.

Down

There are many ways to teach a dog to Down, or Lie Down. I prefer to teach the command from a standing rather than sitting position for three reasons. First, Down can be a life-saving command—even more than Come. Suppose your dog gets away from you and is on the other side of a busy street. A car is coming. You don't want to call your dog, because he might be hit. If he responds to Down no matter where he is, whether he's moving or standing still, you can make him safe even in such a frightening situation.

The other two reasons I teach Down from a standing position aren't so dramatic. One is that teaching it from a sitting position requires two commands—Sit and then Down. Not a big deal, but I'd rather just give one command most of the time. The other reason is that if you decide to train your dog for obedience competition beyond the Novice level (see Chapter 23), you'll have to teach him a "moving down" in which he lies down from a trot. If he sits first and then lies down, he'll creep forward a little. If he just drops into a down position, he won't creep forward. If you're thinking of competing eventually, you'll find it's easier to teach Down without the Sit right from the start. So here's how I teach Down.

Start with your dog standing. If he's a puppy, or a small dog, you may want to kneel in the beginning. Hold a treat in your hand, let your dog know it's there, and slowly move your hand under your dog's head, toward and then between his front legs, lowering it as you go. As his head follows the treat, he should fold himself downward. If necessary, gently guide his rear down; then praise him and give him the treat as soon as he's completely down. If he steps backwards instead of lying down, move your hand with the treat a little faster—that will get his head and neck down faster and he should go down.

If he continues to leave his butt up in the air once his shoulders are down, and he doesn't drop it with a light touch from your hand, don't try to force him down. You want him to learn to put his body in the right position, and he'll learn faster if he has to do it himself.

 Chew on This

If you teach your dog nothing else, teach him to lie down and stay on command. In some situations, Down is safer and more effective than Come.

Besides, a dog's natural response to force is to resist—if you push down on his butt, he'll push up against you. It's amazing how much resistance even a small dog can muster! Instead of forcing him down, keep a treat close to the ground with one hand, and with your other arm cradle your dog's hind legs from behind. Gently move your arm forward around the hind legs until he folds down. Once he's all the way down, praise and give him the treat. Then release him. Slowly increase the amount of time he has to stay down before getting the treat.

Stay

"Stay" is a useful command. It tells your dog not to move from whatever position he's in, whether he's standing on the vet's examining table, sitting on the back seat of the car, or lying on his bed in the family room.

I start teaching Stay in the down position. It's the easiest position for a dog to hold, so if he learns to stay in the down, stays in other positions will be easier. Once your dog lies down on command, start to teach him this extension of the down. Have your leash on the dog. When he is completely down, praise and reward him; then tell him Stay. If he starts to get up, put him back in the down position and praise him, but don't give him a treat. Tell him Stay again. If he stays down a few seconds, praise, reward, and release. Start with very short stays—less than a minute—and stay close to your dog. Very slowly increase the time until he will stay about five minutes with you standing close to him.

When he's solid for five minutes, put him in the down stay, and take a step away from him. Shorten the time to 30 seconds, and slowly build the time up again to 5 minutes. Repeat this process, always reducing the amount of time and building it back up each time you increase the distance between you and your dog. If you hit a point at which he starts popping up before the time is up, shorten the distance for a few days until he's solid again at that distance and time. Then increase the distance by one or two steps, and shorten the time.

Always remember to release your dog from the stay when you're finished. Don't let him decide for himself that he's done. If he does that after 10 minutes, why not after 1?

When your dog seems to understand the idea of the stay when he's lying down, repeat the same process with him in a sit. Remain very close and keep the time very short to begin with. Slowly increase the time, then increase the distance and shorten the time, and then slowly lengthen the time again.

You can have your dog practice down stays and sit stays while you're doing other things. Just don't forget that you told him to do something and let him wander off two minutes later! If you want him to be reliable about following commands, you need to be reliable and consistent about giving them, enforcing them, and releasing him from them.

Leave It!

"Leave It" is a useful command in many circumstances. It enables you to tell your dog not to touch that pretty Poodle at obedience class, that tuna sandwich you set on the coffee table while you get the remote control, and that disgusting pile of what's-it just off the trail at the park.

To teach Leave It successfully, you need to make sure that following your command is more rewarding than getting "it" would be. So when you start to teach the command, you need to reward the dog for leaving the object of his desire, and the reward has to be worthwhile in his eyes (or mouth!). You also have to have enough control of the situation to prevent your dog from getting "it," because if he does, then he has been rewarded for ignoring you.

Begin with a setup. Put something that you know your dog will find interesting on the floor or a low table. It could be a ball (not one of his regular toys—something he's never seen before), a bit of food, a stuffed toy, or anything else he'll probably try to investigate or pick up. Have some especially yummy treats in your pocket or training pouch. Put your dog on leash. Walk your dog near "it," making sure the leash is short enough to let you keep him from getting it. As soon as he shows interest in it, say "Leave it!" and walk quickly away—he'll have to follow you because of the leash. (You can also simply give a quick tug on the leash and reward him, but at first I like to keep moving so the dog refocuses quickly.) As soon as your dog looks at you instead of "it," praise him and give him a treat. Make a big fuss about what a good dog he is. Repeat the process three or four times, and then quit. A couple sessions a day will soon have your dog responding to Leave It, but beware of a couple of pitfalls.

If your dog manages to get "it" before you get him away, you need to get it back if possible. If "it" is a toy, take it away from him, put it back where it was, and repeat the training routine—making sure he doesn't get it again! If "it" is food, you need to get it away from him if possible. *Caution—do not* try to take food away if your dog growls or has a tendency to guard food—in fact, if that's the case, don't use food for teaching Leave It. You could get bitten. Get some help to get the guarding behavior under control (see Chapter 20). *Do not let a child attempt to take food or anything your dog guards away from him!*

Eventually, you won't need treats to reinforce your dog for leaving things, but do always praise him and maybe pet him for obeying this command. You know how hard temptation is to resist!

Canine Good Citizen® (CGC) Tests

The Canine Good Citizen® (CGC) program was developed by the American Kennel Club (AKC) as a way to promote and reward well-behaved dogs as members of the community. To earn the CGC® certificate, your dog must pass the CGC® test, which includes the following 10 parts:

- Accepting a friendly stranger—the dog must allow a friendly stranger to approach and speak to the handler, as might happen on a walk.

- Sitting politely for petting—the dog must allow a friendly stranger to pet his head and body while he sits quietly.

🏠 Appearance and grooming—the dog must allow someone other than the handler to groom and examine him, and must show by his grooming and appearance that he is well cared for.

🏠 Out for a walk—the dog must walk quietly on leash, making turns and at least two stops.

🏠 Walking through a crowd to show that the dog is polite and under control around people in public.

🏠 Sit and Down on command and Stay in place.

🏠 Coming when called—the dog must stay on command and then come when called from a distance of 10 feet.

🏠 Reaction to another dog—the dog must show no more than casual interest in another dog.

🏠 Reaction to distraction—the dog must remain calm when faced with common distractions (for instance, a chair falling over or a jogger running by.

🏠 Supervised separation—the dog must remain calm and polite when left with the evaluator while his handler goes out of sight for three minutes.

The CGC test is performed entirely on a leash, and the dog must wear a properly fitted buckle or slip (choke) collar made of leather, fabric, or chain. You must bring written proof of rabies vaccination and should bring your dog's brush or comb.

If your dog fails any part of the 10-point test, he fails the test. He also fails if he eliminates during testing. (Elimination is allowable during the supervised separation when that part of the test is held outdoors.) A dog that growls, snaps, bites, attacks, or tries to attack a person or another dog will be dismissed from the test.

If you try the CGC test and don't quite make it, don't be discouraged. Think of it as an opportunity to see what you and your dog need to work on. Then do some more training, and try again!

(Photo by Close Encounters of the Furry Kind)

This Golden Retriever is proud to be an AKC Canine Good Citizen®.

Childproof Your Dog and Bite-Proof Your Kids

If you got your dog as a companion for your children, you need to know that happy canine and child relationships don't happen by accident. Young puppies play rough and have sharp teeth and claws. They aren't born knowing how to behave with their new human companions. They're used to playing with their littermates—puppies play with their mouths and feet, they play rough, and they like to make each other squeal. Your puppy needs to learn that teeth do not belong on human skin.

Neither do children automatically know how to "play nice" with puppies and dogs. They need to be taught that ears aren't for pulling and eyes aren't for poking. If you have an adult dog—or adopt one—the same rules apply. Too many people assume that nice dogs will put up with anything a kid dishes out. That's not fair to the dog, and it's not necessarily true. All too often we hear about a dog that bit a child "without warning." Very few dogs bite without warning, but if the child doesn't understand the dog's signals and neither do the adults who should be in charge, the dog may eventually nip.

All interaction between puppies and children should be *closely* supervised by a responsible adult. That doesn't mean watching out the window while they play in the yard—it means being in a position to intervene immediately if necessary. Teach your puppy to sit or lie down for petting, and teach your children how to interact with the pup without getting him all excited. See Appendix B for some excellent books on raising children and puppies together.

Older dogs and older children don't usually need such close supervision, but both need training. For your dog, that means at least basic obedience training and lots of socialization from puppyhood on. Children should be taught to understand that dogs are not toys but living creatures who feel pain. Don't assume that because a dog and child know one another there's no risk of a bite. Most children who are bitten know the dogs that bite them and are on the dogs' home turf. A child will often take more chances with a dog he knows, and dogs are more confident and more protective in their own homes.

Children are much more likely than adults to be bitten, and boys get bitten more often than girls. Most bites happen because the children weren't taught how to behave around dogs. You can increase your child's safety with dogs—at home and in public—by teaching them these basic rules for interacting with dogs. Even if you don't have kids, teach your neighbor kids—everyone benefits when kids know how to be safe around dogs.

🐾 If you see a dog you don't know and he's with someone, ask if it's okay to pet the dog. Some dogs don't like kids or are afraid of them. If the answer is yes, then approach the dog calmly and quietly, and …

- Always let the dog sniff your open hand before you try to pet her. *Never* reach suddenly over a dog's head without letting her sniff—you may frighten her and she may bite because she's afraid.

- If you see a dog running loose or in her yard alone, do not approach the dog. *Never* try to approach or pet a dog that doesn't have a person with her.

- Don't tease dogs, even if they are tied or inside a fence or car. Teasing is mean. Besides, the dog could get loose and bite you. Don't shout at dogs and don't pretend to bark or growl at them.

- Don't grab food, toys, bones, or other things away from a dog.

- Don't bother a dog that's eating, sleeping, or caring for puppies.

- Never stare at a dog's eyes, especially if you don't know the dog.

- Never run away from a dog—he'll probably chase you and might bite.

- If a dog barks, growls, or shows you her teeth, puts her ears back against her neck, and walks on stiff legs with her hair sticking out, she's telling you she's angry and she'll bite if you come closer. If you see a dog acting like that, look away from the dog's face and walk very slowly sideways until the dog relaxes or you're out of sight.

- If a dog comes close to you, "be a tree"—look up, not at the dog, and cross your arms with your hands on your shoulders.

- If a dog attacks you, "be a ball"—curl up on the ground on your knees with your face tucked onto your legs and your arms around your head. Lie still and don't scream.

- If you get bitten, tell an adult right away. Try to remember where you were when you got bitten, where the dog lives if you know or which way he went if he was loose, who else was around when he bit you, and what the dog looked like.

- If you see a dogfight, don't try to break it up! Stay away from the dogs, and find an adult to help.

The Least You Need to Know

🏠 A few simple "rules" make all dog training easier and more effective.

🏠 Every dog should learn to Come, Sit, Lie Down, Stay, and Leave It on command.

🏠 The AKC CGC® test rewards responsible dog ownership and well-behaved dogs.

🏠 Kids and dogs make a great combination, but both need to learn how to behave with one another.

Chapter 20

Dealing with Problem Behaviors

In This Chapter

- 🏠 Understanding why your dog does what he does
- 🏠 Preventing behavior problems
- 🏠 Correcting common behavior problems
- 🏠 Getting help when you can't fix it alone

Most behaviors of dogs are either instinctive or learned. The most effective way to deal with behavior problems is to understand a bit about canine behavior and instincts, and use that knowledge to prevent unwanted behaviors before they occur. When we can't do that, the next best approach is to keep the unwanted behavior from occurring and replace it with a behavior we can live with.

Preventing Problem Behaviors

Nobody's perfect, not even your dog. But with some careful planning and quick responses, you can prevent most problem behaviors and get rid of most others fairly easily.

Remember in Chapter 2 when I talked about breeds being developed for specific purposes? If your dog has been bred for generations to dig vermin out of holes, it really should be no surprise when she tunnels under your turnips. If the generations before her were designed to run down and kill rabbits, you shouldn't be surprised if she goes after bunnies, squirrels, and cats. If you know what your dog's genes are telling her to do, you will better understand some of her behaviors, and you'll be able to decide how to channel her instincts into outlets that are acceptable to both of you.

The next step is to keep control of things. If your puppy isn't trustworthy in your absence because she likes to chew and rip things up, then don't leave her loose. If you have a crate, use it. If you don't have a crate, get one and crate-train your dog (see Chapter 15). If your dog digs holes when she's alone in the yard for 20 minutes, don't leave her alone in the yard for more than 15 minutes. If she loves to chase rabbits and butterflies, and won't come back when you call, don't let her off her leash (see also Chapter 19).

A tired dog is a good dog. Be sure your dog gets plenty of exercise—and again, look to her breed to determine what "plenty" is. If she was bred to be a lap warmer, then a 20-minute walk or game of fetch in the yard may be all she needs. If her ancestors were bred to work all day long herding and guarding livestock or accompanying their owners on hunts, then she probably needs at least an hour of running exercise every day—maybe more. Remember—sending your dog to the backyard by herself is not going to do the trick (see Chapter 13).

Minds need exercise, too. A dog that lacks mental stimulation will make her own, and you probably won't like the results. Some dog toys are designed to provide mental stimulation. For instance, hard plastic cubes that dispense bits of food on a random basis as the dog rolls them around provide lots of entertainment (and noise, so don't give your dog one to play with at bedtime). Training for obedience, agility, tricks, or tracking—anything that requires your dog to think and learn—will help relieve boredom and the behavior problems it causes.

Training, especially obedience training, makes for a better companion across the board. Even if you aren't working on a specific behavior problem in your training sessions, a dog that learns to behave and obey in one setting often acts better in other settings. Undoubtedly, that's due in part to the use of physical and mental energy in training sessions, but it's also because a well-trained dog is a secure dog that knows and trusts you, her trainer (see Chapters 18 and 19).

Before you start trying to solve a behavior problem, review the basics of dog training I mentioned in Chapter 19. It's just as important to be clear, consistent, and patient when correcting an unwanted behavior as when teaching your dog to sit or lie down.

Grrrrowls

Dog owners are responsible for a lot of their dogs' misbehavior. Being sure your dog gets plenty of exercise and mental stimulation will go a long way toward preventing problems.

(Photo by Close Encounters of the Furry Kind)

A well-trained dog is a wonderful companion.

Correcting Some Common Problems

When your puppy or dog does something you don't like, you need to teach her not to do it. Here are three general ideas that should help you deal with most problems.

Number one: Figure out why your dog is doing what she's doing. Is she following some deep instinct bred into her for many generations? Is she bored and full of energy? Has she discovered that this behavior gets her what she wants? If she barks in her crate and you let her out, she'll try that again next time—and she'll bark longer and louder because if it worked once, it'll work again eventually.

Number two: Be sure that you're the one who's in charge. I had a Lab years ago that trained me to go get him a biscuit. I thought it was cute at first—he'd come and bark at me, I'd get up and follow him, he'd point to the dog biscuit box and bark again, and I'd deliver. Then I asked myself, "Who's training whom here?" Aha! I changed the rules of the game. If he came and barked at me, I told him "Sit" or "Down" and maybe a few other commands. Then sometimes I'd have a brilliant idea—"How 'bout a goodie?" Then I'd have him respond to another command—sometimes the ever popular "balance-the-biscuit-on-your-nose trick"—before giving him a biscuit. Other times I'd just praise and give him a belly rub. He still enjoyed the game, but I was back in charge.

If you have a dog that tends to be a little pushy, make him earn what he wants by responding to various commands. You don't have to bore the both of you with "Sit" and "Down" forever. Teach him some tricks (see Appendix B for resources), and have him do one. He'll be a happier dog if he's sure you're in charge.

Number three: Whenever possible, give your dog an alternative behavior to replace the one you don't like. I'll make some suggestions later for specific problem behaviors, but we can't cover everything, so hold this thought—*it's much easier to teach your dog to do something than to teach her to do nothing.*

Jumping on People

Believe it or not, your dog's goal in jumping on you is not to plant big, muddy paw prints on your shirt. So why does he jump up? Well, mostly because he likes you, and because you probably reward him for it part of the time by petting him, pushing him (which he sees as play), and paying attention to him.

If you really want your dog to stop jumping, you need to be absolutely consistent about not rewarding him. Never put your hands on him to push him down and then pet him—the petting is what he wants. Don't try to knee him in the chest. Unless you're more coordinated than most people, you won't connect, and if you do connect, you could injure your dog. Here are two approaches that are safe and effective if you and everyone else in the family is consistent.

One technique that works with some dogs is to completely ignore him when he's jumping. Wear old clothes for this one! When your dog jumps up, don't say a word. Fold your arms over your chest, turn your back on the dog, and look up. He may continue to try for a bit, especially if he's used to getting a more fun response from you. But eventually he'll decide that his jumping turns you into a very boring sort of person, and he'll quit. When he does quit, quietly have him sit or stand and pet him. Stay calm—you don't want to get him all excited. If he does jump up again, go into boring mode. This method requires patience from you, but it does work and is especially effective with puppies. Once your dog is convinced that jumping on you never gets him what he wants, he'll be reliable about staying off.

Another approach is to give your dog a positive command—Sit or Down—before he jumps, and reward him for obeying the command. The problem with this is two-fold. First, he has to know the command, so the technique isn't reliable with young puppies or with dogs who aren't really trained to respond to commands reliably. Second, your dog may decide that if he jumps on you, you'll talk to him and reward him—what a fun game!

Mouthing and Biting

Puppies use their mouths to explore their world. They also use their mouths to play with other dogs. It's quite normal for a puppy to try to use his mouth to play with you as well, but he needs to learn that he must never put his teeth on a person.

Here are two methods that work well with most puppies. One is to stop playing with the puppy the instant he mouths you. Just say "Ow!" and get up and ignore him for a minute or so. Then come back and play with him again, rubbing his tummy, throwing a toy for him to chase, whatever. If he puts his mouth on you, ignore him again. Many puppies will catch on very quickly. Others are more persistent. If your pup doesn't get it, don't just ignore him, but leave him completely alone for a minute or so. Then return. Again, it may take a few sessions, but if you and other members of your family are consistent and if mouthing just never pays off, he'll quit.

Chew on This _____

Mouthing, although annoying and even painful with those sharp puppy teeth, is a normal part of puppy behavior. Growling, guarding, and aggressiveness in a puppy are something else entirely. If your puppy shows signs of aggression, speak to his breeder and to your veterinarian. Don't ignore aggression in a puppy—get qualified professional help or return the pup to the breeder.

Aggressive biting is something else entirely. If your puppy or dog bares his teeth or snaps at you or any other member of your family, or if he guards his food, toys, bed, or anything else from you, ask your veterinarian or obedience instructor for a referral, and talk to a qualified dog trainer or behaviorist who is qualified to deal with aggression. Do not wait! Dogs don't bluff. If your dog threatens you, take him seriously, and if he bites you or anyone else, get help immediately.

Destructive Chewing

Chewing is one of the great pleasures of life for many dogs. A nice, raw knucklebone or a good, hard chew toy can be the canine version of curling up with a good book. But if your dog doesn't limit his pleasures to things he's supposed to chew, he can cause a lot of damage and even hurt himself.

Puppies in particular are champion chewers. Puppies begin to lose their *deciduous* (baby) teeth and get their permanent teeth when they are four or five months old. During this time, your puppy's mouth will be sore and he'll probably want to chew anything and everything to relieve the discomfort. Here are a few things you can do help him—and you and your things—get through teething:

- 🏠 Give your puppy ice cubes or "soupsicles" (low-sodium chicken or beef broth frozen into ice cubes).

- 🏠 Give him high-quality chew toys made for dogs.

- 🏠 Give him raw carrots.

- 🏠 If you feed dry food, soak his food in water for about 20 minutes before feeding him.

- 🏠 When you can't watch him, confine him.

- 🏠 Put anything you don't want chewed and anything that might hurt your puppy out of his reach.

Prevention is by far the best way to deal with chewing. If your puppy or dog likes to chew things and rip things up, then he should never—I repeat, never—be allowed to be loose unsupervised with access to things he might like to have in his mouth. Crate-train your dog, and confine him to his crate when you can't watch him. Give him a nice legal chew toy or bone to play with in the crate. I don't advocate locking a dog up for long hours in a crate—four hours at a time should be about the maximum. If you have to be gone longer than that on a regular basis, arrange to have someone come in during the day to let him out for a while.

When you're with your dog, keep an eye on him. If he picks up something he shouldn't have, gently take it from him while you say "Leave it" and give him one of his own toys. Be patient—it may take him a little while to learn what's his and what isn't. After all, he thinks, "your stuff all smells like you, and it's right there, and you're not using it, so maybe it's okay if I have a little chew?" Just teach him, and he'll catch on.

Pulling on the Leash

Going for a walk should be pleasant for you as well as for your dog. But there's nothing fun about being hauled down the street by a determined canine. Even a small dog can pull like crazy—and a big dog can dislocate your entire body! Besides, having control of your dog on leash is important for your safety and his.

If you're starting with a puppy, or your dog is small or reasonably easy to restrain, try the "no forward progress" approach first. When your dog starts to pull, stop in your tracks and stand still until he stops pulling. It may take him a few seconds to realize that you've stopped walking—that's okay. When he stops pulling, praise him and continue walking. If he pulls, stop. Don't worry if you don't walk too far for a few days. The important thing is to let your dog know that pulling is counterproductive.

If that doesn't work on your dog, try a little stronger version of the same technique. This time, instead of stopping in your tracks, you change directions. Set your hands together in front of your waist with the leash grasped in one hand. This will keep you from jerking your dog. The idea is for him to correct himself, not for you to pull on him. As soon as he starts to pull, turn and walk in another direction. Don't stop and wait for him, and don't say anything to him until he catches up with you. Then praise him and occasionally give him a treat. Most dogs learn quickly to pay attention to where you are, and not to pull ahead.

Chew on This
Always praise your dog when he does what you want.

Some puppies and dogs, though, are just so strong and eager to see the world that they need more control. If your dog is one of these eager beavers, consider trying a head halter or pinch collar (see Chapter 18). These training tools need to fit your dog properly to be effective, and you need to learn to use them properly. A good basic obedience class (or some private lessons with a good instructor) is the best way for you to learn about both the right equipment for your dog and about training in general.

Bark, Bark, Bark!

Barking, howling, whining, growling—it's all dog talk. Barking is a natural means of communication for a dog. A bark can be a warning, a greeting, or an invitation to play. Your dog's tendency to bark a little or a lot is partly inherited. Some breeds bark a lot; others bark very little. Your dog may also have learned that barking gets him what he wants—he barks and you let him in, let him out, feed him, talk to him, play with him. Barking becomes a behavioral problem when it goes on too long or too frequently.

Dogs become problem barkers for many reasons. The first step in controlling excessive barking is to find the reason your dog barks so much. A dog that spends too much time alone may become a problem barker, particularly if he doesn't get enough exercise. Sights and sounds in your dog's environment may trigger barking—not usually a problem unless it's too frequent or lasts too long. Dogs with separation anxiety (see the following "Separation Anxiety" section) are often problem barkers. Aggressive dogs and highly territorial dogs may bark at anyone or anything that comes near. Barking is hard to stop because it's self-rewarding. You can usually reduce nuisance barking, though, with time and effort.

If your dog seems to be barking out of boredom or to get your attention, you may be able to slow him down by giving him what he wants—on your terms, of course. Make sure he gets enough exercise every day. Take him through an obedience class. Even if he doesn't bark in class and you don't directly address the problem there, training often helps problems of all sorts. Besides, if he's lonely and bored, he'll love spending time with you in class and practicing outside of class. Don't leave your dog outdoors when you're not home. Let your neighbors know that you're trying to solve the problem. Most people will give you a little leeway if they know you're trying.

If your dog is barking to warn away intruders on "his" territory, obedience will help as well. When your dog starts to bark at someone, tell him "Down" and make sure he obeys. The down position is a submissive position and should give you control over the barking. When he's quiet, praise and reward him for "good quiet."

Teach your dog that having people around is good for him. Have a friend walk by your yard. Have a tasty treat ready. If he stays quiet, praise him and reward him. If he barks, tell him "Down," and when he's quiet, praise and reward. Have your friend come a bit closer and repeat the process. It may take several sessions (and several friends so that he learns that the rule applies to everyone), but eventually he should be much more tolerant of people walking near your yard. If he barks indoors, have him lie down and be quiet, and praise and reward him. Be consistent—don't encourage him to bark one time and discourage him the next.

Various types of "bark collars" are available. They work by administering a "punishment" in the form of an electrical shock, a spray of citronella (which dogs don't like) aimed at the dog's nose, or a high-pitched sound. Although bark collars may seem like an easy solution to problem barking, they don't address the cause of the barking. If your dog barks because he's bored, he may simply replace the noise with a different behavior like digging or destructiveness. If he barks to defend his territory, he may associate the shock or other punishment from the collar with the person he sees as a threat, and he may become aggressive. If he barks because he's afraid or anxious, a collar that punishes him will frighten him more.

Digging

Digging is an instinct for all dogs. Some breeds—terrier breeds and Dachshunds in particular—were bred to dig vermin and game out of holes in the ground, so they're even more eager to dig than the average dog.

One way to stop a determined digger from tearing up your whole yard is to give him his own digging range. Pick a spot for him, preferably a shady spot with loose sand or sandy soil (it's cleaner than clay or loam). If necessary, consider making him a sandbox for digging. Bury a treat or toy that your dog likes, then bring him to the spot, and when he notices the scent of the treat, encourage him to dig. You dig a little with your hands if necessary to give him the idea. Praise him when he digs, and when he reaches the treat or toy. Repeat a few times over the next few days. If you see your dog digging somewhere else, tell him "Leave it," take him to his spot, and encourage him to dig there. He'll get the idea after a few days.

Aside from being there and stopping him, there are ways to discourage your dog from digging. Some of these methods work with some dogs but not all. If your dog tends to dig in one spot, maybe near a gate, you may be able to discourage him by filling in his hole with rocks or concrete. I stopped my dog from digging up one section of a flower garden by burying chicken wire about three inches deep. It didn't interfere with the plant roots, and my dog didn't like hitting that wire with his feet.

Some people use chemicals and other substances to discourage digging. Black pepper sprinkled on the area stops some dogs. Some people bury mothballs, but they are toxic and they don't make your yard smell too great. Several commercial products are available that are supposed to stop digging, but they don't always work, and they don't provide your dog with an alternative. If he was digging out of boredom, he'll find something else to do, and it may not be any more agreeable to you than the digging was. Retraining and redirecting energy is the best solution.

(Photo by Close Encounters of the Furry Kind)

Obedience training and lots of exercise go a long way toward preventing behavior problems.

Separation Anxiety

A dog with separation anxiety becomes worried and agitated whenever she thinks her owner is going to leave. Once she's alone, she may bark or howl, salivate or even vomit, urinate and sometimes defecate, pace the floor, or become destructive.

To treat separation anxiety, you first need to make sure your dog and your belongings are safe when you're not there. Crate-train your dog, and crate her when you leave. Many dogs feel safe in their crates, and an anxious dog often feels more secure when she doesn't have to worry about where to be in the house. If you crate her with a bone or chew toy, she'll have something to do but won't cause any damage.

Teach your dog the Stay command (see Chapter 19). Have her stay for varying lengths of time while you're home with her, working up to half an hour or longer. Praise and reward her for staying and becoming relaxed. Have her spend some time in her crate while you're home, too, so that it's a safe place whether you're there or not.

Don't make a fuss over your dog when you leave or come home. That just teaches her that your absence really is something to fret about. When you're preparing to leave, put her in her crate a few minutes ahead of time to give her a chance to relax. Give her something wonderful that she gets only when you're about to leave—a hollow bone or rubber chew toy stuffed with peanut butter and kibble, for instance. Once she's crated, ignore her. When you come home, don't let her out right away—let her settle down and get used to your being home. Make your coming and going very matter of fact.

Figure out what makes your dog most relaxed and comfortable. If she likes to look out the window, place her crate where she can see out. If that seems to make her more anxious, then put her crate where she can't look out. Sometimes leaving a radio on to soft music and talk helps a dog relax. Some dogs seem happier if they have a little something of their owner—maybe an old sweatshirt with your smell on it. I had a dog that always took one of my walking shoes to his bed when I was gone. He didn't chew it; he just had it with him.

If you have to be gone long hours, consider having someone come in during the day to give your dog a break. Just having to "hold it" for 9 or 10 hours could make some dogs anxious—I know it would me! If your dog doesn't think your leaving means he'll be all by himself for so long, he may not be quite so worried.

If you can't solve your dog's separation anxiety problem, speak to your veterinarian or a qualified animal behaviorist. They can help you evaluate your dog's situation and set up a treatment plan. If absolutely necessary, you can try an anti-anxiety medication to break the cycle, but drugs are not a long-term solution.

Aggression

Canine aggression comes about due to any of a number of causes. Some dogs just have bad temperaments. Some have medical problems that cause behavioral changes. Aggression can be directed at people, at other animals, or both. An aggressive dog—one that threatens to bite, tries to bite, or does bite—is dangerous. If your dog behaves aggressively, you need to get qualified professional help immediately.

Start with a physical exam by your veterinarian. Be sure she knows about the aggression problem. Have a full thyroid panel run (not just a thyroid screening), as low thyroid sometimes causes aggressive behavior. Ask your vet about other tests you may want to have run. Be aware that even if a physical cause is found, it may be difficult or impossible to control your dog's aggressive behavior reliably enough to make him a safe pet. Altering cuts down on aggression if it's done before sexual maturity. It may help an older dog in some cases, but not all.

Here's the bottom line on aggression: No matter what the cause, and no matter how much you love your dog, if you cannot manage your dog's aggression so that he will never pose a threat to any child, to your neighbors or visitors to your home, or to anyone else's pet, then you should seriously consider having him humanely euthanized. It's a terribly sad and difficult decision to have to make, but sometimes it is the responsible and loving choice. How would you feel if your dog attacked and maimed a child or killed your neighbor's dog? A single dog bite is painful and can cause a lot of damage. An attack by an aggressive dog is devastating. Get help and do what you can to fix the problem, but if it can't be fixed, release your dog from the demons that provoke him, and keep everyone safe.

The Least You Need to Know

- 🐾 Dogs behave as they do because of both instinct and learning.
- 🐾 Many behavior problems can be prevented with proper care and training.
- 🐾 Most common behavior problems can be solved through training and understanding.
- 🐾 Sometimes professional help is needed to deal with problem behaviors.

Part 6

Things to Do with Your Dog

Dogs just wanna have fun, no doubt about it! And if you're like most dog owners, you want to have fun with your dog. I'll suggest lots of ways to do that in this section. We'll start with a look at how you can keep your dog safe on the road—or in the airways—and how you can help protect the rights of all of us who like to go places with our dogs. We'll also look at what to do when your pup would be better off not going.

There's more to having fun with your dog than just taking a walk or a drive, though. Thousands of people, mostly amateurs, compete in dog shows, sporting trials, agility and flying disc events, and other organized activities each year. If you're less competitive, you might want to join the ranks of your fellow dog owners who take up noncompetitive activities such as backpacking or therapy visits with their dogs. We'll survey many of the possibilities, from plain old walking the dog to world-class competition.

Chapter 21

Roving with Rover

In This Chapter

- 🏠 Taking your dog along—or not
- 🏠 Being a responsible dog owner on the road
- 🏠 Planning for your dog's safety and comfort on the road or in the air
- 🏠 Leaving your dog safe at home

If you want to take your dog with you on a trip, plan ahead. Be sure your dog will be welcome. Some motels, campgrounds, parks, and other destinations allow well-behaved dogs and their responsible owners—but some don't. Unfortunately, careless and inconsiderate dog owners have caused enough problems that dogs have been banned from some motels, parks, and other places.

Be considerate of those who will follow you. No one likes to step in dog poop! It's probably the biggest reason that dogs are banned from many public places. Clean up after your dog so that he'll be welcome back. It's very simple to keep some plastic bags handy, and they're easy to use and easy to deposit in waste receptacles. Just turn the bag inside out, put your hand in, pick up the feces, pull the bag back to right side out, and seal it. I keep a roll of inexpensive one-gallon plastic bags with my leashes at home, and another in the car, so they're always handy.

Exercise your dog before you leave so that he can expend some energy and empty his bladder and bowels. If possible, feed and water your dog at least three hours before departure. If that isn't feasible,

Grrrrowls

Dog feces is offensive in public places and can spread diseases and parasites. Always clean up after your dog.

feed a smaller portion than normal, let him have a drink, and plan to stop in an hour or so to let him relieve himself. If you're driving, stop about every three hours to give your dog a drink of water and to let him relieve himself again.

Lodging for People and Dogs

Many motels and some bed and breakfasts allow dogs, but not all. When making reservations, always verify the motel's dog policy, even if you've found information in a book or online. Policies change. Some motels require a deposit or charge an additional fee for dogs, so ask about such charges and refund policies before you check in. Ask if there is a preferred area for taking your dog out to potty. Leaving dog feces on motel grounds is the height of rudeness.

Don't let your dog cause damage or disturb other guests. Bring your dog's crate in and let him sleep in it. The crate is a little bit of home in this strange place. Dogs shouldn't be left alone in motel rooms, even if they're normally well behaved. Even the most reliable dog may become anxious and bark, chew something, or have a lapse in potty manners. A crate will protect the motel's property, but I've known normally quiet dogs to bark bark bark when left crated in a strange room. Remember, too, that the next guest may not suffer dog hair as fondly as we dog people do. Bring a sheet or blanket from home to cover the bed before you allow your dog onto it.

Packing for Rover

Changes in food can cause digestive upsets, so it's best to bring your dog's regular food along unless you're sure you'll be able to purchase her brand wherever you're going. There are ways to simplify feeding during your trip. If I'm traveling with just one dog, I measure individual portions into self-sealing sandwich bags, which I store in a plastic box with a secure lid. If more than one dog is coming along, I measure enough food for all meals into a plastic box, then tuck the measuring cup in on top. I always take at least one extra meal per dog "just in case."

Changes in water can also cause tummy problems, so try not to let your dog drink local water at different places. If you won't be gone too long, take water from home. Distilled water is a safe, inexpensive, readily available alternative, if you'll be gone longer.

If you don't travel with your dog all that often, then you may just want to take her regular dishes from home. If you hit the road together frequently, though, you'll probably want a set of travel dishes. I recommend stainless-steel bowls, one for food and one for water. They're durable and easy to clean.

Be sure your dog's collar fits properly, and that an up-to-date and readable identification tag, rabies tag, and license are attached to it. The name tag should include your name, address, telephone number, and the words "Call Collect" in case your dog is found away from home. Although most people put the dog's name first, I consider it optional and leave it off if there isn't room on the tag. A found dog doesn't really care what people call him, as long as they call his home, so the priority is to enable yourself to be located. Some people also put "reward" on their dogs' tags, thinking that it increases the chance of the dog's return. In this cyberworld of ours, you might want to include your e-mail address, too.

Temporary tags are available from pet supply stores, so if you plan to be somewhere for a few days you might consider attaching a tag with your temporary address to the collar. When I'm showing my dogs, I attach a temporary tag with my name, motel name and phone number, and the dates I'll be there. Of course, the dog's permanent tag remains on the collar. You might also want to consider a permanent form of identification for your dog, such as a microchip or tattoo.

Chew on This _____

The essential information to put on your dog's name tag includes the following:

- 🏠 Your name
- 🏠 Your address
- 🏠 Your telephone number
- 🏠 The words "Call Collect"

Optional information includes the following:

- 🏠 Dog's name
- 🏠 "Reward"
- 🏠 E-mail address

Collars, especially collars with tags, can get caught in the wire of a crate or crate door. If your dog is traveling in a crate, remove the collar when she's crated. Teach your dog not to charge out of a crate so that you'll be able to put her collar and leash on safely when you stop. If she hasn't quite mastered the slow crate departure, then situate your crate so that you can open it and put her collar and leash on before you open the car. If your dog has a tendency to become frightened in new situations, or to slip out of her collar, get her a martingale-style collar (see Chapter 18), which will tighten when pulled and can't be slipped. Also pack an extra leash and collar—they always break or get lost at the most inconvenient times.

Pack first-aid supplies for your dog. You could take your doggy first-aid kit from home (see Chapter 11) or pack a dual-purpose one for you and your dog. If your dog is on medication, you need to pack enough for the trip, of course. Keep a copy of her rabies certificate and vaccination record in a safe place. Some states require proof of rabies vaccination.

If your dog likes toys, take a few of her favorites along. Chew toys are good for relieving stress.

Don't forget the poop bags!

Automobile Safety

We've all seen dogs hanging their heads out car windows or riding in the backs of pickup trucks. Dogs that travel that way are at risk of serious injury or even death. Dust and other airborne debris traveling at the speed of a moving vehicle can cause serious damage to eyes and ears. Worse, dogs sometimes jump from a window or truck bed. If they luck out and land safely, they still may be struck by another vehicle, or run and become lost. Many dogs are killed or badly injured this way every year. We practice auto safety for our children and ourselves. Our dogs deserve as much.

(Photo by Close Encounters of the Furry Kind)

This German Shepherd Dog is buckled up for a safe trip.

The safest way for a dog to travel is in a secure crate. If you are involved in an accident, your pup is much safer in a crate than loose or even in a safety harness. The crate, especially a plastic airline crate, will protect your dog from injuries on impact and keep the dog secure in the aftermath. More than one dog has survived a car accident and then been killed on the road when he slips out an open car door. If you are injured in an accident, emergency personnel won't have to worry about getting past your dog to help you if he's crated.

A doggy seatbelt—a harness arrangement that fastens to the car's seatbelt—is a reasonably good alternative to a crate, although it won't provide as much protection.

Before you decide to take your dog along on a trip, whether it's a 20-minute errand or a 2-week vacation, be sure that he can go with you when you leave the car. In only a few minutes, the temperature in a closed car can rise high enough to kill your dog or cause permanent damage, even with the windows partially open. Try sitting in a closed car with the window just cracked. If you're uncomfortable, your dog will be more so because he isn't as efficient as a human being at cooling himself. Hyperthermia, or overheating, can be fatal (see Chapter 11). If you won't be able to take your dog out of the car with you, leave him at home.

Not all dogs enjoy car rides. Some are so afraid of the car that they drool, shake, or vomit. Sometimes the car itself frightens the dog—the noise, motion, and vibration take some getting used to. Some dogs are afraid of the car

> **Grrrrowls**
> Never let your dog ride in the front seat of a vehicle with air bags. Dogs, like small children, can be killed or injured by deploying air bags.

> **Chew on This**
> When the outside temperature is 78°F, a closed car will reach 90° F in 5 minutes, and 110°F in 25 minutes. Even a few minutes in a hot car can kill your dog or cause irreversible damage.

because they only ever ride in it to go to the vet! (How would you like the car if you only used it to go to the dentist?) Let's see how you can help your dog get past his fear.

Make the car itself a pleasant place. Sit in the car with your dog for short periods without the car running. Give her a few treats (or feed her a regular meal), pet her, talk to her, and then quit. Don't make a big fuss, pet, or play with her when you get out—you want the car to be nicer than getting away from the car. Do this every day for a few days if necessary. When she seems comfortable with being in the car, repeat the procedure with her in her crate or seat belt. When she's relaxed about that, do the same thing with the car running. Don't go anywhere yet, just let her get used to the noise, vibration, and smell of a running car. Then move on to very short trips—maybe around the block. Once you start driving with her, begin to play with her when you stop so that she learns that the car is a magic carpet to good things. Slowly increase the length of the trips. Take her to fun places—a park for a walk, maybe out for an ice cream cone. Most dogs quickly decide that going in the car is great fun and are disappointed when they can't go.

Flying Rover: Airline Travel

Many dogs fly around the United States and abroad every year. Some are on their way to new homes, but many travel with their families for one reason or another. If your dog needs to fly somewhere, he'll have to go as cargo unless he's small enough to qualify for in-cabin travel. Dogs in the cabin must fit into a small carrier that can slide under the seat. Puppies must be eight weeks old to fly on commercial airplanes. The exceptions are for service dogs and certified search and rescue dogs, which are allowed in the cabin.

Although some rules govern all air transport for dogs, every airline has its own rules. Not all airlines accept dogs. Check with the airline you plan to use for booking requirements, prices, restrictions, and other information. Find out whether your dog needs a reservation. All airlines require that the dog be confined in an airline-approved crate that's big enough for the dog to stand, lie down, and turn around. It must be lined with absorbent bedding, and water and food bowls must be securely attached inside, usually to the door so that the water dish can be refilled without opening the crate. Dogs cannot fly as cargo when the outside temperature is too hot or too cold—the exact temperature depends on the airline's regulations and the breed of dog.

Try to use direct flights so that your dog will not have to change planes. If that's not possible, then fly your dog "counter-to-counter" rather than cargo. Counter-to-counter service, which goes by different names with different airlines, costs more than straight cargo, but requires your dog to be loaded onto the airplane closer to departure time, to be offloaded faster at the destination, and to be hand-delivered from one plane to the next if a change is required.

You'll need to get a health certificate from your veterinarian within 10 days prior to traveling. In some cases, a temperature acclimatization statement is also required, so check with the airline. The health certificate must meet the requirements of the states or nations of departure and destination and of the individual airline. The certificate will be fastened to the crate for transport, but keep copies of the certificate and your dog's rabies and other vaccination records with you as well.

Before you decide to take your dog abroad with you, be aware that many countries have mandatory quarantine periods. Hawaii does as well. Unless you will be staying a long time, it's usually better to leave your dog safely at home in these cases.

BowWOW

Great Britain, Australia, New Zealand, and some other countries around the world, as well as Hawaii, have mandatory quarantine periods of up to six months for incoming dogs. If you're traveling abroad, your dog may be better off at home.

Tranquilizers and sedatives are usually not recommended for dogs traveling by air because they decrease the body's ability to regulate temperature and may have other dangerous effects. Use them only if your veterinarian recommends them specifically for air travel.

Follow the identification advice I gave in the "Packing for Rover" section. Be sure to attach complete identification information to the crate. I always tape a statement to the top of the crate that says something like this: "Hello. My name is Spot. I'm going on vacation with my family. I might be a little scared, so please be gentle with me." I think that when the dog in the carrier has a name, he becomes more important to the baggage handlers who load and unload him from the airplane.

Attach a sealed sandwich bag with one or two portions of food to the top of the crate. Use clear packing tape so that airline personnel can see what's in the bag. Feed your dog and give him water about four hours before departure, and be sure to walk him before he needs to be loaded so that he can relieve himself.

(Photo by Close Encounters of the Furry Kind)

A crate provides safe and familiar accommodations for your dog when traveling.

If you haven't already crate-trained your dog, plan to do so well ahead of time so that the crate will be a familiar refuge, not a frightening new experience (see Chapter 15). If your dog's afraid of loud noises or gets nervous in unfamiliar surroundings, make a few advance trips to the airport and walk him around outside so that he can get used to the sights, sounds, and smells.

> **Chew on This** _____
>
> To make your dog's flying experience better for both of you …
>
> - Book on direct, nonstop flights when possible.
> - Use counter-to-counter service if your dog must change planes.
> - In the summer, schedule flights early in the morning or in the evening.
> - If you're traveling and your dog is in cargo, ask the flight attendant to notify the pilot that there's a dog on board.

When you load your dog into his crate, be sure the crate door is secure top and bottom. Do not put a lock on the door—in an emergency, airline personnel may need to get to your dog. If you want a little extra security, you could run a small bungee cord from the door to a side vent.

When Rover Can't Go

Sometimes the dog just can't go along on a trip. Some people are lucky enough to have dog-loving relatives or friends close by who don't mind an extra set of four feet for a few days. If you're not one of the lucky ones, then you'll need to board your dog or hire a pet sitter. Whatever option you choose, make reservations well in advance. Good caretakers are often booked months ahead.

Boarding Your Dog

Some veterinary hospitals have boarding facilities for clients' dogs. If your dog has medical problems and requires special care, boarding at the vet's may be a good idea. On the other hand, good boarding kennels can handle most routine support for dogs with special needs. Consider your dog's overall comfort, the quality of care and attention he'll receive, and the length of his stay. A weekend in a smallish kennel with a few daily walks isn't so bad, but if you're going to be gone a week or two, a place with indoor/outdoor runs and room to stretch his legs may be better for your dog.

To find a good boarding facility, ask your family, friends, obedience instructor, and veterinarian for recommendations. When you have the choices narrowed down, make an appointment and tour the facility. It should be clean and free of feces. Kennel runs should be separated from adjacent runs by a solid wall to prevent contact or fighting with the dog next door. Your dog should have his own private run, unless you're boarding two dogs that get along, in which case you may want them to "room" together. Find out how much time your dog will spend outdoors and how often, where, and for how long he'll be walked. Find out who will handle him and have access to him.

Ask how often the kennels are cleaned and whether they are disinfected between boarders. Kennels and cages should have good dog-proof latches, and should be covered and secure at the bottom to prevent escape. The kennel area should also be surrounded by a fence in case your dog gets loose when the kennel is opened. Ask about security to prevent theft or vandalism, and about fire safety.

With multiple dogs congregated in a small space, disease prevention should be a high priority. Food and water bowls should be cleaned and sterilized daily. If your dog has special dietary needs, ask whether they can accommodate him with a different schedule or his own food. Good boarding facilities require that their guests be vaccinated against common communicable diseases. Find out which vaccinations they require. (Ask your vet, too, if she recommends any other vaccines for your dog while boarding.) If you give your own shots for diseases other than rabies (which must be given by a veterinarian), ask whether your vaccinations are acceptable. Find out what the procedures are in case your dog needs veterinary care in your absence. They should also have an emergency plan in place and someone should be on-site at night and on weekends. Use your judgment about whether you are comfortable with the quality of care. If you're not, take your dog somewhere else.

You'll need to know when you can drop your dog off and pick him up, and be sure that there will be no problem if you're delayed for some reason. You may want to call and check on your dog, so ask about a good time for that.

Some kennels offer extras—more walks, more play times, daily brushing, a bath before going home. Before you decide, ask exactly what is covered in the basic boarding fee—sometimes the extras aren't worth the extra charge.

At-Home Dog Sitters

A pet sitter who comes to your home may be a good alternative to a boarding kennel, depending on your situation. Some sitters will actually stay in your home and take care of your plants, newspapers, mail, and house while you're gone. Others stop in a specified number of times each day to check on things. If you're interested in finding a pet sitter, ask your veterinarian, obedience instructor, and friends for recommendations.

When you have the choices narrowed down, invite the sitter to your home for an interview. Make sure your pets interview her, too! You want to know that she's comfortable with your animals, and that they're comfortable with her. Find out how often she will visit and when. Find out what she's willing to do with your dog—give medication, take him for walks, play and cuddle, groom—and what other tasks she's willing to take on. Ask about her experience both with dogs and as a pet sitter, and get references. Find out whether she's bonded, and whether she's affiliated with one of the national pet sitters' organizations. Discuss emergency procedures, and find out whether she is trained in canine first aid. Does her vehicle look well maintained and reliable? Does she have a crate in which to transport your dog to a vet if necessary? As with all other pet-care professionals, you should feel comfortable with any sitter you hire, and she and your dog should appear to like one another.

The Least You Need to Know

- Traveling with your dog can be fun for both of you.
- Responsible behavior from all dog owners makes our dogs welcome wherever we go.
- Packing canine essentials makes travel safer and easier.
- Safety should come first when taking your dog in the car.
- Your dog can fly the friendly skies if necessary.
- Sometimes it's better to leave your dog in good hands at home.

Chapter 22

Just You and Your Dog

In This Chapter

- Enjoying one-on-one activities with your dog
- Keeping your dog safe in the great outdoors
- Helping your dog be a good canine citizen wherever he goes
- Volunteering doggy smiles to spread some cheer

If you want to keep yourself active and involved in the world outside your home, there's no better partner and motivator than a dog. Whatever your idea of a good outing—whether a leisurely walk around the block or an all-day athletic adventure—the right dog will happily keep you company. Not every dog is suited to every activity, of course, but any reasonably healthy dog enjoys getting out to do *something*.

Walking the Dog

What could be simpler or more fun than heading out the door with your dog on a leash? Walking (or jogging or running) is a great way to keep you and your dog in shape. You can walk as far as you both are up to, and you can continue at home or away. As simple as it is to walk the dog, though, a little planning and a few precautions can make your outings more pleasant and a lot safer.

Before you start any exercise program, physical checkups for both of you may be in order. Make sure your dog's nails are trimmed short and that his pads are in good condition. You may want to trim any long hair between his pads to give him better traction and prevent small debris from collecting between the pads and injuring his feet. If your dog is overweight or out of shape, ask your vet about a diet and an appropriate distance to walk in the beginning. Start slowly and build up.

Whoever walks the dog should be able to control the dog. If a child—your own or a visitor—wants to walk your dog, the same rule applies: If the child can't control the dog under all circumstances, don't let him walk the dog without a responsible adult. Anyone taking a dog for an outing should be capable of making reasonable decisions, too, so even if your dog is tiny and your seven-year-old can control him, consider carefully whether turning them loose together is a good idea. Some walking hazards (encounters with stray dogs, for instance) are difficult even for adults to manage.

Always keep your dog on leash in public places. Make sure your dog's collar fits properly so that she can't slip out of it. If she has a tendency to try to slip her collar off, get a martingale-style collar that tightens when the dog pulls against the leash. Check your leash periodically, too, to be sure the bolt for the collar is securely stitched in place and that the leash is in good condition. Keep a firm grip on your leash, but if your dog weighs more than about 10 pounds, I *do not* recommend slipping the loop over your wrist. A quick leap by a squirrel-happy canine can break your wrist, and if your dog is very big, she could even pull you down. I've seen it happen! Teach children, too, never to slide their hand through the loop, and never ever to slip a leash around their neck or waist.

Doggerel

A brachycephalic dog has a broad, short skull. Pugs and Pekinese are brachycephalic. Because the muzzle is shortened, a brachycephalic dog typically has trouble lowering its body temperature by panting and is therefore more prone to heatstroke than other longer-muzzled breeds.

(Photo by Close Encounters of the Furry Kind)

What could be more natural than hiking the great outdoors with canine companionship?

If it's hot out, keep walks short or postpone them until evening. Concrete and blacktop get very hot in the sun and can easily burn your dog's foot pads. In addition, excess heat can cause heatstroke (see Chapter 11). Dogs can sunburn, too, especially if they have light-colored skin or hair. Avoid areas that may have been sprayed with pesticides or insecticides. If your dog does walk though such a place, wash his feet with warm water and dog shampoo when you get home to prevent absorption or ingestion of toxic chemicals.

If you like to walk before sunrise or after sunset, put a reflective collar or vest on your dog, and wear light colors or a reflective vest yourself.

Cold-weather walking also calls for precautions. Keep the hair between your dog's pads trimmed to prevent accumulation of ice

BowWOW _____

A little petroleum jelly rubbed into the bottoms of your dog's feet will help prevent ice balls from forming between her pads if you're hiking in snow.

balls (see Chapter 16). If your community puts salt or other chemicals on sidewalks and streets, always wash your dog's feet with warm water after walks. The chemicals can irritate his feet and can be hazardous if he licks them off.

Hiking and Backpacking with Fido

Tramping through nature is a lot more fun with a friend, and most dogs are naturals. They're not only energetic and always ready for a good time, but they notice and draw our attention to things we might overlook. They definitely remind us to stop and smell the roses—and the moss, and the deer droppings, and the stream banks, and the raccoon tracks .... Your dog will also alert you to approaching people and animals.

Your dog can learn to carry his own food and water in a backpack (build him up gradually to carrying weight). He can also be a good citizen and carry his feces back in baggies for proper disposal so that public areas will continue to be open to well-mannered dogs and their responsible owners.

Plan carefully, whether you and your dog are headed out for a morning's hike or a week-long backpacking adventure. Learn about local regulations and follow them. Be sure that dogs are allowed where you plan to hike. Dogs are not allowed in many national and state parks. If dogs are permitted, then keep your dog under control at all times. Many areas require your dog to be leashed for his own safety, for the comfort of your fellow hikers, and for the protection of wildlife.

Your dog should wear a collar that is in good condition and that fits properly. His license, identification tag or tags, and rabies tag should be fastened to it. Since your leash is likely to get wet and dirty, you may find a nylon leash better than leather for hiking. Each has its pros and cons. Nylon is rougher on the hands and can burn your skin, but it dries faster and is machine washable. Leather is easier on the hands and skin, but not waterproof. However, if you clean and condition your leather leashes regularly, they will hold up well. Retractable leashes tend to get tangled around trees, bushes, and sometimes other people and dogs. Besides, many parks require dogs to be on leashes six feet or shorter. Tuck a spare collar and leash into your pack in case the ones you're using break.

Teach your dog to sit or lie down quietly at the side of the trail to allow other hikers to pass you. Dogs can be very intimidating for non-dog people, but well-mannered dogs and responsible dog owners make great ambassadors. Never take a dog out on the trail if you can't control him, or if there's any chance that he will injure a person or someone else's dog.

Always be sure your dog's vaccinations are up-to-date before going into natural areas. Ask your veterinarian about recommended vaccines beyond the basics for your day-to-day environment, especially if you're going to another area. Consider effective tick controls as well.

Your dog should, of course, be in good health before going hiking or backpacking. Trim his nails nice and short. Be sure that his pads and feet are in good condition, and trim the hair between his pads to keep them from collecting burrs, debris, or, in winter, ice balls. If your dog is not accustomed to long, rigorous walks, start with short hikes and slowly increase the distance as he (and you!) gains better physical condition.

Bring plenty of water for both of you and a bowl for your dog. Collapsible bowls are available from dog supply stores and are easy to transport. Drinking at regular intervals will prevent dehydration and help prevent overheating. Try to keep your dog from drinking from streams and other water sources along the way. Many are contaminated with bacteria and chemicals that can make your dog ill. If you'll be out for more than an hour or two, bring a little food or treats. Of course, if you're backpacking and camping, you'll need to bring enough food for your dog's regular meals plus a bit extra.

Remember that heatstroke is potentially fatal and that dogs can overheat quickly. Hike in the early morning or evening, and avoid the hottest parts of the day. If you will be at higher altitudes than your normal environment, allow extra time for breaks, and see that both you and your dog drink lots of water. Proper hydration helps fend off altitude sickness.

Pack a first-aid kit, including tweezers in case your dog gets a thorn in his pad. Some antiseptic cleansing towels are a good idea, as well as a topical antibiotic. A small towel can come in handy if your dog gets wet and muddy.

Unfortunately, not all dog owners are responsible. It's always possible to encounter an aggressive dog off-leash when you're hiking. Pepper sprays, which are sold under various brand names, are inexpensive and are available in many sporting goods stores. The spray is effective, but won't cause permanent injury. The drawback is that if you spray into the wind, you'll be the one with the pepper spray in your face, so be careful. We're all reluctant, of course, to hurt a dog (although we might be sorely tempted to squirt the irresponsible owner!), but it makes a lot more sense to stop an aggressor with pepper spray than to be bitten or to allow your own dog to be attacked.

Swimming

Swimming is great exercise for a dog, and many dogs love the water. Dogs swim in swimming pools, lakes, ponds, and the ocean. Dogs run on beaches and ride in boats. But as with most physical activities, swimming comes with a few dangers, and it's up to you to keep your dog safe.

Be cautious about water that may be contaminated with chemicals. Many parks, golf courses, subdivisions, and other sites treat their ponds to control algae. Even if the pond itself isn't treated, it may contain fertilizers, pesticides, and herbicides from drainage run-off from the surrounding area. Dogs can become ill or even die from ingesting the chemicals. The chemicals may also cause skin irritations.

Swimming pools are a bit better, but still present their own dangers. If you own a pool, fence it off securely from the rest of the yard and don't let your dog have access to the pool area unless you are present. Most dogs can't climb out the side of a pool or up a ladder, so teach yours where the steps are so that he can get out of the water. Even good swimmers drown in pools when they become exhausted and can't find a way out.

BowWOW

Despite their hair, dogs can get sunburned. So how can you take your dog with you for a day of sand and sun and still keep him safe? First, get a sunscreen made for dogs, and use it according to directions. Use an umbrella made to block the sun's rays. The potential for dangerous sun exposure is highest between 10 A.M. and 3 P.M., so avoid prolonged exposure during those hours. You'll both be healthier for it!

If your dog has been swimming in chlorinated water, give him a quick bath to remove the chlorine, which can dry his coat and make him sick if he licks himself.

Some beaches allow dogs, and playing in the waves can be great fun. Be sure that dogs are allowed, follow the rules, and clean up after your dog. Remember, the canines aren't the only ones going barefoot on the beach! When you're finished for the day, check your dog carefully for burrs and stickers from beach vegetation. A bath is a good idea, too. Lakes that allow motor boats often have a fair amount of petroleum in the water, and your dog doesn't need to ingest that from his coat. If he's been swimming in the ocean, you need to remove the salt from his coat and skin to prevent irritation.

No matter where your dog does her swimming, be sure to clean and dry her ears afterwards. Water retained in the ears makes a terrific environment for bacteria and yeast to grow (see Chapter 16).

Lots of dogs enjoy boating. If you plan to take your dog for a cruise, get her a life preserver. Even if she knows how to swim, if she jumps or falls out of the boat it may take a while for you to get

back to pick her up. A life preserver will keep her afloat if she gets tired (or is injured jumping or falling from the boat). The bright colors of the life preserver will also make her easier to see in the water.

Of course, you want to prevent your dog from going into the water when you don't want her to, so keep a leash on her and either hold the leash or fasten it securely in the boat. Make sure she doesn't have enough leash to jump over the side.

 Grrrrowls

If you're traveling to Florida with your dog, be aware that alligators can and do attack and kill dogs. Dogs are attacked far more often than people, probably because dogs look more like the wild animals that make up the gators' natural diet. Don't allow your dog to swim in ponds, lakes, or canals. Keep your dog away from the banks as well, especially where there is heavy vegetation.

Before you take him out on a boat, make sure you'll be able to haul your dog back in if necessary. Lifting a reasonably large dog straight up out of the water isn't easy. Be sure, too, that you can provide some shade for your dog to keep him cool and prevent sunburn. Take along plenty of fresh water to prevent dehydration.

Skijoring

Enough fun in the hot sun—what about winter sports for Rover and you? If you enjoy cross-country skiing, then skijoring may be the thing for you. Skijoring is a demanding sport that combines dog sledding and cross-country skiing. The dog, on a tugline, pulls the skier over the snow as they exercise together. Both dog and skier have to be athletic and fit for skijoring. Some people compete in skijoring events, but most enthusiasts simply enjoy heading out into the snowy world with their dogs.

So what do you need for skijoring, besides the ability to ski cross-country and a sense of adventure? A suitable dog, of course. Many medium to large dogs (40 pounds or more) are suitable for hobby skijoring. If you want to compete and win, then you'll probably want to get a dog from a responsible breeder who produces good sled dogs (see Chapter 5).

Skate skis are usually recommended for skijoring. Classic skis may be better for ungroomed trails, but their length makes turns at high speed more difficult. Avoid skis with metal edges that can injure a dog.

You'll need a pulling harness that fits your dog properly, a pulling belt for yourself, and a tugline to connect your belt to your dog's harness. Tuglines are normally about 10 feet long and should include a bungee cord to absorb shocks. (See Appendix D for sources of equipment.)

Before you hit the trail on skis, you need to train your dog to follow basic commands. Directional commands and a stop command are essential for safe skijoring, so be sure your dog responds reliably to those. You'll probably find some additional commands useful as well.

Dog-Assisted Therapy

If you and your dog both like people and enjoy volunteering, you might enjoy dog-assisted therapy work. Therapy dogs come from all walks of canine life, from the tiny to the tall, from stock dogs and hunting dogs to conformation champions to simply cherished companions. Whatever their other roles in life, therapy dogs share several essential qualities—they like people and are friendly, they're reliable in unusual environments, they take things in stride, and they enjoy being petted, smooched, hugged, and talked to by all sorts of people.

What exactly does a therapy dog do? Sometimes he just sits or lies quietly, being petted and listening to story after story about a nursing home resident's former dogs. Sometimes he visits elementary schools to help teach children about humane care of animals. He may work with disabled children. He may volunteer at a hospital, where he might visit patients in pediatrics, oncology, and other wards, including hospice centers. At least one hospital has found that having a therapy dog in the emergency room has a calming effect on patients and on doctors, nurses, and staff members working in the high-stress environment.

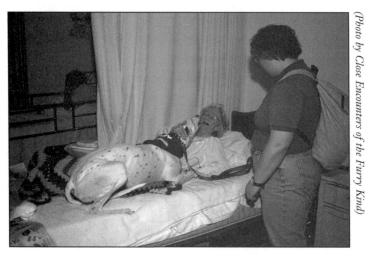

(Photo by Close Encounters of the Furry Kind)

Therapy dogs touch the hands and hearts of the people they visit.

Therapy dogs should not be confused with *service dogs*, who work as guide dogs for the blind, hearing dogs for the deaf, seizure-alert dogs, general assistance dogs, and so on. Service dogs go through intensive training in order to perform their jobs. Therapy dogs don't require intensive training, but they must have basic obedience training and be reliable. They can't jump on people or onto beds uninvited, or ever put their mouths on people. Most therapy dogs also know commands such as *Paws On* (put your paws up on a bed or chair) and *Paws Off* (put your paws back on the floor). Some also know a few people-pleasing tricks.

Several organizations test and certify therapy dogs (see Appendix D). You can make therapy visits to many places without being certified, but there are advantages to making your dog "official." Certification gives your dog and you more credibility and some independent assurance that your dog has the temperament and training needed to make him a good therapy dog. In addition, most certifying organizations provide insurance to cover any accidental damage your dog might cause during official therapy visits. Each organization has rules designed to make therapy visits safe, comfortable, and enjoyable for everyone—residents, patients, staff, and the volunteer handler and dog.

Many dog-and-handler teams work alone or with one or two other teams. Recreation directors in nursing homes and other facilities are often delighted to make space on the calendar for therapy dog visits, so it's usually fairly easy to find a "workplace" close to home. If you'd rather not go it alone, look for a local therapy group. Many obedience and kennel clubs have therapy groups that visit nursing homes, hospitals, and schools. Some hospitals and nursing homes have their own programs and usually welcome new volunteers.

The Least You Need to Know

- A variety of noncompetitive outdoor activities are good for body and soul—human and canine alike.

- Dogs aren't welcome everywhere, so plan ahead.

- Proper equipment and training make roving with Rover fun and safe.

- The responsible dog owner keeps his dogs from being a nuisance.

Chapter 23

Organized Dog Sports

In This Chapter

- 🏠 Enhancing your relationship with your dog through sports
- 🏠 Finding the right sport for you and your dog
- 🏠 Exploring specialized sports that test your dog's instincts
- 🏠 Remembering the real reason you have a dog

As your dog's training progresses, you may find, like many people, that you really enjoy the process as well as the results. You may also find that you enjoy being with other people who enjoy training their dogs. If so, you may want to try some of the following activities. Whether you get involved to compete or just for fun, training and practicing will strengthen the bond between you and your dog as you come to understand one another better. The activity will also channel some of that doggie energy into safe, nondestructive, and even productive activity.

Whatever You Say! Obedience Competition

The sport of *obedience* is meant to demonstrate teamwork between dog and handler, and the usefulness of the companion dog. Several registries (see Chapter 2) offer competitive obedience programs in which dogs can earn titles and other honors. Some are restricted to purebred dogs, while others accept mixed-breed dogs as well.

The American Kennel Club (AKC) offers obedience titles for purebred dogs. To be eligible for AKC obedience competition, your dog must be registered with the AKC, or have an *Individual Limited Privileges* (ILP) number. The United Kennel Club (UKC) offers an obedience titling program that is open to purebred and mixed-breed dogs. To participate, your dog must be registered with the UKC or with the American Mixed Breed Obedience Registry (AMBOR). You can obtain a Single Registration Application for your dog directly from the UKC. AMBOR offers registration of altered mixed-breed dogs and, under some circumstances, rare breed as well as other purebred dogs. AMBOR awards titles to AMBOR-registered dogs competing in obedience at UKC and Australian Shepherd Club of America (ASCA) events. In addition to obedience, AMBOR offers titles in the following sports for AMBOR-registered dogs who successfully compete in such events under licensed judges: agility, backpacking, Canine Good Citizen, carting, field trials, flyball, Frisbee, gameness, German working titles, herding instinct, Schutzhund, sledding, temperament tested, therapy dog, tracking, versatility, water trial, and working.

Doggerel

If your dog is not registered with the AKC but is altered and appears to be a purebred member of an AKC-recognized breed, you can apply for an **Individual Limited Privileges** (ILP) number. The ILP will enable you to enter your dog in AKC obedience, agility, tracking, and other sporting events.

The ASCA opens its obedience, agility, and tracking programs to all breeds and mixed-breeds. To participate, your dog must be registered with ASCA, either on regular registration or with a Limited Exhibition Privileges (LEP) number, or with the AKC, UKC, AMBOR, or Canadian Kennel Club (CKC).

Earning Titles

The requirements for individual titles vary slightly from one competition program to another, but in general, at each level the dog needs three **legs.** To earn a leg, he must score 50 percent on each exercise and have a total score of at least 170 out of 200 possible points. Each level of obedience is meant to test and demonstrate the following skills:

- At the **Novice** level, your dog may earn the **CD** title. To do so, he must heel on and off leash at normal, slow, and fast speeds; wait where you tell him and come when called; stay on command in both a sit and a down position with other dogs; and stand for a physical examination. Novice A is for dogs who have not earned a CD and handlers who have never handled a dog to a CD. Novice B is for dogs who have not earned the CD shown by handlers who have handled other dogs to their CDs.

- At the **Open** level (for dogs who have earned the CD), your dog earns the **CDX** title. To do so, he must heel off leash and stay in a group while you are out of his sight. He must drop to a down position on command while coming to you, jump obstacles, and retrieve a dumbbell. Open A is for dogs that have not earned their CDXs. Open B is for dogs who have their CDXs but are continuing to compete for experience, to earn the OTCH or UDX (see following), or just for fun.

- At the **Utility** level (open to dogs who have earned the CDX), your dog earns the **UD** title. To do so, he must heel off leash in an intricate pattern, respond to hand signals, jump, and find articles by your scent. Utility A is for dogs that do not have their UDs. Utility B is for dogs that have their UDs but are continuing to compete for experience, to earn the OTCH or UDX (see below), or just for fun.

- Dogs who have earned the UD may compete in Open B and Utility B classes to earn points toward the title of **OTCH.**

- The **UDX** is awarded to a dog who has his UD and who earns qualifying scores in both Open B and Utility B classes at 10 shows.

Setting Your Goals

One nice thing about obedience as a sport is that you can set your own goals. If you're competitive by nature, have a smart, responsive dog, and are willing to put in lots of hours of training, you can shoot for high scores, High in Trial (HIT) awards, and national honors. If you aren't so competitive, or your dog isn't up to the rigors of serious training, you can enjoy going into the ring with your dog, achieving your qualifying scores, and obtaining the dog's titles.

(Photo by Close Encounters of the Furry Kind)

Dogs of all sizes enjoy agility.

Over and Under: Dog Agility

Over the past two decades, *agility* has become an extremely popular sport for dogs, handlers, and spectators alike. Agility requires the dog to negotiate a course of jumps, tunnels, and other obstacles in the proper order and within a specified time limit. You can do agility just for fun with simple homemade equipment, or you can compete for titles and other awards. Whatever you choose, the name of this game is fun!

Several organizations sponsor agility competition at all levels, from novice through advanced. The rules, procedures, obstacles, and jump heights vary among organizations, so be sure to read the appropriate rule book before entering your dog in competition.

The AKC offers titles for Novice Agility (NA), Open Agility (OA), Agility Excellent (AX), and Master Agility Excellent (MX).

The United States Dog Agility Association (USDAA) promotes agility competition through major tournament events, including its Grand Prix of Dog Agility championships. The organization offers eight different titles: Agility Dog® (AD), Advanced Agility Dog® (AAD), Master Agility Dog® (MAD), Jumpers Master (JM), Gamblers Master (GM), Snooker Master (SM), Relay Master (RM), and Agility Dog Champion (ADCH). The USDAA recognizes the Agility Top Ten annually, and sponsors the Dog Agility Masters® team pentathlon championship to promote agility as a team sport, and the $4,000 Dog Agility Steeplechase championship to exhibit speed in performance. The USDAA offers a Veterans Program for dogs 7 years of age or older and a Junior Handler Program for handlers 18 years of age and under.

The North American Dog Agility Council (NADAC) offers Certificates of Achievement for Regular, Jumpers, and Gamblers classes. NADAC awards the Agility Trial Champion (NATCH) title to dogs that have earned a minimum of 200 points in the Regular Agility Classes at the Elite level after earning an Elite Agility Certificate, 100 points in the Gamblers classes at the Elite level after earning a Gamblers Certificate-Elite, and 100 points in the Jumpers classes at the Elite level after earning a Jumpers Certificate-Elite. Classes are offered in the Standard Division, Veterans Division, and Junior Handlers Division.

ASCA's agility program, like its obedience program, is open to all breeds and mixed-breeds. ASCA offers Novice-, Open-, and Elite-level competition and titles in Regular Agility, Jumpers, and Gamblers divisions, as well as the ATCH title. Special classes in all divisions and at all levels are offered for veteran dogs (seven years or older) and junior handlers.

The UKC offers an agility competition program open to UKC- and AMBOR-registered dogs. UKC agility dogs can earn titles at four levels of competence, beginning with the Agility I (U-AGI) and progressing to the Agility II (U-AGII), Agility Champion (U-ACH), and Agility Champion Excellent Title (U-ACHX).

Sniff Out Some Fun: Tracking

Tracking is an activity in which your dog just does what comes naturally—he follows his nose. Even if you don't want to pursue a tracking title, training your dog to track on a specified trail can be lots of fun, and you and your dog will both get lots of exercise. The best way to train is with one or more other people and their dogs. If you can find a tracking club, that's even better.

The AKC offers Tracking Tests that demonstrate the dog's ability to recognize and follow human scent. Before you and your dog can enter a Tracking Test, you have to get a written statement from an AKC tracking judge who certifies that your dog has passed a certification test within the 12 months prior to the date of the tracking test. When your dog has passed two Tracking Tests under two different judges, he will be awarded the title of Tracking Dog (TD). He can then proceed to the Tracking Dog Excellent Tracking Test, and when he passes that twice under two judges, he will be awarded the title of Tracking Dog Excellent (TDX). He can also earn the Variable Surface Tracking (VST) dog title by passing the Variable Surface Tracking Test. If he earns all three titles, he will be a Champion Tracker.

ASCA also offers the titles TD and TDX to Australian Shepherds as well as to other purebred and mixed-breed dogs registered with their appropriate registries.

Flying Dogs, Flying Discs

If you want excitement, watch dogs practicing or competing in *flyball*, a sport invented in the late 1970s in California. Dogs love flyball! They run relay races as four-dog teams, with each team member racing down a lane over a series of four hurdles. The dog hits a peddle on a spring-loaded flyball box. The box releases a tennis ball, which the dog snatches in the air and carries full tilt back to the starting line. The first team to have all four dogs run without errors wins the heat.

The North American Flyball Association (NAFA) governs flyball competition in North America. Each dog earns points towards flyball titles on the basis of the team's time. Titles are Flyball Dog (FD), Flyball Dog Excellent (FDX), Flyball Dog Champion (FDCh), Flyball Master (FM), Flyball Master Excellent (FMX), Flyball Master Champion (FMCh), and Flyball Grand Champion (FGDCh).

Many people also enjoy training their dogs to leap and catch flying discs. Quite a few organizations at local, national, and international levels sponsor canine disk events, so for up-to-date comprehensive information, an Internet search may be your best bet.

The International Disc Dog Handlers' Association (IDDHA) sanctions canine disc events and competitions worldwide. IDDHA offers test and titling programs. A handler and dog must first demonstrate the basic ability to work as a team by successfully completing the test program. Then they may seek titles, including the Basic Disc Dog (BDD), Advanced Disc Dog (ADD), Master Disc Dog (MDD), Combined Skills Freestyle Title (CSF), and Disc Dog Expert (DDX).

Skyhoundz, another flying disc organization, offers competition in two divisions, Sport and Open. In Open, teams compete for invitations to the World Championships.

Grrrrowls

> Pushing a dog too hard too fast in any sport is dangerous. If you want to play disc sports with your dog, start slowly and take your time. Practice throwing the disc without your dog. Don't encourage a young dog to leap into the air for the disc—if he injures an open growth plate in a leg, he'll have lifelong problems (see Chapter 13). Teach him to chase the disc thrown low or rolled along the ground, and when he's ready, start slowly teaching him to jump for the disc.

Dancing with Dogs

Canine musical freestyle combines dog obedience and dance into a beautiful display of teamwork and rapport between dog and handler. Handlers and sometimes dogs wear costumes to enhance the choreographed routines they perform to music. Both partners are judged in competition, with an emphasis on teamwork between the handler and the dog. Big or small, from a Bloodhound dancing to "Blue Suede Shoes" to a Chihuahua doing the Mexican Hat Dance, all sorts of dogs and owners enjoy cutting a rug together.

The World Canine Freestyle Organization (WCFO) offers titles for dog-and-handler teams. In the Singles Division (one dog and one handler), titles are Freestyle Dog (W-FD), Freestyle Dog Excellent (W-FDX), Freestyle Dog Master (W-FDM), and Champion Freestyle Dog (W-Ch.FD). The Pairs Division is for two dogs and two handlers, and the titles are W-PFD, W-PFDX, W-PFDM, and W-PCh.FD, with "P" indicating "pairs." Team competition is also available for multiple dogs and handlers (each handler having one dog). Team titles are W-TD, W-FDX, W-TFDM, and W-TCh.FD.

Strut Your Stuff: Conformation Shows

If you're like many Americans, you've watched the Westminster and other dog shows on television. Those are *conformation* shows, in which the dog is judged against his breed standard to see how well he conforms to that standard of excellence.

(Photo by Close Encounters of the Furry Kind)

These Collies are competing for points toward their championships in a conformation show.

The traditional purpose of the show ring was to evaluate the quality of potential breeding stock, so altered animals are excluded from AKC and UKC competition.

In 2001, ASCA initiated a program for awarding a title of champion—the A-CH—to Australian Shepherds that have been spayed or neutered. The requirements are identical to those for the ASCA Champion (CH), except for the reproductive status of the competitors. A few other individual breed registries also allow altered dogs to compete in conformation classes. It's an idea whose time has come. Many people who would enjoy competing with their dogs in conformation prefer not to live with a sexually intact animal and have no desire to be involved with dog breeding. Altered conformation gives them the best of both worlds.

At a show, each breed is judged separately, dogs (males) against dogs, and bitches (females) against bitches. The best representative of each sex earns points toward the championship. Each animal must be registered with the registry that sanctions the show, whether it is the AKC, the UKC, the States Kennel Club (SKC), the International All Breed Kennel Club of America (IABKC), or an individual breed registry.

If you don't have a dog yet and think you'd like to try showing in conformation, explain your desires to breeders you contact. It's unlikely that a breeder will entrust a truly outstanding pup to a beginner, but many breeders will sell you a good-quality dog with the potential to *finish*. You can learn the ropes from that dog and find out if you like showing.

If you already have a purebred dog but aren't certain he's show quality, you'll need to evaluate him carefully and honestly. We all love our dogs and think each one is the prettiest dog in the world. And it's true, because there's nothing more beautiful than an honest, faithful companion. But there's a world of difference between being sweet and pretty, and being show quality, so try not to let your emotions get in the way of an honest look at your dog's faults and virtues. Evaluate your dog carefully in light of the breed standard. Have someone who knows the breed well—a breeder or show judge if possible—evaluate your dog and go over the evaluation with you. Make sure the evaluator understands that you want an honest opinion.

Doggerel

A finished dog is one that has completed the requirements and been awarded the title of Champion in the conformation ring.

If your dog measures up to the breed standard, start training. Showing a dog in the conformation ring is harder than it looks. Contact local training clubs to find out about handling classes in your area. Go to some shows and watch the handlers as well as the dogs. Pay attention to what the good handlers do to make their dogs look like winners in the ring. Read books and magazine articles on show handling (see Appendix B). If possible, attend a few shows with an experienced exhibitor or your dog's breeder. Offer to help out in exchange for guidance. A knowledgeable mentor is worth her weight in blue ribbons.

When you're ready to try out your new handling skills, start with something small—a "puppy match." Despite the name, puppy matches are open to adult dogs that don't have major points toward their championships. Wins at matches don't count toward titles, but you can practice your handling, and you and your dog can get used to the ring environment without the pressures of a point show.

Specialized Sports for Specialized Dogs

In Chapter 2, we saw that each dog breed was originally developed for a purpose. Today many sports have developed with those original purposes in mind. Competitors use their inherited instincts and abilities, whether herding livestock, helping as hunters, or working as draft animals, in competition.

Snow Sports

If you have a northern breed and you enjoy being out in the snow, consider hitching your dog or dogs to a sled and heading out for a brisk run. Some enthusiasts maintain multiple dogs because they enjoy *mushing*, or running teams of dogs with sleds. Others participate in skijoring, a form of cross-country skiing in which the skier is pulled at a fast clip by one, two, or three dogs (see Chapter 22). Both sports make for thrills, spills, and adventures. Most of the national breed clubs for the various sled dog breeds offer testing and titling programs. There are also

Doggerel
The term **mushing,** meaning "driving a team of sled dogs," comes from the French *marche*, or "walk."

independent multibreed organizations that sponsor training, tests, and sled dog races.

Herding Events

Was your dog born to handle livestock? The AKC, the American Herding Breeds Association (AHBA), and ASCA all offer herding events (eligible breeds vary among the organizations). If your dog is eligible and you'd like to try herding, contact your local breed club, herding club, or kennel club for information on instructors and clinics in your area.

(Photo by Close Encounters of the Furry Kind)

Some sports test specific abilities for which certain breeds were developed. This Pembroke Welsh Corgi lives up to his herding heritage.

Earthdog Events

Do you have a "varmint dog"—a *terrier* or Dachshund originally developed to go into underground dens or tunnels in pursuit of their quarry? The AKC offers the Earthdog test program to show the dog's ability to follow and "work" its quarry. Earthdog titles can be earned at four class levels: Introduction to Quarry (for beginning handlers and dogs), Junior Earthdog, Senior Earthdog, and Master Earthdog. The quarry can be either two adult rats, which are caged for protection from the dogs, or an artificial quarry located behind a barrier.

Doggerel

The word **Terrier** comes from the Latin *terra,* or "ground." A Terrier is a dog that digs in the ground.

Lure Coursing

If you own a *sighthound,* you may want to try lure coursing. Coursing dogs follow an artificial lure around a course on an open field and are scored on speed, enthusiasm, agility, endurance, and ability to follow the lure. Coursing is a great way to exercise a sighthound physically and mentally. The AKC offers lure-coursing titles for eligible dogs, and local clubs offer noncompetitive lure-coursing clinics and practice runs.

BowWOW

Hounds come in two basic types. The scenthounds hunt by following the scent of their quarry on the ground or in the air. They usually hunt in packs. **Sighthounds,** on the other hand, find their prey visually and chase it down, usually alone, in pairs, or in groups of three and four.

Weight Pull Events

Some dogs were born to pull. The International Weight Pull Association (IWPA) is one of several organizations that promotes the sport of pulling, in which dogs compete to see who can pull the most weight in relation to the dog's own weight for a distance of 16 feet. The IWPA sanctions some 100 weight pull events a year in the United States and Canada. Most dogs competing in weight pulls are from the Working Group, but IWPA pulls are open to all dogs, mixed-breed or purebred. Some other organizations, including several working breeds' national breed clubs, also sponsor weight pull events.

Field Events

Even if you aren't interested in hunting, if you have a sporting breed dog, you might enjoy doing some field training with him. Much of the training can even be done without game birds, although in order to earn titles, your dog will have to deal with real birds. Field events for sporting breeds include tests and field trials. Hunt Tests are non-competitive events designed to test the dog's instinct and ability to perform the jobs for which his breed was developed. Field Trials do the same, but are competitive. The AKC offers field events for pointing breeds, retrievers, spaniels, Beagles, Basset Hounds, and Dachshunds. Dogs work toward earning the Field Champion (FC) and Amateur Field Champion (AFC) titles in the various field events.

The AKC offers Pointing Breed Hunt Tests and Field Trials for the pointing breeds. The dogs are run in braces (pairs) on a course on which birds are released so that the dogs can demonstrate their ability to find birds and point, and then retrieve the downed birds. In Retriever hunting tests and field trials, Retrievers and Irish Water Spaniels are tested on their ability to "mark" (remember) the location of downed birds and to retrieve those birds to their handlers. At the higher levels, dogs are required to mark multiple birds and to do "blind retrieves" (find unmarked birds—that is, birds they don't see fall).

Doggerel

A **Dual Champion** is a dog that has earned the title Champion of Record (CH) in the conformation ring and has also earned the title of Field Champion (FC) or Herding Champion (HC).

The Hunting Retriever Club (HRC), affiliated with the UKC, offers Hunt Tests at which dogs earn points toward titles awarded by the UKC. The North American Hunting Retriever Association (NAHRA) works to educate the public about the use of purebred

Retrievers as conservation animals and to promote Retriever field testing. NAHRA tests are not competitive. Each dog competes against a standard of performance to earn a title.

Spaniels are judged on their ability to hunt, flush, and retrieve game on land and water. AKC Hunt Tests are open to Clumber, Cocker, English Cocker, English Springer, Field, Sussex, and Welsh Springer Spaniels. Field Trials are open only to Cocker, English Cocker, and English Springer Spaniels.

Field Trials are also offered for Beagles, Basset Hounds, and Dachshunds, but there are no Hunting Tests for them. The AKC sanctions three types of Beagle Trials. A Brace Trial involves running Beagles in braces of two or three dogs who trail a rabbit. The Small Pack Option (SPO) involves running packs of seven hounds in pursuit of rabbits, while in a Large Pack trial, all the dogs in the class are turned loose to find and track hares. Events for Basset Hounds and Dachshunds are run much like the Beagle Brace Trials.

Many other competitive and noncompetitive titling programs are available for sporting dogs through national breed clubs and other organizations. Check with your breeder and your local breed club. A search of the Internet may also yield lots of up-to-date information about local and national programs and events.

Whatever Your Sport ...

Whatever sport you may decide to pursue with your dog, please don't lose sight of the reason you got a dog in the first place. Winning is great. But the real joy should be found on the path we take in pursuit of glory. We make mistakes and our dogs will make mistakes. So what? The real prize to be won in dog sports is the time we spend teaching our dogs, learning from them, and enjoying one another's company, win or lose.

The Least You Need to Know

- If you enjoy working with your dog, consider trying a dog sport.

- Many dog sports are open to all breeds and mixed-breeds.

- Some sports are specialized and open only to dogs of certain breeds.

- Many dogs do well at more than one sport.

- Win or lose, your dog is still your best friend.

Part

All Good Things Must End

The short life span of a dog seems to prove the adage that the good die young. Still, many dogs live well into their second decades. You can expect physical and mental changes as your dog ages, of course, and most of them are fairly predictable. We'll take a look at what you can do to keep your dog fit and healthy well into his senior years so that both of you can enjoy as much time together as possible.

Unfortunately, even the best of care can't keep your dog with you forever. As he prepares to make his final journey, you may have to make some hard choices. I'll make some suggestions to help you face the end of your dog's life, and reflect on what I think are good ways to honor the memory of your time together.

Chapter 24

Dogs Grow Old, Too

In This Chapter

- 🏠 Understanding changes as your dog ages
- 🏠 Caring for your dog in his later years
- 🏠 Dealing with age-related physical and mental problems
- 🏠 Working with your veterinarian to keep your older dog healthy and fit
- 🏠 Deciding whether to introduce a new pet

When will your dog become a senior citizen? That depends on his breed, his genes, and his life history, but generally a dog from reasonably healthy, long-lived bloodlines who has had good health care, exercise, and nutrition throughout his life should still be going strong at 9 or 10 years of age—much older in many breeds. In general, large dogs tend to have shorter life expectancies than small dogs.

Changes You Can Expect as Your Dog Ages

Change is a normal part of the aging process. Not every dog will experience every possible age-related change, of course. As I write this, I have two 10-year-old male Australian Shepherds lying beside my desk They are aging differently. The way your individual dog ages will be affected by his general health and environment, and his family heritage. His breed or combination of breeds will also play a role in the changes you should expect. Some breeds tend to be more prone to heart problems, for instance, while others are susceptible to cancer.

BowWOW

Here's how your mature dog's age translates into human years:

Approximate Age in Years	Equivalent Age in Humans	Approximate Age in Years	Equivalent Age in Humans
5	40	11	72
6	45	12	77
7	50	13	82
8	55	14	88
9	61	15	93
10	66	16	99

You and your veterinarian can help your aging dog as changes occur. Regular checkups to diagnose problems early, and changes in your dog's care and environment, may help him live longer and healthier. Even if he seems to be in terrific health, when your dog reaches about five and six years old, talk to your vet about early screening in addition to regular examinations.

Grrrrowls

Schedule a visit to the vet if your dog has any of the following:

- Sudden loss of weight or appetite
- Increased food intake without weight gain
- Increased drinking
- Diarrhea or vomiting lasting more than a day
- Coughing after exercise, or lasting more than a few minutes
- Excessive panting

Screening tests can detect subtle changes, and help prevent some age-related problems (see Chapter 10). Recommended tests will depend on your dog's breed, current health, and health history. Your vet may suggest blood tests, x-rays, or even an electrocardiogram. Sudden weight gain or loss, increased appetite without weight gain, increased drinking, diarrhea or vomiting, coughing, or excessive panting all call for a trip to the vet. Remember, too, that arthritis, thyroid imbalance, excess weight, and other conditions can cause symptoms similar to aging, and treatment may give your dog several more good years.

Changes in Nutritional Needs

An older dog generally requires fewer calories than he did when he was younger. If you continue to feed him as much as you used to, he'll get fat. Don't let that happen! Obesity is a serious health threat and can contribute to many problems, including heart disease, arthritis, and other debilitating conditions.

Some older dogs require nutritional supplements. Speak to your veterinarian and read about canine nutrition to determine which, if any, supplements may help your dog age more comfortably.

Changes in Skin, Coat, and Nails

Many dogs get gray hair as they age, particularly on the muzzle and around the eyes. Their coats may also become thinner, although that can be a sign of problems other than advancing age. If your dog's coat changes suddenly or substantially, tell your veterinarian. Regular grooming will let you check for lumps, bumps, and other signs of potential trouble. Benign tumors and fatty deposits are common in older dogs, but cancerous tumors can also occur. Have any new bumps or suspicious areas on the skin checked by your veterinarian.

Your dog's nails may become more brittle as he gets older. If that happens, speak to your vet about nutritional supplements that may help. You may need to trim your dog's nails more frequently as he becomes less active. If your dog's nails are very brittle, be careful when clipping or consider learning to use a grinder. You don't want a nail to split into the quick. Ouch!

Arthritis and Muscular Problems

Arthritis is common in older dogs. Its effect on your dog's life can vary from mild stiffness after sleeping to debilitating pain that keeps him from doing many things he used to do with ease.

Many people find that glucosamine and other supplements seem to make their arthritic dogs more comfortable. Anti-inflammatory pain relievers are often recommended as well. Consult your veterinarian before treating your dog, though, as some medications may interfere with one another or be harmful if your dog has other medical conditions. Special "egg-crate" orthopedic beds designed to distribute weight evenly may make your dog more comfortable.

Dental Disease

Dental disease is common in older dogs. Routine dental care is more important than ever for dogs as they age (see Chapter 9). Don't assume that your dog should have bad breath—he shouldn't. Bad breath often indicates gum disease, which can affect the heart, lungs, kidney, and other organs and contribute to life-threatening complications.

Proper oral hygiene will protect your aging dog from gum disease and also give your veterinarian a chance to examine your dog's mouth for telltale signs of disease. Professional tooth cleaning should be scheduled at least once a year or more frequently if necessary. Regular brushing at home will also help maintain your dog's oral health, as will chew toys designed to help keep teeth and gums clean and healthy.

Heart, Kidney, and Liver Problems

As your dog ages, his internal organs may lose some of their ability to function properly. His heart will probably become less efficient, and the heart valves—particularly the mitral valve—will lose elasticity.

Some changes are a normal part of aging, but if your dog had indications of heart problems when younger, or if his breed is prone to heart problems, talk to your vet about screening and care as he ages. Radiographs (x-rays), electrocardiograms (EKGs), and echocardiograms are used to diagnose heart disease.

The risk of kidney and liver disease also increases as your dog ages. Unfortunately, by the time symptoms of a kidney or liver problem become noticeable, the disease may be well advanced. Speak to your vet about including screening tests for kidney and liver functions as part of your aging dog's regular exams. If your dog needs to be anesthetized for any reason, pre-anesthesia screening is also advisable.

Loss of Hearing

Your dog may experience hearing loss as he ages. Most people don't notice the first indications of hearing loss in a dog because the signs tend to be subtle. Dogs use many cues to interact with us besides their hearing—they watch us, they know our patterns (probably better than we do), and they continue to interact effectively. By the time you do notice, your dog may already have experienced considerable, irreversible hearing loss.

Don't despair if your dog can't hear as well as he used to. Many people successfully teach their dogs to respond to hand signals and light signals in place of voice signals. For instance, you could use a flashlight to call your dog in from the yard. Even in daylight he'll be able to see a flashing light unless he's also lost his vision to age. If you start teaching these new communication skills before your dog loses his hearing, all the better.

Eye and Vision Changes

Changes in the eye are also common in aging dogs. If your dog's breed, or one of his breeds if he's a mix, is prone to inherited eye disease (see Chapter 3), consider taking your dog to a veterinary ophthalmologist for a thorough eye exam once every year or two. Other changes are simply a normal function of aging or in some cases the result of injury or other diseases.

Nuclear sclerosis, a condition in which the lens looks cloudy, is common in older dogs. It has little or no effect on the dog's vision. People sometimes mistake nuclear sclerosis for cataracts, which do cause vision loss. If you are in doubt, check with your veterinarian. In fact, an ophthalmic examination should be part of your dog's regular geriatric checkup. If you notice changes in the way your dog's eyes look, or if he seems to have vision problems between his regular exams, take him for a checkup. Changes in the eye sometimes indicate other health problems.

Sex-Related Changes

Prostate disease occurs in approximately 80 percent of unneutered male dogs 8 years of age and older. Although prostate cancer is not common in dogs, an enlarged prostate can cause your dog problems with urination and defecation. A check of his prostate gland should be part of your older male dog's annual physical exam.

Cancerous mammary (breast) tumors are the most common tumors found in unspayed bitches. In fact, breast cancer occurs as frequently in dogs as it does in people. It is also common for non-malignant fibrous tissue to develop in the mammary glands, causing them to harden. If your doggy girl is not spayed or was spayed after having one or more heat cycles, an examination of her mammary glands should be part of her annual check-up. You can also check for lumps during belly rubs—which you know she'll enjoy.

BowWOW

Altering your pet will increase his chances of living longer and healthier. Neutering eliminates risk of testicular cancer and reduces the risk of prostate disease in males; spaying eliminates a female's risk of ovarian cancer and greatly reduces her risk of breast cancer.

Cognitive Dysfunction

More than half of dogs over 10 years of age will experience some signs of *canine cognitive dysfunction* (CCD), which is characterized by a number of behavioral changes ranging from confusion to changes in long-established behavior patterns. If you think your dog may have CCD, talk to your veterinarian. There are drugs now that can alleviate some of the symptoms, but it's important to rule out other problems first.

BowWOW

Possible signs of CCD include the following:

- 🏠 Becoming confused or disoriented in familiar surroundings
- 🏠 Inability to recognize familiar people and animals
- 🏠 Forgetting housetraining
- 🏠 Inability to pay attention
- 🏠 Pacing, insomnia, or altered sleep patterns
- 🏠 Staring at nothing
- 🏠 Lower activity level

Not all age-related behavior changes indicate CCD. Let's look at some of the more common changes your dog may experience.

Aggression

Some older dogs show signs of aggression. In many cases, aggression is a reflexive response to pain. If your dog has lost his hearing or vision, he may be startled at times and snap. If he's not as spry as he used to be, he may fight back when he can't get away from something that's bothering or hurting him, such as a puppy or even a child. If your dog has a nervous system problem or is on certain medications, he may not know what he's doing.

The first step in solving the problem is to find its source. If your dog's behavior changes, take him in for an exam. If he's on medication, ask your vet if there could be behavioral side effects. If no medical cause can be found, consider talking to a qualified animal behaviorist who is familiar with canine geriatric problems. Ask your veterinarian for a referral.

Loss of Housetraining

Some older dogs have accidents in the house, even though they've been reliably housetrained for years. Some medical problems may directly affect the dog's ability to control elimination. Other problems make elimination painful and make the dog reluctant to go until he really can't hold it any longer, and he soils the house.

You can help your vet diagnose a medical problem. Write down as much information as possible about when accidents occur, including whether you're home, how often your dog needs to eliminate, his posture while eliminating, any sounds he makes that might indicate pain, unusual characteristics of the urine or stool, how much urine or stool your dog passed, and changes in your dog's food or water intake.

Sometimes the solutions to inappropriate elimination are easy. A ramp in place of stairs may make it easier for a dog who has trouble walking to get in and out. Medications help with some medical problems. If your dog needs to go more frequently now than when he was younger, see if you can arrange to get him out more often. If you can't figure out what to do, again, talk to your vet. Your buddy isn't the first old dog with this problem, and your vet may have some excellent suggestions based on the specifics of your dog's problem.

Routine Health Care for Your Older Dog

Good routine care goes a long way toward keeping a dog healthy at any age, but becomes ever more critical the older your dog gets. Let's look at some of the things you can do.

Regular Veterinary Examinations

It's important for your aging dog to see the vet at least once a year for a checkup, and at other times if you see signs of problems. Much of the examination is the same as it was when your dog was younger. As part of these regular exams, your veterinarian will normally examine your dog's teeth, gums, tongue, and throat. She will also perform a rectal exam, checking the inner pelvic area, internal lymph nodes, colon, and, if your dog is male, the prostate. A routine ophthalmic (eye) exam is part of the geriatric exam, too, and your vet will look for obvious symptoms of developing cataracts, glaucoma, blocked tear ducts, and other age-related eye problems.

(Photo by Close Encounters of the Furry Kind)

Some older dogs enjoy the company of puppies, as the author's 10-year-old dog, Dustin, enjoys his 4-week-old son.

Your vet may recommend additional screening tests, including a *urinalysis* and a *blood count*, two fairly simple tests that can provide lots of information for now and the future. She may suggest a *chemistry panel*, which is useful in diagnosing diabetes mellitus, liver disease, kidney disease, and several hormonal diseases. If your dog has a heart murmur, or if he's a member of a breed with a high risk of heart disease, your vet may recommend an EKG or echocardiogram.

A thyroid screening test or complete thyroid panel may be recommended. If your dog has symptoms or a history of heart, lung, kidney, liver, or gastrointestinal disease, or if your dog has had cancer, your vet may recommend radiographs (x-rays).

Preventive Health Care

Many veterinarians now feel that dogs should not be revaccinated annually for everything (refer to Chapter 9). Excessive vaccination can compromise the immune system, leading to more problems than the vaccines prevent. Speak to your veterinarian about your senior dog's need for vaccinations.

If heartworm is a problem where you live, your older dog should continue to be tested annually, and he should remain on heartworm prevention unless your veterinarian advises you otherwise.

(Photo by Close Encounters of the Furry Kind)

There's no friend quite like an old friend.

Parasites can compromise an older dog's health and make him uncomfortable. Talk to your vet about flea and tick controls that are appropriate for your dog, especially if he has any health problems. As part of your dog's annual examination, be sure to have your vet check a fecal sample and treat for internal parasites if necessary.

Good Grooming for the Senior Citizen

Healthy skin and coat can help keep the rest of the dog healthy. Ten to 15 minutes of daily brushing will stimulate your dog's circulation, help keep his skin and coat healthy and clean, and give you a chance to check him for early signs of trouble. Don't forget his nails.

Occasionally, a bath may be in order for your senior. Use warm water in a warm room. You don't want him to get chilled. Use a mild dog shampoo, rinse thoroughly, and towel him as dry as possible. Keep him in a warm place until he's completely dry.

Chew on This

Here are eight tips for keeping your older dog healthy:

- Take your dog to the vet for regular examinations.
- Discuss your dog's vaccination schedule with your vet, and avoid over- or undervaccinating.
- Tell your vet right away if you notice changes in your dog's behavior or physical condition.
- Feed your dog a high-quality food, and don't let him get fat.
- Give your dog regular exercise appropriate to his condition.
- Take care of your dog's dental health.
- Keep your dog free of parasites, and keep his living quarters clean.
- Remember that your old dog still loves you, and love him back.

Don't forget, either, that your old dog's soul needs grooming as much as his body does. Grooming should be a loving time between you and your dog. He'll revel in your gentle touch. He'll listen as you talk. Tell him you still love him—he may not know the words, but he knows what they mean.

Keeping Your Older Dog Safe and Comfy

As your dog gets older, he'll become less able to regulate his body temperature. He may not want to give up his old ways, so it's up to you to control his exposure to the weather. Cold and dampness can chill an older dog who played in the snow for hours when he was younger. In hot weather, he may be more susceptible to heat stroke than he used to be, so be sure your dog has shade (or bring him into your air-conditioned house). He should have access to clean water at all times, summer and winter.

Your dog may need some new bedding as he gets older. Watch him to see what sort of bed he seems to like. Pet supply stores carry dog beds in a wide range of styles and sizes. Despite their creaky old joints, some dogs still choose to sleep on the cold, hard floor. And, of course, *your* bed may be the most comfy and inviting of all!

Feeding the Aging Canine

Most dog food manufacturers now offer "light" and "senior" lines of foods with lower calories and lower protein content. Unless your dog is overweight or has a medical problem, though, there's no scientific evidence that geriatric foods are any better for older dogs than regular food. If your dog is holding a proper weight, if his skin and coat are healthy, and if he has reasonable energy for his age, then there's probably no good reason to change his food just because he's aging.

Many elderly dogs have problems with dehydration, which can contribute to more serious problems. If your dog has trouble getting around, he may not be visiting his water bowl often enough. An extra water bowl or two in different parts of the house will make it easier for him to get a drink. Try to monitor his water intake, and if he hasn't been drinking, take his bowl to him and offer him a drink. Be sure his water is always fresh and clean to help his kidneys stay in good working order.

As your dog's energy level drops and his metabolism slows with age, he may begin to put on weight. If that's the case, cut back a little on the amount of food you're feeding him. If he still seems to be hungry, there are ways to add volume without adding calories to his meals (see Chapter 12).

Your dog may become less interested in food as he ages, perhaps because his senses of smell and taste aren't as keen as they once were. If his lack of interest is leading to poor nutrition, making his food more appealing may encourage him to eat. Warm food is more fragrant—and more appetizing—than cold, so you might try serving it at room temperature or slightly warmer. Don't make it hot—you don't want him to burn his mouth. Adding a bit of water or unsalted broth, or plain yogurt or cottage cheese, may also revive his appetite.

Chew on This

You can make an inexpensive elevated feeding table for your dog with a plastic container or wastebasket that stands about as high as your dog's chest, and with a bowl that has a rim. Measure the outside perimeter of the bowl at the top just under the rim. Cut a circle the same size into the bottom of your plastic stand. Turn the stand upside down, and insert the bowl into the hole. The rim should hold it in place, and your dog should be able to eat more comfortably.

Make sure a physical problem isn't interfering with your dog's ability to eat. If he's arthritic, bending his neck downward may put pressure on sore joints, making meal time painful. Pet supply stores offer elevated bowls that may help, or you can make a stand for food and water bowls. Dental problems can also cause a dog to stop eating properly, so check his teeth, gums, tongue, cheeks, and the roof of his mouth. If changes in your dog's eating behavior are sudden, or if he's barely eating or is losing a lot of weight, a visit to the vet is definitely in order.

Should You Get a New Dog Now?

You may be considering adding a younger dog to your family while your older dog is still around. That usually works out fine, but before you proceed, think about a few things.

Many older dogs enjoy having a younger dog around. Some even seem to develop a new lease on life with a new friend to "talk" to. It's up to you to make sure he doesn't get carried away and hurt himself in his renewed enthusiasm for life. If your older dog is ill or suffers from arthritis or other problems that limit his ability to interact safely and effectively with a younger dog—particularly a puppy—it may be better to wait a while. If you really don't want to wait, then make sure your new dog can't pester or hurt the old guy. Fair is fair, after all! Your old dog has been your friend for years, and he's earned the right to be comfortable, safe, and well loved until the end.

Activities for Your Older Dog

Your dog will undoubtedly slow down some as he gets older, but he still needs reasonable exercise to stay physically, mentally, and emotionally fit. A proper diet combined with exercise appropriate to your dog's general health and condition will help keep him a healthy weight and will tone his muscles. It will help his cardiovascular and digestive systems stay healthy. Exercise will prevent boredom and depression, and help your old friend lead the life of a happy senior citizen.

If your dog hasn't been on a regular exercise program, have him checked out by your vet before beginning one. Then see to it that he gets out and about every day, within proper limits for his health and condition. When he gets caught up in the fun, he may not acknowledge his limitations. It's up to you to monitor his activity and keep him from overdoing it.

Watch for signs of overexertion, especially when the weather is hot or cold. Coughing or shortness of breath during or after exercise can indicate heart problems, so report them to your vet. If your dog has arthritis or other orthopedic problems, talk to your vet about appropriate exercise. Swimming is good for dogs with joint problems, but risky for a dog with heart disease. An older dog can become chilled more easily than he did when younger, too, so he should swim only in reasonably warm water and in fair weather. Walks on leash are less stressful than running and playing, and better for dogs with many medical problems. Two or three short walks a day may be better than one long one.

If your dog is healthy and physically fit, there's no reason he can't remain active. Many older dogs are involved in therapy work, visiting nursing homes, hospitals, and schools. In fact, senior dogs are often more reliable and less rambunctious than their younger counterparts. Older dogs can also participate in obedience or other sports, many of which offer senior or veterans classes or divisions for dogs over seven years old. If your dog doesn't seem to enjoy an activity, or if it's too taxing, don't force him. But if he's having a good time and he's physically capable, there's no reason he shouldn't keep on keepin' on.

The Least You Need to Know

- Change is a normal part of the aging process.
- Good veterinary care is essential to maintaining your aging dog's good health.
- Moderate exercise and good nutrition are also important to your dog's physical and mental condition.
- Your elderly dog continues to love and need you.

Chapter 25

Saying Farewell

In This Chapter

- 🏠 Facing the end of your dog's life
- 🏠 Making the decision to euthanize
- 🏠 Dealing with your loss
- 🏠 Moving into the future

It's never easy to think about saying farewell to a beloved companion. Unfortunately, one of the prices we pay for the joy of living with dogs is that eventually they leave us.

Many dogs age gracefully into their teens, but elderly dogs can also experience problems and illnesses that come with advanced age (see Chapter 24). Some of these problems are minor and have little effect on the dog's overall quality of life. Others are more devastating, and we have to make some difficult and painful decisions.

Considering the Quality of Life

We are sometimes faced with this heartbreaking choice for a younger dog, too. Injury or disease can take the joy out of living and replace it with pain at any age. Sometimes the kindest thing we can do is let go.

Your dog's overall quality of life should be the most significant element in the difficult process of deciding to euthanize. Does he seem to be in pain or depressed much of the time? Does he still enjoy simple pleasures, like eating or being petted? Does he still respond to you normally, or has he become withdrawn and disinterested? If your dog is in severe pain, or clearly has more bad days than good ones, it may be time to talk to your veterinarian about euthanasia. There's no question that it's a difficult thing to decide. But euthanasia is a far better alternative than letting your dog suffer with no hope of relief.

Doggerel

Euthanasia, the act of humanely ending a life, offers a gentle passage and freedom from pain and is a final gift we can give our dogs.

Making Important Decisions

A number of factors may influence your decision to euthanize your dog. You need to weigh all the factors in making the right choice for your dog, yourself, and your family.

Your dog's health, of course, is the most important factor. Unless your dog is in severe, acute pain, you'll have some time to decide. Talk to your veterinarian about your dog's condition, treatment options, and chance for recovery. Cost may also be a factor, and you shouldn't feel guilty or embarrassed if you simply cannot afford the recommended treatment. Unfortunately, medical care can be extremely expensive, for dogs as well as for people, and most of us have financial limits. Long-term care for a very sick animal can also take a serious emotional toll on you and other family members, including other pets. If you have a big, heavy dog, that may be a factor as well. It's one thing to carry a small dog out for potty breaks or to clean up after a small dog that is incontinent. It's quite another with a big, heavy dog. If you aren't up to the financial, physical, and emotional costs of long-term care, be honest about that with yourself and your vet. It doesn't mean you love your dog any less, and it doesn't make you a bad person. Everyone's situation is different. Do what is right for you and your dog.

If you're not ready to let go, but your dog is terminally ill, you may be interested to know that some veterinary hospitals and organizations are beginning to offer home hospice care. Pet hospice care is designed to keep terminally ill pets comfortable at home until family members come to terms with the pending loss. If hospice care interests you, ask your vet or closest veterinary school about your options.

Chew on This

The American Association of Human-Animal Bond Veterinarians offers information on home hospice care for terminally ill animals on its website at www.members.aol.com/guyh7/hospice.htm. Or ask your veterinarian for more information.

If you decide that euthanization is the best option, you and your family should discuss in advance where and when the procedure will take place. Some vets will come to your home, especially if you're a long-time client and the dog is very ill. If you decide to go to the veterinarian's office, you'll probably want to arrange a time when the clinic is not busy, and when you don't have to rush back to work or other obligations. Be gentle with yourself and give yourself time and space to grieve.

You also need to decide who will be there. Family members will probably want to say good-bye, and each may want to do it a little differently. Everyone should have a chance to say farewell, both before and after euthanasia has been performed. Talking it all out will make it easier on everyone when the time comes.

Many people are afraid that euthanization will be frightening or painful for the dog. I've been present to say farewell to quite a few dogs and can tell you that every one of them went gently and quietly, secure in knowing that they were well loved even at the end. The process is virtually painless.

It may help you make a decision if you understand what happens during euthanasia. It is usually done by injection of a concentrated solution of pentobarbital, which causes the heart to stop. It is injected directly into a vein and usually works in a few seconds.

BowWOW _____

Just this side of Heaven is a place called Rainbow Bridge.

When an animal dies that has been especially close to someone here, that pet goes to Rainbow Bridge. There are meadows and hills for all of our special friends so they can run and play together. There is plenty of food and water and sunshine, and our friends are warm and comfortable. All the animals who had been ill and old are restored to health and vigor; those who were hurt or maimed are made whole and strong again, just as we remember them in our dreams of days and times gone by.

The animals are happy and content, except for one small thing: They miss someone very special to them who had to be left behind.

They all run and play together, but the day comes when one suddenly stops and looks into the distance. The bright eyes are intent; the eager body quivers. Suddenly he begins to break away from the group, flying over the green grass, his legs carrying him faster and faster. You have been spotted, and when you and your special friend finally meet, you cling together in joyous reunion, never to be parted again. The happy kisses rain upon your face; your hands again caress the beloved head, and you look once more into the trusting eyes of your pet, so long gone from your life but never absent from your heart.

Then you cross Rainbow Bridge together.

—Anonymous

Muscles may contract or relax after death has occurred, and cause movements. Sometimes the animal passes urine and feces because of the relaxation. Sometimes air is pushed out of the lungs, making it seem that the dog is gasping. There is no pain associated with these movements, and no awareness on the part of your dog. He's already gone. But knowing what to expect will help you decide who in the family should be present, and also help whoever will be there to be prepared.

Some people simply cannot face being there for the process, but if you can, your dog will usually be more relaxed if you hold him and whisper farewell while the injection is given. If you cannot handle being there, that's okay. You'll probably get all sorts of advice, but ultimately the decision is yours. Do what's best for you—that will be best for your dog. You're not abandoning him; you're placing him in gentle hands that can guide him on his way. He has known your love, and he will take it with him.

Young children probably shouldn't be present during the actual euthanization, but they should be helped to prepare for the loss of their pet. (See Appendixes B and C for resources on talking to children about death.) Be sure that each child has a chance to say good-bye before and possibly after the dog dies.

Chew on This

Creating a scrapbook or photo album, or keeping a bit of hair, a collar, or a nametag as a memento, helps many people deal with the loss of a beloved dog.

Some people want time with their dog after the procedure to say a final good-bye. If you or members of your family feel a need for some solitary time, tell your vet. People often want to keep a memento—a lock of hair, a collar, or a name tag, for instance. Be sure that all family members have an opportunity to express what they want to do to say good-bye and what, if anything, they want to keep.

You should decide in advance how you want to handle the body. There are a number of options, depending on your preferences, your finances, and the services offered where you live. Speak to your veterinarian in advance. You may want to have your dog cremated and the ashes returned to you to keep, or perhaps to bury or scatter in your dog's favorite spot. It's also possible to have your dog cremated with other pets. The ashes would not be returned to you in that case. Burial is also an option. You may want to bury him at home, but make sure that is legal where you live. Pet cemeteries are available in many communities. Whatever you choose, your veterinarian can help you with the arrangements.

Dealing with Loss

Be kind to yourself after the euthanasia. Try to plan something to do for the rest of the day with someone who understands your grief. Don't share your feelings with anyone who you think won't understand. The last thing you need is for someone to say, "It was just a dog." The dogs we live with and love are part of our Selves, and you have a right to your feelings.

Ceremonies can help. Consider burying your dog's remains or perhaps his collar and a favorite toy for a sense of closure. When we lost our first Australian Shepherd, my husband and I buried his ashes and planted a Gentle Shepherd day lily over the spot. We hung his tags on a hook by the lily. When we moved, the lily came with us, and so did our memories. I know people—adults as well as children—who take comfort in assembling a photo album or scrapbook about their dog. Going through pictures of him as a puppy, an adolescent, and an adult can help soften grief with happy memories. Many people make a donation to a rescue group or a local humane society in honor of their dog. If your dog died of an inherited disease, you might want to make a donation to canine health research in his name. You will know what feels right to you.

Chew on This

Losing a pet is one of the most stressful events we can experience. Be sure to take good care of yourself and your family members during the mourning period.

Grrrrowls

Not everyone understands the pain of losing a dog. Avoid anyone who may demean your grief, and be kind to yourself as you mourn your friend.

Losing a pet is one of the saddest and most stressful experiences in our lives. Some people don't understand this. Don't let them embarrass you or demean your grief. You and other members of your family need to talk to someone who understands in order to begin healing. If you don't know anyone you feel you can confide in, consider calling one of the following services. They will understand what you're going through. They'll listen, and they'll offer suggestions to help you through this difficult time.

Pet Loss Grief Counseling Services

California

🏠 530-752-4200, or toll-free 1-800-565-1526. Staffed by University of California-Davis veterinary students.

Florida

🏠 352-392-4700; then dial 1 and 4080. Staffed by University of Florida veterinary students.

Illinois

🏠 630-603-3994. Staffed by Chicago Veterinary Medical Association veterinarians and staff. Leave voice-mail message; calls will be returned 7 P.M. to 9 P.M. (CT).

🏠 217-244-2273 or toll-free 1-877-394-2273 (CARE). Staffed by University of Illinois veterinary students. Leave voicemail message; calls will be returned 7 P.M. to 9 P.M. (CT), Tuesdays, Thursdays, and Sundays.

Iowa

🏠 1-888-ISU-PLSH. Hosted by the Iowa State University College of Veterinary Medicine.

Maryland and Virginia

🏠 540-231-8038. Staffed by Virginia-Maryland Regional College of Veterinary Medicine students.

Massachusetts

🏠 508-839-7966. Staffed by Tufts University veterinary students.

Michigan

🏠 517-432-2696. Staffed by Michigan State University veterinary students.

New York

🏠 607-253-3932. Staffed by Cornell University veterinary students.

Ohio

🏠 614-292-1823. Staffed by The Ohio State University veterinary students.

Washington

🏠 509-335-5704. Hosted by Washington State University's College of Veterinary Medicine.

Moving On

Sometimes it's hard to imagine ever loving another dog as much as one you've loved and lost. We're all different in our need for time to grieve, and even in how we grieve. You will have to decide what's best for you.

When you're ready, look for a new dog. Don't try to replace the old one—you'll only disappoint yourself and rob both dogs of their distinction as individuals. If you focus too much on looking for identical traits in the two, you'll be likely to miss out on the wonderful little things that make your new dog special in his own right. If you love the breed of your first dog, then by all means get another of the same breed. But don't expect the new one to be the same as the old. He can't be your old dog; he can only be himself. If looking at a face, coat, and color similar to what your old friend had will be difficult for you, then consider a different breed, or the same breed but a different sex or color.

I've often heard people say that they'll never have another dog because they loved the other one so much. I find that idea even sadder than the death of a dog. You can never replace a dog who's gone before, but you can love another one, and he can love you. I think the best tribute we can give to the dogs we've loved before is the faith in their species that sends us out to look for another to love and care for. Dogs are social animals. They don't want us to be alone.

BowWOW

The one best place to bury a good dog is in the heart of his master.
—Ben Hur Lampman

(Photo by Close Encounters of the Furry Kind)

Whatever your beliefs about a hereafter, honor your dog in your own way.

The Least You Need to Know

- As your dog ages, you may have to weigh your desire to keep him against the quality of his life.

- Euthanasia offers a gentle means of releasing a dog from pain and discomfort.

- All family members should have a chance to say good-bye and to grieve in their own ways.

- Help is available if you have trouble dealing with the loss of your dog.

- Don't be afraid to give your love to another dog when the time is right.

Doggy Dictionary

acquired diseases or **conditions**   Diseases or conditions that develop as a result of aging, illness, or accident.

airscenting   A process by which a dog follows scent as it travels on the air.

alpha   The term used for the socially dominant male and female animal in a pack. Among dogs, dominance determines who is alpha, not age, sex, or even size.

backyard breeder (BYB)   A person who produces puppies, accidentally or intentionally, without health clearances for the parents or pups, and with little if any knowledge of the breed standard, genetics, or effective methods of raising puppies.

biddability   The degree to which a dog wants to do as you bid him.

bitch   The correct term for a female canine.

brachycephalic   The term for dogs that have short, broad skulls and short muzzles. Pugs and Pekinese are brachycephalic.

breed   A group of animals that are fairly homogeneous in size, looks, personality, instincts, and other traits, and are all members of one species.

breed standard   A written set of characteristics that define the hypothetical ideal specimen of a breed.

call name   The name you call your dog informally (*see* registered name).

Canine Brucellosis   A bacterial disease spread primarily through sexual contact with an infected animal. Brucellosis causes abortion or early death of infected puppies and serious problems in infected adults. It may be passed from an infected dog to people.

colostrum   A highly concentrated mixture of antibodies, protein, vitamins, electrolytes, nutrients, and fluid produced by the mother's breasts during the first 36 to 48 hours after birth.

congenital diseases or **conditions**   Diseases or conditions that are present at birth and may or may not be inherited.

cornea   The clear membrane that covers the surface of the eye.

crates   Cages for dogs. They're used for potty training, safe travel, and confinement if the dog is injured or ill.

crossbred   Refers to the offspring of two purebreds of different breeds.

dam   Refers to a dog's mother.

deciduous teeth   Commonly called "baby teeth," the deciduous teeth are replaced by permanent teeth starting when a puppy is four or five months old.

dew claws   The small toes located above the feet on the inside of the legs. In many breeds the dew claws are customarily removed.

dog trainer   Someone who works directly with dogs, teaching them various commands and then teaching the owners how to use the commands with their dogs (*see* obedience instructors).

dominance hierarchy   A social system in which an *alpha* is socially dominant, and each animal in the group occupies a specific rank.

double coats   The combination of a protective outer coat over a soft, dense, warm undercoat.

Dual Champion   A dog that has earned the title Champion of Record in the conformation ring and has the title of Field Champion (FC) or Herding Champion (HC).

expressed   Genetic traits that occur in the individual. A person with blue eyes expresses the gene for blue eyes.

fear imprint periods   Periods that occur in puppies at about 8 weeks, 5 to 6 months, and 18 months. Puppies are very sensitive to being frightened during those times.

fractures   Breaks in bones. A *closed fracture* is one in which the bone is fractured, but the skin over the break is unbroken. In a *compound fracture*, the broken bone protrudes through the skin, creating risk of infection. *Epiphyseal fractures* occur in the growth plates or epiphyseal plates of young dogs that are still growing. If the bone is cracked but not broken, the dog has a *greenstick fracture*.

genetic traits   Characteristics that an individual inherits from his or her parents. Every puppy inherits one gene for each of his traits from each of his parents. If the two genes are the same, then the pup is *homozygous* for that trait. If the two genes are different, the pup is *heterozygous* for that trait.

genotype   An individual's genetic makeup, or all the traits the individual has inherited from his or her parents (*see* phenotype).

gingivitis   Inflammation of the gum (*see* periodontal disease).

growth plates   Also known as *epiphyseal plates* or the epiphysis, they are soft areas of immature bone from which growth occurs in puppies.

heat   The time in a bitch's reproductive cycle when she bleeds and then becomes fertile and receptive to male dogs. A *silent heat* is a heat cycle in which the bitch doesn't bleed or bleeds so little that the owner never knows. A *standing heat* is the period, usually after the bleeding stops, when the bitch is fertile and receptive to males.

hobby breeder   A hobby breeder may be (1) a small-time breeder of puppies for distribution through pet stores, or (2) a responsible, serious breeder who places puppies carefully and directly with individual buyers. If someone tells you he's a hobby breeder, be sure you know which definition he has in mind.

humane traps   Wire cages used to catch animals without hurting them.

idiopathic epilepsy   A condition in which seizures occur for no identifiable reason. It is believed to be inherited.

incomplete proteins   Proteins that lack some amino acids needed by dogs (or people). Most plants provide incomplete proteins.

Individual Limited Privileges (ILP) number   Allows an unregistered purebred dog of a breed recognized by the American Kennel Club (AKC) to compete in AKC obedience, agility, tracking, and other sporting events.

intermediate host   An animal in which a parasite's larvae live until they reach the final host. Once the larvae reach the final host, the adult parasites develop.

larvae   Animals in a special feeding stage in their life cycle.

mixed-breed   A dog with more than two breeds in his background. Also called random-bred, mutt, or mongrel.

mode of inheritance   The way in which a trait is passed from parent to offspring.

mush   Means "to drive a team of sled dogs," from the French *marche*, or "walk."

nuclear sclerosis   A condition in which the lens of the eye appears to be cloudy. It is common in older dogs and rarely affects vision.

obedience instructors   Instructors who teach you to train your dog (*see* dog trainers).

pedigree   A family tree for a dog.

pet wholesalers   Brokers who buy puppies in quantity from puppy mills and resell them, usually to pet stores.

phenotype   An individual's expressed traits, the ones we can determine with our normal senses (*see* genotype).

periodontal disease   Gum disease. Food particles and bacteria form *plaque* along the gum line. Plaque can form *tartar* (*calculus*), which irritates the gums and causes bad breath and *gingivitis*. If tartar builds up under the gums, it causes periodontal disease, leading to tooth loss, abscesses, infection, and bone loss. Bacteria from infected gums enter the bloodstream and can infect the heart valves, liver, and kidneys. Proper dental care can prevent or stop the progress of periodontal disease.

positive reinforcement   The process of rewarding your dog with something he likes for doing what you want him to do.

praise word   A word you use to tell your dog he's done well.

puppy mills   Businesses that produce puppies strictly to make money. Puppy millers don't care about physical traits, sound genetic health, good temperament, or where the puppies end up once they are paid for, and they do not socialize them for proper mental and social development.

Rainbow Bridge   Refers to a heavenly place that dogs are said to go when they die to wait for the people they love.

registered name   The name that appears on your dog's registration papers and the certificates for any titles he earns in competition (*see* call name).

release word   A word you use to tell your dog that he's finished with whatever you told him to do—he's "off duty," at least for the moment.

rescue   Refers to (1) a dog fostered and placed into a new home by volunteers who work with one or two breeds, or (2) the process of taking in homeless or unwanted dogs and placing them in new homes.

scent articles Items that a lost person has touched or worn. Scent articles are often used to "show" a tracking dog the scent of the missing person so that the dog knows who he's trying to find. Scent articles in obedience are metal and leather items used to test the dog's ability to detect his handler's scent.

search and rescue (SAR) Refers to dogs who are trained to search for victims of a disaster or for people who are lost.

selective breeding The practice of carefully matching a sire and dam in order to perpetuate desirable traits, and reduce or eliminate undesirable traits, in their offspring.

service dogs Highly trained, full-time partners for people with disabilities. Service dogs include guide dogs for the blind, hearing dogs, seizure-alert dogs, and general assistance dogs. Service dogs have the legal right to accompany their people wherever they go.

sire A dog's father.

terrier A dog that digs, from the Latin *terra*, or "ground."

territorial Animals that mark certain areas as their own. Dogs mark territory by urinating around the perimeter. Some dogs defend their territory by barking or behaving aggressively.

therapy dogs Dogs that visit nursing homes, hospitals, hospices, schools, and other environments to make people a little happier. Therapy dogs have no special legal status.

trailing dogs Dogs that follow scent left on the ground by a person or animal.

whelp Used as a verb, *to whelp* means to give birth to puppies. Used as a noun, *whelp* means a newborn puppy.

Further Reading

Bookstores and libraries abound with books on everything dog. The reading suggestions I've provided here are necessarily limited, but I recommend you poke around your local library, bookstore, or on-line bookseller, especially those that specialize in dog books. Then curl up with your resident canine and enjoy a good read!

Specialized Sources for Dog Books and Videos

Note: Most of the books I recommend here are also available from regular booksellers.

Alpine Publications, Inc.
PO Box 7027
Loveland, CO 80537
Orders: 1-800-777-7257
Customer Service: 970-667-2017
www.alpinepub.com

Barrons Educational Series, Inc.
250 Wireless Boulevard
Hauppauge, NY 11788
1-800-645-3476
www.barronseduc.com/pets-dogs.html

4M Dog Books
1280 Pacific Street
Union City, CA 94587-2030
1-800-487-9867
www.4Mdogbooks.com

Dogwise
PO Box 2778
Wenatchee, WA 98807
1-800-776-2665
www.dogwise.com

Dog Lovers Bookshop
PO Box 117, Gracie Station
New York, NY 10028
Phone and fax: 212-369-7554
www.dogbooks.com

PetBook Express
www.petbookexpress.com

ePetBooks
www.epetbooks.com

Pet Books Online
www.petbooksonline.com

Apogee Videos (videos on first aid for dogs and cats)
www.apogeevideo.com

Recommended Reading for All Dog Owners

Caras, Roger A. *A Dog Is Listening: The Way Some of Our Closest Friends View Us.* New York: Simon & Schuster, 1992.

Donaldson, Jean. *The Culture Class: A Revolutionary New Way of Understanding the Relationship Between Humans and Domestic Dogs.* Berkeley, CA: James and Kenneth Publishers, 1996.

Dog Breeds

The Complete Dog Book, 19th Edition. New York: American Kennel Club, 1997.

Flamholtz, Cathy J. *A Celebration of Rare Breeds.* OTR Publications, 1986.

Kilcommons, Brian, and Sarah Wilson. *Paws to Consider: Choosing the Right Dog for You and Your Family.* New York: Warner Books, 1999.

Walkowicz, Chris. *The Perfect Match: A Dog Buyer's Guide.* New York: Howell, 1996.

Training

Kilcommons, Brian, and Sarah Wilson. *Childproofing Your Dog: A Complete Guide to Preparing Your Dog for the Children in Your Life.* New York: Warner Books, 1994.

———. *Good Owners, Great Dogs.* New York: Warner Books, 1999.

McConnell, Patricia. *Beginning Family Dog Training.* Black Earth, WI: Dog's Best Friend, 1996.

Pryor, Karen. *Clicker Training for Dogs.* Waltham, MA: Sunshine Books, 2001.

Rescue and Adoption

Benjamin, Carol Lea. *The Chosen Puppy: How to Select and Raise a Great Puppy from an Animal Shelter.* New York: Howell, 1990.

———. *Second Hand Dog.* St. Paul, MN: Hungry Minds, 1994.

Boneham, Sheila W., Ph.D. *Breed Rescue: How to Start and Run a Successful Program.* Loveland, CO: Alpine, 1998.

Palika, Liz. *Save That Dog!: Adopting a Purebred Rescue Dog.* St. Paul, MN: Hungry Minds, 1997.

Appendix C

Dogs Online

Many, many websites are devoted to dogs and related topics, and they change every day. I've listed a few sites that I think are useful. Most of them have links to other sites. If you're looking for information on a specific topic, say "lameness in dogs" or "agility" or "Yorkshire Terriers," a search by topic will yield an amazing number of links. Have fun surfing!

Dogs in General

Dog Owners Guide
www.canismajor.com/dog/index.html

Purebred Dogs

American Kennel Club (AKC)
www.akc.org

United Kennel Club (UKC)
www.ukcdogs.com

Rescue

Breed Rescue Discussion List
www.groups.yahoo.com/group/BreedRescue/

National Breed Club Rescue Network
www.akc.org/breeds/rescue.cfm

Training

Dr. P's Dog Training Library
www.uwsp.edu/psych/dog/library.htm

Karen Pryor's
Clickertraining.com
www.clickertraining.com

Clicker Solutions
www.clickersolutions.com

Equipment and Supplies

J and J Dog Supplies
www.jandjdog.com

PetSmart.com
www.etsmart.com

SitStay.Com
www.sitstay.com

Veterinary and Emergency Information

American Veterinary Medical
Association (AVMA)
www.avma.org

AVMA Poison Guide
www.avma.org/pubhlth/
poisgde.asp#acet

Animal Disaster Preparedness
www.cyberpet.com/cyberdog/
articles/general/artad1d.htm

Canine Health Online
www.caninehealthonline.org

Canine Hip and Elbow
Dysplasia Resources
www.workingdogs.com/doc0090.
htm

Canine Eye Registry Foundation
(CERF)
www.vet.purdue.edu/~yshen/
cerf.html

Pet-Helpers Emergency
Disaster Care
www.pet-helpers.com

University of Pennsylvania Hip
Improvement Program
(PennHIP)
www.vet.upenn.edu/
ResearchCenters/pennhip

Traveling with Fido

Find a Place to Stay
www.petswelcome.com

Pet-friendly Lodging
www.petswelcome.com

See Appendixes B and D for
additional website listings.

Major Doggy Organizations

Registries and Competition Programs

American Kennel Club (AKC)
5580 Centerview Drive
Suite 200
Raleigh, NC 27606
919-233-9767
www.akc.org
e-mail: info@akc.org

American Herding Breeds Association (AHBA)
1548 Victoria Way
Pacifica, CA 94044
415-355-9563
www.ahba-herding.org

American Mixed Breed Obedience Registry (AMBOR)
179 Niblick Road #113
Paso Robles, CA 93446
805-226-9275
www.amborusa.org

American Rare Breed Association
9921 Frank Tippett Road
Cheltenham, MD 20623
301-868-5718
Fax: 301-868-6409
www.arba.org

Australian Shepherd Club of America (ASCA)
PO Box 3790
Bryan, TX 77805-3790
916-778-1082
www.asca.org

North American Dog Agility Council (NADAC)
HCR 2, Box 277
St. Maries, ID 83861
208-689-3803
www.nadac.com

United Kennel Club (UKC)
100 East Kilgore Road
Kalamazoo, MI 49001-5593
616-343-9020
www.ukcdogs.com

United States Dog Agility Association (USDAA)
PO Box 850995
Richardson, TX 75085-0955
972-231-9700
www.usdaa.com

Dog Trainers and Obedience Instructors

Association of Pet Dog Trainers (APDT)
17000 Commerce Parkway, Suite C
Mt. Laurel, NJ 08054
1-800-PET-DOGS
www.apdt.com

National Association of Dog Obedience Instructors (NADOI)
Attn: Corresponding Secretary
PMB #369
729 Grapevine Highway, Suite 369
Hurst, TX 76054-2085
www.nadoi.org

Dog-Assisted Therapy

Therapy Dogs Incorporated
PO Box 5868
Cheyenne, WY 82003
877-843-7364
www.therapydogs.com

Therapy Dogs International, Inc.
88 Bartley Road
Flanders, NJ 07836
973-252-9800
Fax: 973-252-7171
www.tdi-dog.org

Delta Society Pet Partners Programs
289 Perimeter Road East
Renton, WA 98055
206-226-7357
www.deltasociety.org

Canine Health

Institute for Genetic Disease Control (GDC)
PO Box 222
Davis, CA 95617
Phone and fax: 530-756-6773
www.vetmed.ucdavis.edu/gdc/gdc.html

Orthopedic Foundation for Animals
2300 East Nifong Boulevard
Columbia, MS 65201-3856
573-442-0418
www.offa.org

Canine Eye Registration Foundation
1248 Lynn Hall
Purdue University
West Lafayette, IN 47907
765-494-8179
www.vet.purdue.edu/~yshen/cerf.html

Index

nails
changes with aging, 335-336
dew claw, 217
grooming, 217
names, registered, 35-36
neighbors, common problems with, 48-54
neutering, 136-138
Novice levels, obedience competitions, 317
nuclear sclerosis, 215, 338
nutrition. *See* food

O

obedience
AMBOR events, 316
classes/schools, 113, 250-252
competitions, 315-316
goals, 318
legs, 316
titles, 316-317
AKC, 316
UKC, 316
obesity, 171-172
obstacles, agility, 7-8
OFA (Orthopedic Foundation for Animals), 33
omega-3 (fatty acid), 148
omega-6 (fatty acid), 148
Open levels, obedience competitions, 317
open tunnels (agility), 9

orthopedic problems, 44, 139-141
canine hip dysplasia, 140-141
degenerative joint disease, 140
easing discomfort, 143
elbow dysplasia, 43, 140
hip dysplasia, 41-43
osteochondritis dissecans, 140
osteochondrosis, 43
osteochondrosis dissecans, 43
panosteitis, 141
patellar luxation, 44, 141
rheumatoid arthritis, 140
Ruptured Anterior Cruciate Ligament, 141
treatments, 142
osteochondrosis (OC), 43
osteochondrosis dissecans (OCD), 43, 140
outdoor dogs, 183-184
oversupplementation, 165
ownership, 11-13
family decision, 7-8
role of dog, 9-11
space, 7
time investment, 5-7

P

panosteitis ("pano"), 141
parasites, 129-135

parvo, vaccinations, 127-129
patella, 44
patellar luxation, 44, 141
pedigrees, 31-35
PennHIP (Pennsylvania Hip Improvement Program), 42
Pet Loss Grief Counseling Services, 355-356
pet stores, 86-87
pet wholesalers (brokers), 85
petroleum jelly, dog's feet, 306
Phenobarbital, seizures, 144
phenotypes, 41
pipe tunnels (agility), 9
plants, incomplete proteins, 164
Pointing Breed Hunt Tests, 328
poisons, 156-157
Polysulfated Glycosaminoglycan (Adequan), 142
positive reinforcement, 196-198
potty training, 200-203
pounds, adoption, 92-98
pregnancies, gestation period, 232
preventive health care, 342-343
Primidone, seizures, 144
prostate diseases, 338
proteins, 164
pupal, 130